God, Father and Creator

A Catechesis on the Creed

Pope John Paul II

With a Foreword
by Joseph H. Casey, SJ

auline
BOOKS & MEDIA
Boston

Library of Congress Cataloging-in-Publication Data

John Paul II, Pope, 1920-
    God, Father, and Creator / Pope John PaulII ; with a foreword by
Joseph H. Casey.
        p.   cm.
    Includes index.
    ISBN 0-8198-3080-1
    1. God—Papal documents. 2. God—Fatherhood—Papal
documents. 3. Creation—Papal documents. 4. Nicene Creed—Papal
documents.   I. Title.
BT102.J63   1996
231—dc20
                                              95-38647
                                              CIP

Reprinted with permission from *L'Osservatore Romano,* English
Edition.

The texts in the Appendix are taken from *The Christian Faith,* edited
by J. Neuner, SJ, and J. Dupuis, SJ, and published by Alba House,
Staten Island, New York, and are used by permission. All rights
reserved.

Cover: Michelangelo Buonarroti. Sistine Chapel, Vatican Palace,
    Vatican State.

Printed and published in the U.S.A. by Pauline Books & Media,
50 Saint Pauls Avenue, Boston MA 02130-3491.

www.pauline.org

Pauline Books & Media is the publishing house of the Daughters of
St. Paul, an international congregation of women religious serving
the Church with the communications media.

3 4 5 6 7 8 9   06 05 04 03 02 01

The following abbreviations are used in the text
to indicate certain documents:

DH   *Dignitatis Humanae* (Declaration on Religious Freedom)

DV   *Dei Verbum* (Dogmatic Constitution on Divine Revelation)

GS   *Gaudium et Spes* (Pastoral Constitution on the Church in the Modern World)

LG   *Lumen Gentium* (Dogmatic Constitution on the Church)

NA   *Nostra Aetate* (Declaration on the Relation of the Church to Non-Christian Religions)

UR   *Unitatis Redintegratio* (Decree on Ecumenism)

DS   indicates citations from Denzinger-Schönmetzer

Contents

The Existence and Nature of God

The Blessed Trinity

God the Creator

Divine Providence

Foreword

"We believe in one God, the Father, the Almighty, maker of heaven and earth, of all that is, seen and unseen." Pope John Paul II's catechesis on the creed, given at his general audiences from 1985 to 1991, will be published in three volumes. Trinitarian in perspective, they will be about God, the Father, the Son and the Holy Spirit. Volume one limits itself to the first statement of the Nicene Creed mentioned above.

Why did the Pope decide to develop a catechesis on the creed? Proposals for an authorized catechism for the universal Church, the first since the Roman Catechism of 1566, were often made, but in vain. This proposal was heard during the Second Vatican Council. It was repeated in reaction to the Dutch catechism in 1966, and at the Synods of Bishops in 1974 and 1977. Aware of widespread concern about the divisions in the Church and about the state of catechetics, John Paul II published his *Catechesis in Our Time* in 1979. Was there any connection between the recommendation for the catechism by the Extraordinary Synod of Bishops in December, 1985 and his catechesis on the creed which began in January of the same year? This recommendation received the Pope's approval and

The Catechism of the Catholic Church was finally published in 1992. The three volumes of John Paul II's talks on the creed correspond to Part One of this catechism. In any event, Pope John Paul II devoted his weekly general audience talks from January 1985 until August 1986 to the first statement of the Nicene Creed.

What a privilege it is to "listen" to the Vicar of Christ on issues vital to human and Christian living. Faith comes alive and the idea of eternal life takes on new vibrancy, not as "immortality" but as the very life of God who is eternal. Baptized, we live with the knowing and loving proper to God—to the extent that children adopted into the divine family can.

John Paul II speaks not only with the authority of the Vicar of Christ but with the human authority of a profoundly intelligent man who has assimilated God's message. He can communicate it because he knows the human heart and contemporary consciousness.

Scholars will appreciate how completely our Pope has integrated Scripture, the famous councils, and Aristotelian-Thomistic insights with 20th century intellectual perspectives. However, other readers will not be put off by recondite concepts or professional jargon. They will be caught up by questions that minds and hearts have always asked. Pope John Paul II touches the heart with such questions and prisms God's answers through contemporary perspectives, obviously awed and delighted by God's revelation.

The four opening talks address catechists, their mission, the need of faith and adequate preparation for their sacred mission. Readers will appreciate the Pope's insights on pedagogical methods, on the primacy of faith, and the transmission of doctrine in the light of "the inseparable connection between Sacred Scripture, Tradition, and the Magisterium." But they will find illuminating and inspiring the explanation of "I believe."

Before he turns to the professed belief in God as Almighty

Father and Creator, the Pope develops "the genetic and organic link between our Christian 'I believe' and that particular initiative of God himself...called revelation." He covers the deposit of faith (Scripture and Tradition), inspiration, relation with other religions, the problem of unbelief, and atheism.

This first of six major divisions, "Revelation and Faith," prepares the audience for the second, "The Existence and Nature of God." Beginning with the profound innate human hunger for God, John Paul II schematizes the traditional proofs of God's existence. He then breathes life into them when he explains how God makes himself known as a personal God— the God of Abraham, Isaac, Jacob, Moses, the prophets, the God revealing himself definitively in Jesus Christ. Scripture reveals our God as eternal, spirit, immense and invisible, the almighty Father and God of the covenant—God who is Love.

The Christian knows God as the Blessed Trinity, Father, Son and Holy Spirit. In this third division John Paul II uncovers the treasures of Scripture and the Church's articulation of Trinitarian revelation. Readers may experience a sense of wonderment and mystery; the doctrine is familiar and the further unfolding of the mystery draws them on while a strange happiness rises in the heart. After all, isn't this what our eternity will be about—knowing and loving the Triune God?

Have you not asked yourself, "Where did I, we, things come from?" "Where are we going?" "What is the meaning of life?" "Are we here by chance, by destiny, or does it all go back to God?" "If to God, why is there so much evil and suffering?" To answer these questions, in the fourth division John Paul II turns to God the Creator. Our God, the Triune God, reveals himself as Creator and provident Father. John Paul II integrates Old and New Testaments, conciliar texts and the ordinary teaching of the Church with the insights of theologians and other Christian thinkers as he lays out what we believe as Christians.

Creation is for the glory of God, yes, but created things have their own legitimate autonomy. Only in the modern age would this distinction emerge. For the same reason the author considers other contemporary concerns: the equal dignity of men and women, their covenantal mission to subdue (not devastate) the universe, human rights based on being created in God's image.

The need and blessing of faith is brought sharply into focus in the next division, "Divine Providence." Lurking in our hearts are the crucial questions, "Is God with us?" "Does God care what is happening?" "Why so much suffering and evil?" "If God is ensuring the providential resolution of human development, are we free?" Because John Paul faces our questions and knows what it means to be "on the razor's edge between hope and despair," readers will share his conviction, "Never does the word of God assume such greatness and attraction as when man's greatest demands confront it." Because of his masterful yet modest confronting of these complex problems, readers will find acceptable the solutions he points to in the body of our faith. God indeed is with us in all his wisdom, bringing good out of evil. All things are to be restored in Christ Jesus our Lord.

Finally in the division, "The Angels," the Pope concludes the treatment of the first statement of the Nicene Creed: "Creator of all things, seen and unseen." He faces the challenge of materialists and rationalists who deny the possibility of angels. Even some modern Christians find talk about angels to be "far away" and "less vital." The Pope knows he must simply hand on the whole of God's revelation with integrity. Although truth about angels clearly is not the central content of the word of God (Jesus Christ is), still, "If one wishes to get rid of the angels, one must radically revise Sacred Scripture itself, and with it, the whole of salvation." He treats what the Church does teach about angels, about the struggle between Satan and Christ, and what will happen when Jesus Christ returns.

We are much indebted to the Daughters of St. Paul for undertaking this work and look forward to the promised volumes.

Joseph H. Casey, SJ
Boston College

CATECHESIS HANDS ON THE FULLNESS OF REVELATION

Every Catechist Must Be Faithful to the Integrity of Revealed Truth

We have recalled how catechesis is a work of the Church which spreads the Good News throughout the world and seeks to deepen its sacramental life through a better knowledge of the mystery of Christ.

Through catechesis, as through the overall work of evangelization, the Church is aware of responding to man's most essential questions, those which each one has already asked or will ask sooner or later in the course of life. Where does man come from? Why does he exist? What are his relationships with God and with the invisible world? How must he behave in order to achieve the goal of life? Why is he subject to suffering and death, and what is his hope?

To these problems catechesis brings God's response. It aims to give an understanding of a doctrine that is not simply the product of certain personal researches, but the truth communicated to us through divine revelation. Therefore, in communicating the truth of salvation, catechesis is concerned with making manifest the fundamental questions arising in man's heart. It shows how God has answered them in his revelation with a gift of truth and life that surpasses man's deepest expectations (cf. 1 Cor 2:6-9). Its role is to give certitude, based on the authority of revelation.

Integrity of content

Far from raising doubts or confusion through the problems it considers, catechesis enlightens the intellect and strengthens it with firm convictions. Certainly, with the answers it supplies, catechesis introduces the human soul more deeply into the mystery of revelation. But this mystery gives light to the mind even if during this earthly life it does not dispel all the shadows. We cannot understand everything, but what is understood is enough to point out the fundamental truths and the meaning of life.

Often, the formulas of catechisms, with a series of questions and answers, have expressed concretely and practically the fundamental structure of catechesis, which can be defined as the meeting between man's question and God's response. It is true that man's question is inspired and already enlightened by divine grace and that God's response is formulated in the limitations and imperfections of human language. But it is truly a matter of questions, typical of man—questions to which catechesis brings divine light.

This means that, though being attentive to the human side of the problem, catechesis is not limited to reflections of a human character nor to investigations of a philosophical, psychological or sociological order, nor to the effort merely to preface revelation. It is aware of having to expound revealed truth and have it understood, a truth which it does not have the power to reduce or attenuate. It seeks to adapt its teaching to the capacity of those who receive it. But it does not claim the right to veil or suppress a part of the truth which God himself has willed to communicate to man.

A problem of faith

It pays to recall here what I stressed in the Apostolic Exhortation *Catechesi Tradendae* concerning the integrity of the content of catechesis: "In order that the sacrificial offering of his or her faith should be perfect, the person who becomes a disciple of Christ has the right to receive the 'word of faith' not in mutilated, falsified or diminished form, but whole and entire, in all its rigor and vigor. Unfaithfulness to the integrity of the message on some point means a dangerous weakening of catechesis and putting at risk the results that Christ and the ecclesial community have a right to expect from it" (n. 30). It can be clearly seen that the message may be difficult to understand and accept. Many ideas contrary to evangelical doctrine are circulating in the world. Some maintain an attitude of opposition to everything that is taught in the name of the Church. In the face of such resistance, one who is dedicated to catechesis could be tempted to retreat, not to expound the Christian message in all its truth and all its demands on life, and to limit himself to some more admissible points. It is then that he must remember that he has been charged with a teaching that surpasses him. He must strive to propose it as he received it. Above all, he must be aware that in his work of catechesis he has at his disposal a divine power that enables him to transmit his faith, and that in the heart of his listeners the Holy Spirit makes the word penetrate to the extent that it is faithful to the truth it has to express.

Role of catechesis

The problem of catechesis is a problem of faith. At the beginning of the Church, who would have thought that a small number of Jesus' disciples would be able to undertake the work of evangelizing and catechizing all mankind? But that is precisely what happened. From the very beginning, the Christian message succeeded in penetrating the mentality of a great number of people. What grace accomplished at that time, and ever afterward throughout the centuries, it continues to accomplish even today.

Catechesis therefore counts on the power of grace to transmit to children and to adults the integral gift of the faith. Every catechist has the duty to communicate the whole Christian message and receives from Christ himself the ability to carry out this mission fully.

General audience of January 9, 1985

The Spirit of Faith Is Essential to Every Christian Catechesis

Catechesis poses some problems of pedagogy. From the Gospel texts we know that even Jesus had to face them. In his preaching to the crowds he used parables to communicate his teaching in a way that suited the intelligence of his listeners. In teaching his disciples he proceeded gradually, taking into account the difficulty they had in understanding. So it was only in the second part of his public life that he expressly announced his sorrowful way and only at the end did he openly declare his identity not only as the Messiah, but as the "Son of God." We note also that, in his most detailed dialogues, he communicated his revelation by answering the questions of his listeners and using language their mentality easily understood. At times, he himself asked questions and posed problems.

Christ has shown us the necessity for catechesis to have a multiform adaptation according to the groups and persons to whom it is given. He has also pointed out to us the nature and the limits of this adaptation. He offered his listeners the whole doctrine he had been sent to teach. In the face of the resistance of those who heard him, he expounded his message with all the demands of faith that it involves. We recall his discourse on the Eucharist on the occasion of the miracle of the multiplication of the loaves. Despite objections and defections, Jesus maintained his doctrine and asked his disciples to accept it (cf. Jn 6:60-69). In transmitting the entirety of his message to his listeners, he counted on the illuminating action of the Holy Spirit, who would later make them understand what they couldn't yet grasp (cf. Jn 14:26; 16:13). Therefore even for us the adaptation of catechesis must not mean the reduction or mutilation of the content of revealed doctrine, but rather the effort to have it accepted with an adherence of faith, under the light and with the power of the Holy Spirit.

Problem of adaptation

Following the example of her only teacher, who is Jesus, the Church in her catechesis has tried to adapt to those to whom she wanted to communicate the light of the Gospel. This effort to adapt is especially evident in recent times, which have been marked by progressive catechetical specialization. In fact, institutes for catechetical training have multiplied, methods of catechesis have been systematically studied, and more effective ways of teaching religion have been proposed. It is to be hoped that this effort will continue and develop further. The problems of adaptation are multiple and difficult. They vary according to place and time, and they will not cease to be posed in the future.

It must be noted that these problems today are linked with the problems of the development of new means of social communication. Alongside the simple and traditional forms of catechesis there is room for a catechetical teaching which utilizes the most modern ways of circulation. The Church cannot but encourage attempts to devise new forms of transmitting the Gospel truth. All the fine initiatives in this field must be viewed favorably. We must congratulate those who have pioneered in this area.

Utilizing new means of teaching

Therefore catechesis is not meant to fossilize in what has been done in the past. As I acknowledged in the Exhortation *Catechesi Tradendae,* catechesis "needs to be continually renewed by a certain broadening of its concept, by the revision of its methods, by the search for suitable language, and by the utilization of new means of transmitting the message" *(CT* 17). We can say that catechesis, like the Church herself, is leaning toward a future better than the past. This future requires an active collaboration of all concerned and a watchful opening to the advances of human society.

The need for renewal requires a constant effort to reflect on the results that have been achieved. We cannot start from the principle that everything that is new is good and fruitful. The important thing is to verify by experience the effectiveness of the way that has been followed. In recent times considerable efforts have been made to develop catechetical methods. But we cannot ignore the fact that in various places there have been frequent complaints about the gaps and the disappointing results of certain new methods. The 1977 Synod did not fail to recognize "the limitations and deficiencies that are in contrast with an undeniable advance in the vitality of catechetical activity and promising initiatives" *(CT* 17). These deficiencies must give rise to a careful review of the means that are employed and the doctrine that is transmitted.

Organic and systematic

The Synod particularly stressed the necessity for an organic and systematic teaching, not an improvised one. If it is true that "routine leads to stagnation, lethargy and eventual paralysis," we must acknowledge that "improvisation begets confusion on the part of those being given catechesis and when these are children, on the part of their parents; it also begets all kinds of deviations, and the fracturing and eventually the complete destruction of unity" *(CT* 17).

In addition to being systematic, with a program and precise goal, three other characteristics of catechetical teaching were recalled at the end of the Synod's discussion. It must "deal with essentials, without any claims to tackle all disputed questions or to transform itself into theological research or scientific exegesis; it must nevertheless be sufficiently complete, not stopping short at the initial proclamation of the Christian mystery such as we have in the *kerygma*; it must be an integral Christian initiation, open to all the other factors of Christian life" *(CT* 21).

The intention to give a complete teaching arises spontaneously from an attitude of faith and love which is loyal to all of revelation and wishes to communicate it. The spirit of faith is essential to every Christian catechesis. The search for and setting up of more adapted methods would not suffice if these were not inspired by this spirit of faith. The scientific aspects of pedagogy could not supply for a lack of faith. In reality, it is faith that pushes the catechist to seek the best method for explaining and transmitting doctrine. It is faith that forms the soul of catechesis and inspires every effort at pedagogy in religious teaching.

Because catechesis is one of the ways to transmit revelation in the Church, it must be regulated in its contents and in its methods by the structure proper to such transmission. This includes the inseparable connection between Sacred Scripture, Tradition and the Magisterium (cf. *DV* 10). In our future instructions we will have occasion to return to this structure.

General audience of January 16, 1985

Adequate Doctrinal Preparation
Is Fundamental for Catechists

The obligation of catechesis implies for the Church an intense work of formation of catechists. Again, Christ's example enlightens us. During his ministry, Jesus devoted himself above all to forming those who were to spread his message throughout the whole world. He dedicated much time to preaching to the crowds, but he reserved more time to the formation of disciples. He had them live in his company in order to inculcate in them the truths of his message. He did this not only by his words, but by his example and his daily contacts. He revealed to his disciples the secrets of his kingdom. He had them enter the mystery of God, whose revelation he himself brought. He stirred up faith in them and gradually developed it with an ever more complete instruction. When he gave them the mission to teach all nations, he was able to entrust this task to them because he had gifted them with the doctrine they were to spread. But the full understanding of that doctrine would come to them from the Holy Spirit, who would give them the divine power of the apostolate.

Receiving this lesson from the master, the Church attaches great importance to the formation of those who have the duty of teaching revealed truth. First among these are the pastors, who by virtue of the priesthood have received the mission to proclaim the Good News in the name of Christ. Then there are all the others who share in the Church's teaching mission, especially catechists, whether full-time or as volunteers. The formation of catechists is an essential element in the common commitment to the development and the vitality of the Church. It is necessary everywhere. Its value is even more significant in certain countries where catechists carry out an important role in Christian communities that lack a sufficient number of priests. In certain places it could be said that the Church is alive thanks to the work of catechists.

The formation of catechists is often undertaken by specialized institutes. It is to be hoped that catechists will be formed more and more in these institutes where they receive both an indispensable doctrinal instruction and training in pedagogical methods.

Doctrinal formation is a fundamental necessity, seeing that catechesis cannot be limited to teaching a minimum of truths that are learned and repeated by rote. If catechists have the mission to inculcate in their listeners the whole Christian doctrine, they must first have learned it well themselves. They must not merely witness to their faith, they must communicate its content. The teaching received in preparation for Baptism, Confirmation or Communion is often insufficient for an exact and profound knowledge of the faith to be transmitted. A more systematic study is indispensable. At times, circumstances have forced those responsible for catechesis to have recourse to the cooperation of people of good will, but who lack an adequate preparation. Such solutions are generally wanting. To assure the future of a solid catechesis it is necessary to entrust this work to catechists who through study have acquired doctrinal competence.

This doctrinal formation is even more necessary in so far as catechists live in a world in which ideas and theories of all kinds abound. These are often incompatible with the Christian message. Catechists must be able to react to what they see and hear, discerning what can be accepted from what must be rejected. If they have assimilated the Christian doctrine and have understood its meaning, they will be able to teach it with fidelity, even maintaining an open spirit.

Doctrinal formation requires an effort of the intellect for learning revealed doctrine, yet it must at the same time deepen the faith. The essential goal of catechesis is the communication of the faith, and this must guide the study of doctrine. A study that would question the faith or that would introduce doubts about revealed truth would not serve catechesis. The development of doctrinal knowledge must coincide with a development of faith. For this reason, institutes of catechetical formation must be considered above all as schools of faith.

The responsibility of the teachers in these institutes is even greater because their teaching will have multiple repercussions through the catechists that they are training. It is the responsibility of the faith that bears its own witness and manifests its ardor in seeking the authentic meaning of all that is given by revelation.

In addition, institutes for catechetical formation have the obligation to develop a missionary spirit in their students. Catechesis cannot be considered a mere professional activity, since it exists in order to spread Christ's message in the world. For this reason it is at the same time a vocation and a mission. It is a vocation, because there is a call from Christ for those who want to devote themselves to this task. It is a mission, because from the very beginning catechesis was established in the Church in order to carry out the command of the Risen Savior: "Go and make disciples of all the nations" (Mt 28:19).

The teaching of Christian doctrine aims not merely at knowledge of truth, but at the spread of faith. It stirs up an allegiance to Christ in the intellect and in the heart and enlarges the Christian community. It must therefore be undertaken as a mission of the Church and a mission for the Church. Catechesis contributes to building up the Mystical Body of Christ, to its growth in faith and charity.

This missionary spirit is expected not only on the part of those catechists who carry out their activity in the so-called mission countries, but also of all the Church's catechists, wherever they are teaching. The missionary spirit inspires catechists to dedicate all their strength and talents to teaching. This makes them more aware of the importance of their work and enables them to face all difficulties with greater confidence in the grace that sustains them.

We therefore hope that progress in the formation of catechists will foster everywhere the development of the Church and the Christian life on the basis of that sincere, convinced and consistent faith to which catechesis is directed.

General audience of March 6, 1985

What Does It Mean to Believe?

The universally known professions of the Christian faith form the first and fundamental reference point for the present catechesis. They are also called "symbols of faith." The Greek word *symbolon* signified the half of an object that had been broken (for example, half of a seal) and which was offered as a sign of recognition. The separated parts were put together in order to prove the bearer's identity. Further meanings of "symbol" come from such things as proofs of identity, letters of credence and also a treaty or contract of which the *symbolon* was the proof. The passage from this meaning to that of a collection or summary of reported and documented things was natural enough. In our case, "symbols" signify the collection of the principal truths of faith—what the Church believes. Systematic catechesis contains instructions on what the Church believes, that is, on the contents of the Christian faith. The "symbols of faith" are the first and fundamental reference point for catechesis.

Symbol of faith

Among the various ancient "symbols of faith" the most authoritative is the Apostles' Creed, the oldest in origin and commonly recited in the "prayers of the Christian." It contains the principal truths of the faith transmitted by the apostles of Jesus Christ. Another ancient and famous symbol is the Nicene-Constantinopolitan Creed, which contains the same truths of the apostolic faith authoritatively explained in the first two ecumenical councils of the universal Church: Nicaea (325) and Constantinople (381). The custom of "symbols of faith" being proclaimed as a result of councils of the Church was resumed even in our century. After the Second Vatican Council, Pope Paul VI proclaimed the profession of faith known as the *Credo of the People of God* (1968). It contains the synthesis of the truths of the Church's faith. It gives special consideration to those teachings which the last Council had expressed, or to those points about which some doubts had appeared in recent years.

The symbols of faith are the principal reference point for the present catechesis. However, they go back to the synthesis of the "deposit of the Word of God," made up of Sacred Scripture and apostolic Tradition, and are only a concise summary of it. Through the professions of faith, therefore, we too propose to go back to that unchangeable "deposit" with the guidance of the interpretation which the Church, assisted by the Holy Spirit, has given it throughout the centuries.

Meaning of "I believe"

Each one of the above-mentioned "symbols" begins with the words "I believe." Each one of them serves not only as an instruction but also as a profession. The contents of this profession are the truths of the Christian faith. All of them are rooted in these first words, "I believe." In this first catechesis, we wish to concentrate precisely on this expression, "I believe."

The expression is used in daily language, even apart from all religious content, especially any Christian content. "I believe you" means that I trust you, and I am convinced that you are telling the truth. "I believe in what you are saying" means that I am convinced that the content of your words corresponds to objective reality.

In this common use of the word "believe," some essential elements are given prominence. "To believe" means to accept and to acknowledge as true and corresponding to reality the content of what is said, that is, the content of the words of another person (or even of more persons) by reason of his (or their) credibility. This credibility determines in a given case the particular authority of the person—the authority of truth.

So then by saying "I believe," we express at the same time a double reference—to the person and to the truth; to the truth in consideration of the person who enjoys special claims to credibility.

Biblical meaning

The words "I believe" appear often in the pages of the Gospel and of all Sacred Scripture. It would be very useful to compare and analyze all the points of the Old and the New Testaments that enable us to grasp the biblical meaning of "to believe." Along with "to believe" we also find the noun "faith" as one of the central expressions of the whole Bible. We find even a certain type of "definition" of faith as, for example, "Faith is confident assurance concerning what we hope for, and conviction about things we do not see" (*fides est sperandarum substantia rerum et argumentum non apparentium*) (Heb 11:1).

These biblical data have been studied, explained, and developed by the Fathers and by theologians over the span of the two thousand years of Christianity. This is attested to by the enormous exegetical and dogmatic literature we have at our disposal. As in the "symbols," so also in all of theology, "to believe"—"faith"—is a fundamental category. It is also the starting point for catechesis, as the first act by which one responds to God's revelation.

In this meeting we will limit ourselves to just one source, which, however, includes all the others. It is the Constitution *Dei Verbum* of the Second Vatican Council. In it we read as follows:

"In his goodness and wisdom, God chose to reveal himself and to make known to us the hidden purpose of his will (cf. Eph 1:9) by which through Christ, the Word made flesh, man has access to the Father in the Holy Spirit and comes to share in the divine nature (cf. Eph 2:18; 2 Pet 1:4)..." *(DV 2)*.

"'The obedience of faith' (Rom 16:26; cf. 1:5; 2 Cor 10:5-6) is to be given to God who reveals, an obedience by which man commits his whole self freely to God, offering 'the full submission of intellect and will to God who reveals' (Vatican I), and freely assenting to the truth revealed by him" *(DV 5)*.

These words of the conciliar document contain the answer to the question, "What does it mean to 'believe?'" The explanation is concise, but it contains a great wealth of content. Consequently we will have to penetrate more fully into this explanation of the Council, which has an importance equal to a so-called technical definition.

One thing is obvious. There is a genetic and organic link between our Christian "I believe" and that particular initiative of God himself which is called revelation.

Therefore catechesis on the creed (faith), must be carried out together with catechesis on divine revelation. Logically and historically revelation comes before faith. Faith is conditioned by revelation. It is man's response to divine revelation.

Henceforth we say that this response is possible and must be given, because God is credible. No one is as credible as he. No one has the authority of truth as he does. In no other case as in faith in God is there verified the conceptual and semantic value of the words that are so common in human language—"I believe," "I believe you."

General audience of March 13, 1985

REVELATION AND FAITH

One Can Know God By
the Natural Light of Human Reason

In our last catechesis, we said that faith is conditioned by revelation and that revelation comes before faith. We therefore will have to try to clarify the notion and verify the reality of revelation (following the Constitution *Dei Verbum* of the Second Vatican Council). However, before this, we wish to concentrate on the subject of faith, that is, on the person who says "I believe," thus responding to God who "in his goodness and wisdom" has willed to "reveal himself to man."

Even before a person utters "I believe," he already has some concept of God that he has acquired by the effort of his intellect. Treating of divine revelation, the Constitution *Dei Verbum* recalls this fact in the following words: "As a sacred Synod has affirmed, 'God, the beginning and end of all things, can be known with certainty from created reality by the light of human reason' (cf. Rom 1:20)" *(DV* 6).

Vatican II is here recalling the doctrine fully presented by the preceding Council, Vatican I. It is in keeping with the whole doctrinal tradition of the Church, which is rooted in Sacred Scripture, in both the Old and the New Testaments.

Recognized through what he has made

A classic text on the subject of the possibility of knowing God—his existence, first of all—from created things is found in St. Paul's Letter to the Romans: "Whatever can be known about God is clear to them: he himself made it so. Since the creation of the world, invisible realities, God's eternal power and divinity, have become visible, recognized through the things he has made. Therefore they are inexcusable" (Rom 1:19-21). The Apostle has in mind here people who "in this perversity of theirs hinder the truth" (Rom 1:18). Sin draws them away from giving glory due to God, whom every person is able to know. He is able to know God's existence and even, to a certain extent, his essence, his perfections and his attributes. The invisible God becomes in a certain way "recognized through the things he has made."

In the Old Testament, the Book of Wisdom proclaims the same doctrine as the Apostle. It speaks about the possibility of arriving at a knowledge of the existence of God from created things. This teaching is found in a somewhat lengthy passage which we would do well to read in its entirety:

"For all those were by nature foolish who were in ignorance of God, and who from the good things seen did not succeed in knowing him who is, and from studying the works did not discern the artisan.

"But either fire, or wind, or the swift air, or the circuit of the stars, or the mighty water, or the luminaries of heaven, the governors of the world, they considered gods. Now if out of joy in their beauty they thought them gods, let them know how far more excellent is the Lord than these; for the original source of beauty fashioned them.

"Or if they were struck by their might and energy, let them from these things realize how much more powerful is he who made them.

"For from the greatness and the beauty of created things their original author, by analogy, is seen.

"But yet, for these the blame is less; for they indeed have gone astray perhaps, though they seek God and wish to find him.

"For they search busily among his works, but are distracted by what they see, because the things seen are fair. But again, not even these are pardonable. For if they so far succeeded in their knowledge that they could speculate about the world, how did they not more quickly find its Lord?" (Wis 13:1-9).

No explanation without First Principle

We find the main thought of this passage also in St. Paul's Letter to the Romans (1:18-21). God can be known through creation—the visible world constitutes for the human intellect the basis for affirming the existence of the invisible Creator. The passage from the Book of Wisdom is fuller. The inspired author argues with the paganism of his time, which attributed divine glory to some creatures. At the same time, he offers us some elements for reflection and judgment that can be valid for every era, including our own. He speaks of the enormous effort expended to learn about the visible universe. He speaks also of those who "seek God and wish to find him." He asks why human wisdom, which enables man to "speculate about the world," does not come to know its Lord. The author of the Book of Wisdom—as St. Paul did—sees some blame in this. But we will have to return to this theme separately.

For now, let us too ask: how is it possible that the immense progress in the knowledge of the universe (the macrocosm and the microcosm), its laws and its happenings, its structures and its energies, does not lead everyone to recognize the First Principle, without whom the world cannot be explained? We will have to examine the difficulties which many people today stumble into. Yet we joyfully note that even today, many true scientists find precisely in scientific knowledge a stimulus to believe, or at least to bow before the mystery.

Man's intellect

Following Tradition, which has its roots in Sacred Scripture of the Old and New Testaments, the Church, in the nineteenth century during the First Vatican Council, recalled and confirmed the doctrine on the possibility with which the human intellect is endowed to know God through creation. In our century, the Second Vatican Council recalled this doctrine anew in the context of the Constitution on Divine Revelation *(Dei Verbum)*. This takes on great importance.

Divine revelation is indeed at the basis of faith, of man's "I believe." At the same time, the passages of Sacred Scripture in which this revelation is found, teach us that man is capable of knowing God by reason alone. He is capable of a certain "knowledge" about God, even though it is indirect and not immediate. Therefore, alongside the "I believe" we find a certain "I know." This "I know" concerns the existence of God and even, to a certain extent, his essence. This intellectual knowledge of God is systematically treated by a science called "natural theology," which is of a philosophical nature and springs from metaphysics, that is, the philosophy of being. It focuses on the knowledge of God as the First Cause, and also as the Last End of the universe.

These questions, as well as the vast philosophical discussion connected with them, cannot be examined within the limits of a brief instruction on the truths of faith. Neither do we intend to take up here in a detailed way those "ways" that guide the human mind in the search for God (the *"Quinque viae"* [five ways] of St. Thomas Aquinas). For this catechesis of ours, it is sufficient to keep in mind that the sources of Christianity speak of the possibility of a rational knowledge of God. Therefore, according to the Church, all our thinking about God, based on faith, also has a "rational" and "intellective" character. Even atheism lies within the sphere of a certain reference to the concept of God. If it denies the existence of God, it must also know whose existence it is denying.

It is clear that knowledge through faith differs from purely rational knowledge. Nevertheless God would not have been able to reveal himself to the human race if it were not already naturally capable of knowing something true about God. Therefore, alongside and in addition to an "I know," which is proper to man's intellect, there is an "I believe," proper to the Christian. With faith the believer has access, even if obscurely, to the mystery of the intimate life of God who reveals himself.

General audience of March 20, 1985

God Who Reveals Himself
Is the Source of Our Faith

Our starting point in the catechesis on God who reveals himself is still the text of the Second Vatican Council: "In his goodness and wisdom, God chose to reveal himself and to make known to us the hidden purpose of his will (cf. Eph 1:9) by which through Christ, the Word made flesh, man might in the Holy Spirit have access to the Father and come to share in the divine nature (cf. Eph 2:18; 2 Pet 1:4). Through this revelation, therefore, the invisible God (cf. Col 1:15; 1 Tim 1:17) out of the abundance of his love speaks to men as friends (cf. Ex 33:11; Jn 15:14-15) and lives among them (cf. Bar 3:38), so that he may invite and take them into fellowship with himself" *(DV 2)*.

But we have already considered the possibility of knowing God through the capacity of human reason alone. According to the constant teaching of the Church, expressed especially in the First Vatican Council (Dogmatic Constitution *Dei Filius* 2) and taken up again in the Second Vatican Council (Dogmatic Constitution *Dei Verbum* 6), human reason has this capacity and possibility: "God, the beginning and end of all things [it says] can be known with certainty from created reality by the light of human reason (cf. Rom 1:20)." However, divine revelation is necessary "that those religious truths, which are by their nature accessible to human reason can be known by all men with ease, with solid certitude, and with no trace of error, even in the present state of the human race."

This knowledge of God through reason, which reaches him "through created things," is in keeping with man's rational nature. It is in keeping also with the original plan of God, who by endowing man with this nature intends that man be able to know him. "God, who through the Word creates all things (cf. Jn 1:3) and keeps them in existence, gives men an enduring witness to himself in created realities (cf. Rom. 1:19-20)" *(DV* 3). This witness is given as a gift and at the same time is left as an object for study on the part of human reason. Through the careful and persevering reading of the witness of created things, human reason is directed toward God and approaches him. This is in a certain sense the "ascending" way. Using the steps of creation, man rises toward God by reading the witness of the being, the truth, the goodness and the beauty that creatures have in themselves.

The way of "knowing"

This way of knowledge, which in a certain sense has its origin in man and in his mind, enables the creature to ascend to the Creator. We can call it the way of "knowing." There is a second way, the way of "faith," which has its origin exclusively in God. These two ways differ from each other, but they meet in man himself and in a certain way mutually complete and help each other.

Unlike knowledge through reason, which begins in "creatures" and which only indirectly leads to God, in the knowledge that comes through faith we draw upon revelation, in which God "makes himself known" directly. God reveals himself. He allows himself to be known, manifesting "the hidden purpose of his will" (Eph 1:9). God's will is that man, by means of Christ, the Word made man, could have access to the Father in the Spirit and be made a sharer in the divine nature. God therefore reveals "himself" to man, at the same time revealing his salvific plan with regard to man. God's mysterious saving plan cannot be known by human reason alone. Even the most clever reading of the witness of God in created things is incapable of revealing to the human mind these supernatural horizons. It does not open up "the way of heavenly salvation" (as the Constitution *Dei Verbum* 3, expresses it), a way that is closely united to "the gift that God makes of himself" to man. In revealing himself, God himself "invites and takes man into fellowship with himself" (cf. *DV* 2).

Accepting as true what God has revealed

Only by keeping these things before our eyes can we understand what faith truly is, what the content of the expression "I believe" is.

If it is precise to say that faith consists in accepting as true what God has revealed, the Second Vatican Council has aptly stressed that it is also a response of the whole person, highlighting its "existential" and "personalistic" dimension. If in fact God "reveals himself" and manifests the saving "hidden purpose of his will," it is right to show to God who reveals himself such an "obedience of faith" through which the whole person freely abandons himself to God by showing him "the full submission of intellect and will" (Vatican I), and "freely assenting to the truth revealed by him" *(DV* 5).

In knowing by faith, man accepts the whole supernatural and salvific content of revelation as true. But at the same time, this fact introduces him into a profound personal relationship with God who reveals himself. If the very content of revelation is the saving "self-communication" of God, then the response of faith is correct to the degree that man—accepting that salvific content as the truth—at the same time "entrusts his whole self to God." Only a complete "abandonment to God" on man's part constitutes an adequate response.

General audience of March 27, 1985

Jesus Is the Definitive Fulfillment of the Revelation of God

Faith—that which is contained in the expression "I believe"—is essentially related to revelation. The response to the fact that God reveals "himself" to man—and at the same time discloses to him the mystery of the eternal will to save man through "sharing the divine nature"—is "abandonment to God" on the part of man, which expresses the "obedience of faith." Faith is the obedience of reason and will to God who reveals. This obedience consists above all in accepting "as the truth" what God reveals. Man remains in harmony with his natural reason in this acceptance of the content of revelation. But through faith, man abandons his whole self to this God who reveals himself to him—and then, while he receives the gift "from on high," he responds to God with the gift of his humanity. Thus, with the obedience of reason and will to God who reveals, a new way of existing in relationship with God begins for the whole human person.

Revelation—and consequently also faith—"goes beyond" man because it opens to him supernatural perspectives. But in these perspectives lies the most profound fulfillment of the aspirations and desires that are rooted in man's spiritual nature—truth, good, love, joy, peace. St. Augustine expressed this reality in the famous phrase: "Our hearts are restless until they rest in you" (St. Augustine, *Confessions,* I, 1). St. Thomas devotes the first questions of the second part of the *Summa Theologica* to demonstrating, as though developing St. Augustine's thought, that the full realization of human perfection, and therefore man's destiny is found only in the vision and in the love of God. For this reason divine revelation meets, in faith, with the human spirit's transcendent capacity for opening to the Word of God.

God communicates himself gradually

The conciliar Constitution *Dei Verbum* notes that this "economy of revelation" has developed from the very beginning of the history of mankind. It "is realized by deeds and words having an inner unity: the deeds wrought by God in the history of salvation manifest and confirm the teaching and realities signified by the words, while the words proclaim the deeds and clarify the mystery contained in them" *(DV* 2). We can say that economy of revelation contains a particular "divine pedagogy." God gradually "communicates himself" to man, introducing him step by step to God's supernatural "self-revelation," right to the summit which is Jesus Christ.

At the same time, the entire economy of revelation is realized as the history of salvation. This process permeates human history from the very beginning. "God, who through the Word creates all things (cf. Jn 1:3) and keeps them in existence, gives men an enduring witness to himself in created realities (cf. Rom 1:19-20). Planning to make known the way of heavenly salvation, he went further and from the start manifested himself to our first parents" *(DV* 3).

Just as from the start the "witness in created realities" speaks to man, drawing his mind toward the invisible Creator, so also from the start there perdures in human history God's self-revelation, which requires a proper response in man's "I believe." This revelation was not interrupted by the sin of our first parents. God, in fact, "after their fall, his promise of redemption aroused in them the hope of being saved (cf. Gen 3:15), and from that time on he ceaselessly kept the human race in his care, to give eternal life to those who perseveringly do good in search of salvation (cf. Rom 2:6-7). Then, at the time he had appointed, he called Abraham in order to make of him a great nation (cf. Gen 12:2). Through the patriarchs, and after them through Moses and the prophets, he taught this nation to acknowledge himself as the one living and true God, provident Father and just judge, and to wait for the Savior promised by him. In this manner he prepared the way for the Gospel down through the centuries" *(DV* 3).

Faith as man's response to the word of divine revelation entered the definitive phase with the coming of Christ, when "in this, the final age," God "has spoken to us through his Son" (Heb 1:1-2).

"Jesus Christ, therefore, the Word made flesh, was sent as 'a man to men.' He 'speaks the words of God' (Jn 3:34), and completes the work of salvation which his Father gave him to do (cf. Jn 5:36; 17:4). To see Jesus is to see his Father (Jn 14:9). For this reason Jesus perfected revelation by fulfilling it through his whole work of making himself present and manifesting himself—through his words and deeds, his signs and wonders, but especially through his death and glorious resurrection from the dead and final sending of the Spirit of truth. Moreover, he confirmed with divine testimony what revelation proclaimed—that God is with us to free us from the darkness of sin and death, and to raise us up to life eternal" *(DV* 4).

In the Christian sense, "to believe" means to accept God's definitive self-revelation in Jesus Christ by responding to it with an "abandonment to God," of which Christ himself is the foundation, the living example and the saving mediator.

Such a faith includes the acceptance of the entire "Christian economy" of salvation as a new and definitive covenant which "will never pass away." As the Council says: "We now await no further new public revelation before the glorious manifestation of our Lord Jesus Christ" *(DV 4)*.

So the Council, which in the Constitution *Dei Verbum* concisely but completely presents to us the whole "pedagogy" of divine revelation, teaches us at the same time what faith is. It teaches what it means "to believe," and particularly "to believe as Christians," as though in answer to the request of Jesus himself: "Have faith in God and faith in me" (Jn 14:1).

General audience of April 3, 1985

The Holy Spirit Constantly Perfects Our Faith So That Revelation May Be Better Understood

We have said many times during these reflections that faith is a particular response on the part of man to the word of God who reveals himself until the definitive revelation in Jesus Christ. Without doubt, this response has a cognitive character. It gives man the possibility of receiving this knowledge (self-knowledge) which God "shares" with him.

The acceptance of this knowledge of God, which in the present life is always partial, provisional and imperfect, gives man the possibility of already participating in the definitive and total truth which will be revealed to him one day in the immediate vision of God. "Abandoning himself completely to God" in response to his self-revelation, man participates in this truth. From such participation there begins a new supernatural life which Jesus calls "eternal life" (Jn 17:3) and which the Letter to the Hebrews defines as "life by faith": "my righteous one shall live by faith" (Heb 10:38).

Originality of faith

If then we wish to deepen our understanding of what faith is, and what the expression "to believe" means, the first thing that strikes us is the originality of faith, in comparison with the rational knowledge of God which starts from "created things."

The originality of faith consists, first of all, in its supernatural character. By faith, man gives his response to "God's self-revelation" and accepts the divine plan of salvation which consists in participation in the nature and intimate life of God himself. Such a response should lead man beyond everything that the human being himself attains by the faculties and the powers of his own nature, both as regards knowledge and will. It is a question of the knowledge of an infinite truth and of the transcendent fulfillment of aspirations to the good and to happiness which are rooted in the will and the heart. It is a matter of "eternal life."

"Through divine revelation," we read in the Constitution *Dei Verbum,* "God chose to show forth and communicate himself and the eternal decisions of his will regarding the salvation of men. That is to say, he chose 'to share with them those divine treasures which totally transcend the understanding of the human mind'" (n. 6). The Constitution is here quoting the words of the First Vatican Council (Dogmatic Constitution *Dei Filius,* n. 12), which underline the supernatural character of faith.

Thus the human response to God's self-revelation, and in particular to his definitive self-revelation in Jesus Christ, is formed interiorly under the enlightening power of God himself. God works in the depths of man's spiritual faculties, and in a certain way, in the whole ensemble of his energies and dispositions. That divine power is called grace, in particular, the grace of faith.

Work of the Spirit

We read again in the same Constitution of the Second Vatican Council: "To make this act of faith, the grace of God and the interior help of the Holy Spirit must precede and assist, moving the heart and turning it to God, opening the eyes of the mind and giving 'joy and ease to everyone in assenting to the truth and believing it' [the words of the Second Council of Orange repeated by the First Vatican Council]. To bring about an ever deeper understanding of revelation the same Holy Spirit constantly brings faith to completion by his gifts" *(DV* 5).

The Constitution *Dei Verbum* speaks succinctly on the subject of the grace of faith. However, this synthetic formulation is complete and reflects the teaching of Jesus himself who said: "No one can come to me unless the Father who sent me draws him" (Jn 6:44). The grace of faith is precisely such an "attraction" exercised by God in regard to man's interior essence, and indirectly in regard to the whole of human subjectivity. It enables man to respond fully to God's "self-revelation" in Jesus Christ, by abandoning himself to God. That grace precedes the act of faith. It stirs up, supports and guides it. Through it, man becomes capable first of all of "believing in God," and in fact believes. Thus prevenient and cooperating grace establishes an interpersonal, supernatural "communion" which is the living structural framework of faith. Through it, man who believes in God, participates in "eternal life": "He knows the Father and him whom he has sent, Jesus Christ" (cf. Jn 17:3) and through charity enters into a relationship of friendship with them (cf. Jn 14:23; 15:15).

Source of supernatural illumination

This grace is the source of the supernatural illumination which "opens the eyes of the mind." The grace of faith particularly embraces the cognitive sphere of the human person and concentrates on it. From this follows the acceptance of the entire content of divine revelation. This revelation contains the mysteries of God and the elements of the plan of human salvation. But at the same time man's cognitive faculty, under the action of the grace of faith, tends to an ever deeper understanding of the contents revealed. This understanding is projected to the total truth promised by Jesus (cf. Jn 16:13), toward "eternal life." This effort of growing understanding finds support in the gifts of the Holy Spirit, especially in those which perfect the supernatural knowledge of faith—knowledge, understanding, wisdom....

From this brief sketch the originality of faith is presented as a supernatural life. Through it, God's "self-revelation" is rooted in the ground of human intelligence, becoming the source of supernatural light. Through it, man participates, in a human measure, but at a level of divine communion, in that knowledge by which God eternally knows himself and every other reality in himself.

General audience of April 10, 1985

Through Faith Man Accepts in a Free and Convincing Manner the Truths Contained in God's Revelation

The originality of faith consists in the essentially supernatural character of knowledge which it derives from God's grace and from the gifts of the Holy Spirit. It must likewise be said that faith possesses its own authentically human originality. We find in it all the characteristics of rational and reasonable conviction in regard to the truth contained in divine revelation. Such conviction, or certainty, corresponds perfectly to the dignity of the person as a rational and free being.

Among the documents of the Second Vatican Council, the *Declaration on Religious Liberty* throws light on this problem. It begins with the words *Dignitatis Humanae*, and we read there among other things:

"It is one of the major tenets of Catholic doctrine that man's response to God in faith must be free: no one therefore is to be forced to embrace the Christian faith against his own will. This doctrine is contained in the word of God and it was constantly proclaimed by the Fathers of the Church. The act of faith is of its very nature a free act. Man, redeemed by Christ the Savior and through Christ Jesus called to be God's adopted son, cannot give his adherence to God revealing himself unless, under the drawing of the Father, he offers to God the reasonable and free submission of faith. It is therefore completely in accord with the nature of faith that in matters religious every manner of coercion on the part of men should be excluded" *(DH* 10).

"God calls men to serve him in spirit and in truth, hence they are bound in conscience but they stand under no compulsion. God has regard for the dignity of the human person whom he himself created and man is to be guided by his own judgment and he is to enjoy freedom. This truth appears at its height in Christ Jesus" *(DH* 11).

Christ bore witness to the truth

Here the conciliar document indicates in what way Christ sought to "stir up and strengthen the faith in the hearers" by excluding all coercion. He bore definitive witness to the truth of his Gospel through the cross and the resurrection, "He refused to impose the truth by force on those who spoke against it.... His rule...is established by witnessing to the truth and by hearing the truth, and it extends its dominion by the love whereby Christ, lifted up on the cross, draws all men to himself" *(DH* 11). Christ then handed on to the apostles the same method of convincing in regard to the truth of the Gospel.

Precisely because of this freedom, faith—which we express by the word "credo"—possesses its own human authenticity and originality, besides the divine. It expresses conviction and certainty about the truth of revelation, by virtue of an act of free will. This structural voluntariness of faith in no way implies that faith is optional and that an attitude of fundamental indifference would be justified. It only means that man is called to respond with the free adherence of his entire being to the invitation and gift of God.

The same conciliar document which deals with the problem

of religious liberty underlines clearly that faith is a matter of conscience.

"It is in accordance with their dignity as persons—that is, beings endowed with reason and free will and therefore privileged to bear personal responsibility—that all men should be at once impelled by nature and also bound by a moral obligation to seek the truth, especially religious truth. They are also bound to adhere to the truth, once it is known, and to order their whole lives in accord with the demands of truth" (DH 2). If this is the essential argument in favor of the right to religious liberty, it is also the fundamental motive for the fact that this same liberty must be correctly understood and observed in social life.

As regards personal decisions, "everybody has the duty and therefore the right to seek the truth in religious matters in order that, through the use of suitable means, he may prudently form judgments of conscience which are sincere and true.

"Truth, however, is to be sought after in a manner proper to the dignity of the human person and his social nature. The inquiry is to be free, carried on with the aid of teaching or instruction, communication and dialogue, in the course of which men explain to one another the truth they have discovered, or think they have discovered, in order thus to assist one another in the quest for truth. Moreover, as the truth is discovered, it is by a personal assent that men are to adhere to it" (DH 3).

In these words we find a very striking characteristic of our "credo" as a profoundly human act corresponding to the dignity of man as a person. This correspondence is expressed in the relationship with the truth by means of the interior freedom and the responsibility of conscience of the believing subject.

This doctrine, drawn from the conciliar declaration on religious liberty (Dignitatis Humanae), also serves to show the importance of a systematic catechesis, for two reasons. First, it makes possible the knowledge of the truth of God's plan of love which is contained in divine revelation. Secondly, it helps to adhere ever more firmly to the truth already known and accepted by faith.

General audience of April 17, 1985

The Transmission
of Divine Revelation

Where can we find what God has revealed, so that we may adhere to it with our convinced and free faith? There is a "sacred deposit," from which the Church draws and communicates its contents to us.

As the Second Vatican Council says: "This sacred Tradition, therefore, and Sacred Scripture of both the Old and New Testaments are like a mirror in which the pilgrim Church on earth looks at God, from whom she has received everything, until she is brought finally to see him as he is, face to face (cf. 1 Jn 3:2)" *(DV 7)*.

With these words the conciliar Constitution synthesizes the problem of the transmission of divine revelation, which is important for the faith of every Christian. Our "credo" should prepare man on earth to see God face to face in eternity. In every stage of history, the "credo" depends on the faithful and inviolable transmission of divine self-revelation, which reached its apex and plenitude in Jesus Christ.

Christ himself "commissioned the apostles to preach to all men that Gospel which is the source of all saving truth and moral teaching" *(DV 7)*. By oral preaching first of all, they carried out the mission entrusted to them. At the same time, some of them "under the inspiration of the same Holy Spirit committed the message of salvation to writing" *(DV* 7). This was done also by some of those in the circle of the apostles (Mark and Luke).

Thus the transmission of divine revelation was carried out in the first generation of Christians. "In order to keep the Gospel forever whole and alive within the Church, the apostles left bishops as their successors, 'handing over' to them 'the authority to teach in their own place'" (according to the expression of St. Irenaeus, cf. *Adv. Haer,* III, 3, 1; *DV* 7).

According to the teaching of the Council, Tradition and Sacred Scripture reciprocally support and complete each other in the transmission of divine revelation in the Church. By these means the new generation of disciples and witnesses of Jesus Christ nourish their faith, because "what was handed on by the apostles includes everything which contributes toward the holiness of life and increase in faith of the people of God" *(DV* 8).

"This tradition which comes from the apostles develops in the Church with the help of the Holy Spirit. For there is a growth in the understanding of the realities and the words which have been handed down. This happens through the contemplation and study made by believers, who treasure these things in their hearts (cf. Lk 2:19, 51) through a penetrating understanding of the spiritual realities which they experience, and through the preaching of those who have received through episcopal succession the sure gift of truth. For as the centuries succeed one another, the Church constantly moves forward toward the fullness of divine truth until the words of God reach their complete fulfillment in her" *(DV* 8).

In this thrust toward the plenitude of divine truth, the Church constantly draws on the one original "deposit," constituted by the apostolic Tradition and Sacred Scripture. "For both of them, flowing from the same divine wellspring, in a

certain way merge into a unity and tend toward the same end"
(DV 9).

Truly God's word

In this regard it is fitting to clarify and emphasize, in the
words of the Council, that "it is not from Sacred Scripture
alone that the Church draws her certainty about everything
which has been revealed" *(DV 9).* This Scripture "is the word
of God inasmuch as it is consigned to writing under the inspiration of the divine Spirit, while sacred Tradition takes the
word of God entrusted by Christ the Lord and the Holy Spirit
to the apostles, and hands it on to their successors in its full
purity, so that led by the light of the Spirit of truth, they may in
proclaiming it preserve this word of God faithfully, explain it,
and make it more widely known" *(DV 9).* "Through the same
tradition the Church's full canon of the sacred books is known,
and the sacred writings themselves are more profoundly understood and unceasingly made active in her" *(DV 8).*

"Sacred Tradition and Sacred Scripture form one sacred
deposit of the word of God, committed to the Church. Holding
fast to this deposit the entire holy people united with their
shepherds remain always steadfast in the teaching of the
apostles" *(DV 10).* Therefore both Scripture and Tradition
must be accepted and honored with equal feelings of devotion
and reverence.

Authentic interpretation

The problem arises here of the authentic interpretation of
the word of God written or handed down by Tradition. This
task has been entrusted "exclusively to the living teaching
office of the Church, whose authority is exercised in the name
of Jesus Christ. This teaching office is not above the word of

God, but serves it, teaching only what has been handed on, listening to it devoutly, guarding it scrupulously and explaining it faithfully in accord with a divine commission and with the help of the Holy Spirit. It draws from this one deposit of faith everything which it presents for belief as divinely revealed" *(DV* 10).

Here then is a further characteristic of faith. In the Christian sense, "to believe" also means to accept the truth revealed by God as it is taught by the Church. But at the same time the Second Vatican Council stated that "The entire body of the faithful, anointed as they are by the Holy One, cannot err in matters of belief. They manifest this special property by means of the whole peoples' supernatural discernment in matters of faith when 'from the bishops down to the last of the lay faithful' they show universal agreement in matters of faith and morals. That discernment in matters of faith is aroused and sustained by the Spirit of truth. It is exercised under the guidance of the sacred teaching authority, in faithful and respectful obedience to which the people of God accepts that which is not just the word of men but truly the word of God. Through it, the people of God adheres unwaveringly 'to the faith given once and for all to the saints,' (cf. Jude 3) penetrates it more deeply with right thinking, and applies it more fully in its life" *(LG* 12).

Vivifying process

Tradition, Sacred Scripture, the Magisterium of the Church and the supernatural sense of faith of the entire People of God form that vivifying process in which divine revelation is transmitted to succeeding generations. "Thus God, who spoke of old, uninterruptedly converses with the bride of his beloved Son; and the Holy Spirit, through whom the living voice of the Gospel resounds in the Church, and through her, in the world, leads unto all truth those who believe and makes

the word of Christ dwell abundantly in them (cf. Col 3:16)"
(*DV* 8).

To believe in the Christian sense means to be willing to
be introduced and led by the Spirit to the plenitude of the truth
in a conscious and voluntary way.

General audience of April 24, 1985

Divine Inspiration
of Sacred Scripture

Today we repeat once again those beautiful words of the conciliar Constitution *Dei Verbum:* "And thus God, who spoke of old, uninterruptedly converses with the bride of his beloved Son [which is the Church]; and the Holy Spirit, through whom the living voice of the Gospel resounds in the Church, and through her, in the world, leads unto all truth those who believe and makes the word of Christ dwell abundantly in them (cf. Col 3:16)" *(DV 8).*

Let us take up again what it means "to believe." To believe in a Christian way means precisely to be led by the Spirit to the entire truth of divine revelation. It means to be a community of the faithful open to the word of the Gospel of Christ. Both are possible in every generation. The living transmission of divine revelation, contained in Tradition and Sacred Scripture, remains integral in the Church, thanks to the special service of the Magisterium, in harmony with the supernatural sense of the faith of the People of God.

Authentic interpretation

To complete this concept of the bond between our Catholic "creed" and its source, the doctrine of the divine inspiration of Sacred Scripture and the authentic interpretation of Scripture is also important. In presenting this doctrine we will follow above all (as in the previous catecheses) the Constitution *Dei Verbum.*

The Council said: "Holy Mother Church, relying on the belief of the apostles, holds that the books of both the Old and New Testaments in their entirety, with all their parts, are sacred and canonical because, having been written under the inspiration of the Holy Spirit (cf. Jn 20:31; 2 Tim 3:16; 2 Pet 1:19-21; 3:15-16), they have God as their author and have been handed on as such to the Church herself" *(DV* 11).

God—as the invisible and transcendent author—"chose men and while employed by him they made use of their powers and abilities, so that...they, as true authors, consigned to writing everything and only those things which he wanted" *(DV* 11). For this purpose the Holy Spirit acted in them and through them (cf. *DV* 11).

Granted this origin, it must be held "that the books of Scripture must be acknowledged as teaching firmly, faithfully, and without error that truth which God wanted put into the sacred writings for the sake of our salvation" *(DV* 11). St. Paul's words in his Letter to Timothy confirm this: "All Scripture is inspired of God and is useful for teaching—for reproof, correction, and training in holiness so that the man of God may be fully competent and equipped for every good work" (2 Tim 3:16-17).

In accordance with the teaching of St. John Chrysostom, the *Constitution on Divine Revelation* expresses admiration for that special "condescension," a "stooping down" as it were by divine Wisdom. "The words of God, expressed in human language, have been made like human discourse, just as the Word of the eternal Father, when he took to himself the flesh of human weakness, was in every way made like men" *(DV* 13).

Constitution lists norms

Some norms concerning the interpretation of Sacred Scripture logically spring from the truth of its divine inspiration. The Constitution *Dei Verbum* lists them briefly:

A primary principle is that "since God speaks in Sacred Scripture through men in human fashion, the interpreter of Sacred Scripture, in order to see clearly what God wanted to communicate to us, should carefully investigate what meaning the sacred writers really intended, and what God wanted to manifest by means of their words" *(DV* 12).

For this end—and this is the second point—it is necessary to take into consideration, among other things, the "literary genres." "For truth is set forth and expressed differently in texts which are variously historical, prophetic, poetic, or of other forms of discourse" *(DV* 12). The meaning of what the author expresses depends precisely on these literary genres, which must therefore be considered against the background of all the circumstances of a given era and a specific culture.

Here, then, is the third principle for a correct interpretation of Sacred Scripture: "For the correct understanding of what the sacred author wanted to assert, due attention must be paid to the customary and characteristic styles of perceiving, speaking, and narrating which prevailed at the time of the sacred writer, and to the pattern men normally employed at that period in their everyday dealings with one another" *(DV* 12).

Its content and unity

These sufficiently detailed indications, given for interpretation of an historical-literary character, demand a deepened relationship with the premises of the doctrine on the divine inspiration of Sacred Scripture. It must be "read and interpreted according to the same Spirit by whom it was written" *(DV* 12).

Therefore, "no less serious attention must be given to the content and unity of the whole of Scripture...the living tradition of the whole Church must be taken into account along with the harmony which exists between elements of the faith" *(DV* 12).

By the "harmony which exists between elements of the faith," we mean the consistency of the individual truths of faith among themselves and with the total plan of revelation and the fullness of the divine economy contained in it.

The task of exegetes, that is, researchers who study Sacred Scripture with appropriate methods, is to contribute, in keeping with the above-mentioned principles, "to a better understanding and explanation of the meaning of Sacred Scripture, so that through preparatory study the judgment of the Church may mature" *(DV* 12). Granted that the Church has "the divine commission and ministry of guarding and interpreting the word of God," whatever concerns "the way of interpreting Scripture is subject finally to the judgment of the Church" *(DV* 12).

This norm is important and decisive for specifying the reciprocal relationship between exegesis (and theology) and the Magisterium of the Church. It is a norm that remains closely related to what we have previously said about the transmission of divine revelation. We must stress once again that the Magisterium makes use of the work of theologians and exegetes and at the same time watches over the results of their studies. The Magisterium is called to safeguard the whole truth contained in divine revelation.

God's providence

To believe in a Christian way means to adhere to this truth by taking advantage of the guarantee of truth which comes to the Church through its institution by Christ himself. This holds true for all the faithful, and also for theologians and exegetes—at the right level and in the proper degree. In this field the merciful providence of God is revealed for everyone. God has willed to grant us not only the gift of his self-revelation, but also the guarantee of its faithful preservation, interpretation and explanation, entrusting it to the hands of the Church.

General audience of May 1, 1985

The Light of Revelation in the Old Testament

As you know, Sacred Scripture is made up of two large collections of books: the Old Testament and the New. The Old Testament, completely compiled before the coming of Christ, is a collection of forty-six books of various kinds. We will list them here by grouping them in such a way as to differentiate them, at least generally, according to each one's character.

The Pentateuch

The first group that we meet is the so-called Pentateuch, made up of Genesis, Exodus, Leviticus, Numbers and Deuteronomy. Almost as a prolongation of the Pentateuch we find the Book of Joshua and then Judges. The concise Book of Ruth in a certain way constitutes the introduction to the following group, historical in character, made up of the two Books of Samuel and the two Books of Kings. Among these books we must include also the two Books of Chronicles, the Book of Ezra and the Book of Nehemiah, which deal with the period of Israel's history after the Babylonian Captivity.

The Books of Tobit, Judith and Esther, although dealing with the history of the Chosen People, have the character of allegorical and moral narrative rather than history properly so called. But the two Books of Maccabees have a historical nature.

Didactic Books

The so-called "Didactic Books" form a group by themselves, and include various kinds of works. The Book of Job, Psalms, and the Song of Songs belong to this group, as do some books that have a sapiential and educational character: the Book of Proverbs, Qoheleth (Ecclesiastes), the Book of Wisdom and the Wisdom of Sirach (Ecclesiasticus).

Finally, the last group in the Old Testament is made up of the "Prophetic Books." The four so-called "major" prophets are distinguished: Isaiah, Jeremiah, Ezechiel and Daniel. Lamentations and the Book of Baruch are added to the Book of Jeremiah. Then come the so-called "minor" prophets: Hosea, Joel, Amos, Abadiah, Jonah, Micah, Nahum, Habakkuk, Zephaniah, Haggai, Zechariah and Malachi.

Plan of salvation

With the exception of the first chapters of Genesis, which deal with the origin of the world and of mankind, the books of the Old Testament, beginning with the call of Abraham, deal with a nation that has been chosen by God. Here is what we read in the Constitution *Dei Verbum:* "In carefully planning and preparing the salvation of the whole human race, the God of infinite love, by a special dispensation, chose for himself a people to whom he would entrust his promises. First he entered into a covenant with Abraham (cf. Gen 15:18) and, through Moses, with the people of Israel (cf. Ex 24:8). To this people which he had acquired for himself, he so manifested himself through words and deeds as the one true and living God that

Israel came to know by experience the ways of God with men. With God himself speaking to them through the mouth of the prophets, Israel daily gained a deeper and clearer understanding of his ways and made them more widely known among the nations (cf. Ps 22:28-29; 96:1-3; Is 2:1-4; Jer 3:17). The plan of salvation, foretold by the sacred authors, recounted and explained by them, is found as the true word of God in the books of the Old Testament; these books, therefore, written under divine inspiration, remain permanently valuable..." *(DV* 14).

The conciliar Constitution then points out the principal purpose of the plan of salvation in the Old Testament: "to prepare for the coming of Christ, the redeemer of all and of the messianic kingdom, to announce this coming by prophecy (cf. Lk 24:44; Jn 5:39; 1 Pet 1:10) and to indicate its meaning through various types (cf. 1 Cor 10:11)" (cf. *DV* 15).

At the same time the books of the Old Testament, in accordance with the state of humanity before Christ, "reveal to all men the knowledge of God and of man and the ways in which God, just and merciful, deals with men. These books, though they also contain some things which are incomplete and temporary, nevertheless show us true divine pedagogy" *(DV* 15). They give expression to a "lively sense of God," "sound wisdom about human life," and finally "a wonderful treasury of prayers in which is present in a hidden way the mystery of our salvation" *(DV* 15). Therefore even the books of the Old Testament must be received by Christians with devotion.

The conciliar Constitution then illustrates the relationship between the Old and the New Testaments in this way: "God, the inspirer and author of both testaments, wisely arranged that the New Testament be hidden in the Old and the Old be made manifest in the New" (according to the words of St. Augustine: *"Novum in Vetere latet, Vetus in Novo patet...")*. "For, though Christ established the New Covenant in his blood (cf. Lk 22:20; 1 Cor 11:25), still the books of the Old Testament with all their parts, caught up into the proclamation of the Gospel, acquire and show forth their full meaning in the New Testament (cf. Mt 5:17; Lk 24:27; Rom 16:25-26; 2 Cor 3:14-16) and in turn shed light on it and explain it" *(DV* 16).

As you see, the Council offers us a precise and clear doctrine, sufficient for our catechesis. This doctrine enables us to take a further step in determining the significance of our faith. "To believe in a Christian way" means to attain, according to the spirit that we have spoken about, the light of divine revelation from the books of the Old Covenant as well.

General audience of May 8, 1985

The New Testament Is a Perpetual and Divine Witness to Christ

Twenty-seven books in the New Testament

The New Testament is of lesser extent than the Old. Under the aspect of historical redaction, the books that make it up were written in a much shorter period of time than those of the Old Testament. It contains twenty-seven books, some of which are very brief.

In first place we list the four Gospels according to Matthew, Mark, Luke and John. Then follows the Acts of the Apostles, whose author is also Luke. The most numerous group contains the apostolic letters, and among these the most numerous are the Letters of St. Paul: one to the Romans, two to the Corinthians, one to the Galatians, one to the Ephesians, one to the Philippians, one to the Colossians, two to the Thessalonians, two to Timothy, one to Titus, and one to Philemon. The so-called *corpus Paulinum* ends with the Letter to the Hebrews, written in Paul's sphere of influence.

Then follow the Letter of St. James, two Letters of St. Peter, three Letters of St. John, and the Letter of St. Jude. The last book of the New Testament is St. John's Apocalypse (Revelation).

Of apostolic origin

With regard to these books, the Constitution *Dei Verbum* has this to say: "It is common knowledge that among all the Scriptures, even those of the New Testament, the Gospels have a special pre-eminence, and rightly so, for they are the principal witness of the life and teaching of the incarnate Word, our Savior.

"The Church has always and everywhere held and continues to hold that the four Gospels are of apostolic origin. For what the apostles preached in fulfillment of the commission of Christ, afterward they themselves and apostolic men, under the inspiration of the divine Spirit, handed on to us in writing: the foundation of faith, namely, the fourfold Gospel, according to Matthew, Mark, Luke and John" *(DV* 18).

What Jesus taught

The conciliar Constitution underlines in a particular way the historicity of the four Gospels. It writes that the Church "has firmly and with absolute constancy held, and continues to hold, that the four Gospels...whose historical character the Church unhesitatingly asserts, faithfully hand on what Jesus Christ, while living among men, really did and taught for their eternal salvation until the day he was taken up into heaven (cf. Acts 1:1-2)" *(DV* 19).

With regard to the way the four Gospels came to be, the conciliar Constitution links it above all with the apostolic teaching that began after the descent of the Holy Spirit on Pentecost. Here is what we read: "Indeed, after the ascension of the Lord the apostles handed on to their hearers what he had said and done. This they did with that clearer understanding which they enjoyed after they had been instructed by the events of Christ's risen life and taught by the light of the Spirit of truth" *(DV* 19). These "events of Christ's risen life" are mainly the resurrection

of the Lord and the descent of the Holy Spirit. We can understand that, in the light of the resurrection, the apostles
definitively believed in Christ. The resurrection cast a basic light
on his death on the cross and also on all that he had done and
proclaimed before his passion. On the day of Pentecost the
apostles were "taught by the light of the Spirit of truth."

The four Gospels

From the oral apostolic teaching we pass to the drafting
of the Gospels, concerning which the conciliar Constitution
says: "The sacred authors wrote the four Gospels, selecting
some things from the many which had been handed on by word
of mouth or in writing, reducing some of them to a synthesis,
explaining some things in view of the situation of their
churches, and preserving the form of proclamation but always
in such fashion that they told us the honest truth about Jesus.
For their intention in writing was that either from their own
memory and recollections, or from the witness of those who
themselves 'from the beginning were eyewitnesses and minis-
ters of the word' we might know 'the truth' concerning those
matters about which we have been instructed (cf. Lk 1:2-4)"
(DV 19).

This concise statement of the Council reflects and briefly
sums up the richness of the investigations and studies that
biblical scholars have not ceased to dedicate to the question of
the origin of the four Gospels. For our catechesis, this summary will suffice.

Concerning the rest of the books of the New Testament,
the conciliar Constitution *Dei Verbum* says the following: "By
the wise plan of God, those matters which concern Christ the
Lord are confirmed, his true teaching is more and more fully
stated, the saving power of the divine work of Christ is
preached, the story is told of the beginnings of the Church and

her marvelous growth, and her glorious fulfillment is foretold" *(DV* 20). This is a brief and concise presentation of the contents of those books, apart from chronological questions, which are of less interest here. We will mention only that scholars place their composition in the second half of the first century.

What counts more for us is the presence of the Lord Jesus and his Spirit in the authors of the New Testament, who are the means through whom God introduces us into the new revelation. "For the Lord Jesus was with his apostles as he had promised (cf. Mt 28:20) and sent them the advocate Spirit who would lead them into the fullness of truth (cf. Jn 16:13)" *(DV* 20). The books of the New Testament introduce us precisely to the way that leads to the fullness of the truth of divine revelation.

Here we have another conclusion for a more complete concept of faith. To believe in a Christian way means to accept God's self-revelation in Jesus Christ, which constitutes the essential content of the New Testament.

The Council tells us: "When the fullness of time arrived (cf. Gal 4:4), the Word was made flesh and dwelt among us in his fullness of grace and truth (cf. Jn 1:14). Christ established the kingdom of God on earth, manifested his Father and himself by deeds and words, and completed his work by his death, resurrection and glorious ascension and by the sending of the Holy Spirit. Having been lifted up from the earth, he draws all men to himself (cf. Jn 12:32, Greek text), he who alone has the words of eternal life (cf. Jn 6:69)" *(DV* 17).

Therefore they provide special support for our faith.

General audience of May 22, 1985

Relations With
Non-Christian Religions

The Christian faith meets in the world with various religions that take their inspiration from other teachers and traditions outside the stream of revelation. We must take their reality into account. As the Council says, "Men expect from the various religions answers to the unsolved riddles of the human condition, which today, even as in former times, deeply stir the hearts of men: What is man? What is the meaning, the aim of our life? What is moral good, what sin? What gives rise to our sorrows and to what intent? Where lies the path to true happiness? What is the truth about death, judgment and retribution beyond the grave? What, finally, is that ultimate and unutterable mystery which engulfs our being, and whence we take our rise, and whither our journey leads us?" *(NA* 1).

With this fact the Council, in the Declaration *Nostra Aetate*, begins to treat of the Church's relations with non-Christian religions. It is significant that the Council spoke out on this subject. To believe in a Christian way means to respond to God's revelation of himself, contained fully in Jesus Christ. But especially in the modern world, this faith does not escape a knowing relationship with non-Christian religions. Each one of them expresses in some way "what men have in common and what draws them to fellowship" *(NA* 1). The Church does not avoid this relationship but rather desires and seeks it.

Against the background of a vast communion in positive values of spirituality and morality, there is outlined above all the relationship of "faith" with "religion" in general, which is a special element in man's earthly existence. In religion man seeks answers to the questions listed above and in different ways establishes his own relationship with the "mystery which engulfs our being." The various non-Christian religions especially express this quest on man's part, while the Christian faith is based on revelation on God's part. And here—notwithstanding some similarities with other religions—lies their essential difference.

Religious knowledge of God

The Declaration *Nostra Aetate* nevertheless attempts to stress the likenesses. We read: "From ancient times down to the present, there is found among various peoples a certain perception of that hidden power which hovers over the course of things and over the events of human history; at times some indeed have come to the recognition of a Supreme Being, or even of a Father. This perception and recognition penetrates their lives with a profound religious sense" *(NA* 2). With regard to this we can recall that right from the early centuries, Christian thinkers loved to see the ineffable presence of the Word in human minds and in the achievements of culture and civilization: "All the writers, in fact, through the inborn seed of the Logos (Word) implanted in them, were capable of a dim glimpse of reality," said St. Justin (II, 13, 3). With other Fathers, he did not hesitate to see in philosophy a kind of "minor revelation."

But here we must define our terms. That "religious sense," that is, the religious knowledge of God on the part of people, goes back to the rational knowledge of which man is capable through his natural powers, as we have seen. At the same time it is distinguished from purely rational speculations by philosophers and thinkers on the subject of the existence of God. It involves the whole person and becomes a life force in him. It is distinguished above all from Christian faith as knowledge based on revelation and a knowing response to the gift of God present and at work in Jesus Christ. I repeat that this necessary distinction does not exclude a similarity and an agreement in positive values. It does not hinder one from recognizing, with the Council, that the various non-Christian religions (among which the conciliar document mentions especially Hinduism and Buddhism, and gives a brief outline of them) "try to counter the restlessness of the human heart, each in its own manner, by proposing 'ways,' comprising teachings, rules of life, and sacred rites" *(NA 2)*.

The document continues: "The Catholic Church rejects nothing that is true and holy in these religions. She regards with sincere reverence those ways of conduct and of life, those precepts and teachings which, though differing in many aspects from the ones she holds and sets forth, nonetheless often reflect a ray of that truth which enlightens all men" *(NA 2)*. My predecessor Paul VI, of happy memory, strikingly underlined the Church's position on this in the Apostolic Exhortation *Evangelii Nuntiandi*. These are his words, which borrow from the texts of the ancient Fathers: "They (non-Christian religions) carry within them the echo of thousands of years of searching for God, a quest which is incomplete but often made with great sincerity and righteousness of heart. They possess an impressive patrimony of deeply religious texts. They have taught generations of people how to pray. They are all impregnated with innumerable 'seeds of the Word' and can constitute a true 'preparation for the Gospel'" *(EN 53)*.

Therefore the Church exhorts Christians and Catholics

that "through dialogue and collaboration with the followers of other religions, carried out with prudence and love and in witness to the Christian faith and life, they recognize, preserve and promote the good things, spiritual and moral, as well as the socio-cultural values found among these men" *(NA* 2).

To believe in a Christian way

We could therefore say that to believe in a Christian way means to accept, profess and proclaim Christ who is "the way, the truth and the life" (Jn 14:6), so much more fully the more that the values of other religions reveal signs, reflections and, as it were, hints of him.

Among non-Christian religions, the religion of the followers of Mohammed deserves special attention by reason of its monotheistic character and its link with the faith of Abraham, whom St. Paul described as the "father...of our (Christian) faith" (cf. Rom 4:16).

The Muslims "adore the one God, living and subsisting in himself; merciful and all-powerful, the Creator of heaven and earth, who has spoken to men; they take pains to submit wholeheartedly to even his inscrutable decrees, just as Abraham, with whom the faith of Islam takes pleasure in linking itself, submitted to God" *(NA* 3). But there is more. The followers of Mohammed even honor Jesus: "Though they do not acknowledge Jesus as God, they revere him as a prophet. They also honor Mary, his virgin mother; at times they even call on her with devotion. In addition, they await the day of judgment when God will render their deserts to all those who have been raised up from the dead. Finally, they value the moral life and worship God especially through prayer, almsgiving and fasting" *(NA* 3).

Among non-Christian religions, the Church has a special relationship with those who profess faith in the Old Testament, the heirs of the patriarchs and prophets of Israel. The Council recalls "the bond that spiritually ties the people of the new covenant to Abraham's stock" *(NA* 4).

This bond, to which we have already referred in the catechesis dedicated to the Old Testament, and which brings us close to the Jewish people, is again emphasized by the Declaration *Nostra Aetate* when it refers to those common beginnings of faith, which are found in the patriarchs, Moses and the prophets. The Church "professes that all who believe in Christ—Abraham's sons according to faith are included in the same patriarch's call, ...the Church, therefore, cannot forget that she received the revelation of the Old Testament through the people with whom God in his inexpressible mercy concluded the ancient covenant" *(NA* 4). From this same people comes "Christ in his human origins" (Rom 9:5), Son of the Virgin Mary, as also his apostles are its sons. This entire spiritual heritage, common to Christians and Jews, constitutes an organic foundation for a mutual relationship, even though a great part of the children of Israel "did not accept the Gospel." Nevertheless the Church (together with the prophets and the Apostle Paul) "awaits that day, known to God alone, on which all peoples will address the Lord in a single voice and 'serve him with one accord' (Zeph 3:9)" *(NA* 4).

As you know, after the Second Vatican Council a pertinent secretariat for relations with non-Christian religions was established. Paul VI saw in these relations one of the ways for the "dialogue of salvation" which the Church must carry on with all persons in today's world (cf. Encyclical *Ecclesiam Suam,* AAS 56, 1964, 654). All of us are called to pray and work that the network of these relations may be strengthened and enlarged, stirring up to an ever greater degree the will for mutual knowledge, collaboration and the quest for the fullness of truth in charity and peace. Our faith itself urges us to do this.

General audience of June 5, 1985

The Problem of
Unbelief and Atheism

To believe, in the Christian sense, means "to accept the invitation to a conversation with God," by abandoning oneself to one's Creator. Such a conscious faith predisposes us also to that "dialogue of salvation" which the Church must carry on with all people in the world today (cf. Paul VI Encyclical *Ecclesiam Suam,* AAS 56 [1964], p. 654), even with non-believers, "Many of our contemporaries...have never recognized this intimate and vital link with God" *(GS* 19), constituted by faith. Therefore, in the Pastoral Constitution *Gaudium et Spes,* the Council also took a stand on the subject of unbelief and atheism. It tells us how mature and aware our faith should be, a faith to which we are frequently called upon to bear witness before non-believers and atheists. Precisely during this present era our faith should be "so well trained that it can see difficulties clearly and master them" *(GS* 21). This is the essential condition for the dialogue of salvation.

Brief analysis of atheism

The conciliar Constitution makes a brief but searching analysis of atheism. In the first place, it observes that this term "is applied to phenomena which are quite distinct from one another. For while God is expressly denied by some [atheism], others believe that man can assert absolutely nothing about him [agnosticism]. Still others use such a method to scrutinize the question of God as to make it seem devoid of meaning [positivism, scientism]. Many, unduly transgressing the limits of the positive sciences, contend that everything can be explained by this kind of scientific reasoning alone, or by contrast, they altogether disallow that there is any absolute truth. Some laud man so extravagantly that their faith in God lapses into a kind of anemia, though they seem more inclined to affirm man than to deny God. Again some form for themselves such a fallacious idea of God that when they repudiate this figment they are by no means rejecting the God of the Gospel. Some never get to the point of raising questions about God, since they seem to experience no religious stirrings nor do they see why they should trouble themselves about religion. Moreover, atheism results not rarely from a violent protest against the evil in this world, or from the absolute character with which certain human values are unduly invested, and which thereby already accords them the stature of God. Modern civilization itself often complicates the approach to God not for any essential reason but because it is so heavily engrossed in earthly affairs" *(GS* 19).

Pragmatic attitude

This Conciliar text indicates, as one can see, the variety and the multiplicity of what is contained under the term "atheism."

Undoubtedly, atheism is often a pragmatic attitude resulting from carelessness or from a lack of interest in religious matters. In many cases, however, this attitude finds its roots in the whole mentality of the world, especially of scientific thought. If it is accepted that the source of cognitive certainty is exclusively the experience of the senses, then all access to reality which transcends the senses is excluded. Such a cognitive attitude is found at the basis of that particular notion which in our time has taken the name of "the theology of the death of God."

So then the motives of atheism and still more frequently of agnosticism today are also of a theoretical-cognitive nature, not merely pragmatic.

The second group of reasons emphasized by the Council is connected with that exaggerated exaltation of man which induces many to forget such an obvious truth that man is a contingent being and limited in existence. The reality of life and of history makes us observe ever anew that if reasons exist to recognize the great dignity and the primacy of man in the visible world, there is still no foundation for regarding him as absolute and rejecting God.

We read in *Gaudium et Spes* that modern atheism "stretches the desires for human independence to such a point that it poses difficulties against any kind of dependence on God. Those who profess atheism of this sort maintain that it gives man freedom to be an end unto himself, the sole artisan and creator of his own history. They claim that this freedom cannot be reconciled with the affirmation of a Lord who is author and purpose of all things, or at least that this freedom makes such an affirmation altogether superfluous. Favoring this doctrine can be the sense of power which modern technical progress generates in man" *(GS* 20).

Today, systematic atheism "anticipates the liberation of man especially through his economic and social emancipation." It combats religion in a programmatic way by stating that religion is an obstacle to such emancipation "by arousing man's hope for a deceptive future life, thereby diverting him from the constructing of the earthly city." When those who hold such views gain control of the state, the Council goes on to say, "they vigorously fight against religion, and promote atheism by using, especially in the education of youth, those means of pressure which public power has at its disposal" *(GS* 20).

This last problem demands that there be set out clearly and firmly the principle of religious freedom emphasized by the Council in the relevant Declaration *Dignitatis Humanae.*

Complete rejection

If we wish to enunciate the fundamental attitude of the Church in regard to atheism, it is clear that she rejects it with "complete firmness" *(GS* 21), because it contrasts with the very essence of the Christian faith which includes the conviction that the existence of God can be reached by reason. However, "While rejecting atheism, root and branch, the Church sincerely professes that all men, believers and unbelievers alike, ought to work for the rightful betterment of this world in which all alike live; such an ideal cannot be realized, however, apart from sincere and prudent dialogue" *(GS* 21).

It is necessary to add that the Church is particularly sensitive to the attitude of those who cannot reconcile the existence of God with the multiple experience of evil and of suffering.

At the same time the Church is aware that what she proclaims—the Gospel and the Christian faith—"is in harmony with the most secret desires of the human heart when it champions the dignity of the human vocation, restoring hope to those who have already despaired of anything higher than their present lot" *(GS* 21).

"She further teaches that a hope related to the end of time does not diminish the importance of intervening duties but rather undergirds the acquittal of them with fresh incentives. By contrast, when a divine instruction and the hope of life eternal are wanting, man's dignity is most grievously lacerated, as current events often attest; riddles of life and death, of guilt and of grief go unsolved with the frequent result that men succumb to despair" *(GS* 21).

On the other hand, while rejecting atheism, the Church "strives to detect in the atheistic mind the hidden causes for the denial of God; conscious of how weighty are the questions which atheism raises, and motivated by love for all men, she believes these questions ought to be examined seriously and more profoundly" *(GS* 21). In particular, she is concerned to make progress "led by the Holy Spirit who renews and purifies her ceaselessly" *(GS* 21), in order to remove from her life whatever might unjustly hurt those who do not believe.

The Church responds

With such an approach the Church once again comes to our aid to answer the question: "What is the faith? What does it mean to believe?" precisely against the background of unbelief and of atheism which at times assumes the form of a programmed struggle against religion, and especially against Christianity. Precisely because of such hostility, the faith should become particularly aware, penetrating and mature, characterized by a deep sense of responsibility and of love in regard to all men. The awareness of the difficulties, of the objections and of the persecutions should awaken a still further readiness to bear witness "to the hope that is in us" (1 Pet 3:15).

General audience of June 12, 1985

The Faith Rooted
in the Word of God

We take up again our discourse on the faith. According to the doctrine contained in the Constitution *Dei Verbum,* the Christian faith is the conscious and free response of man to God's self-revelation which reached its fullness in Jesus Christ. By means of what St. Paul calls "the obedience of faith" (cf. Rom 16:26; 1:5; 2 Cor 10:5-6), the whole of man abandons himself to God, accepting as true what is contained in the word of divine revelation. The faith is the work of grace which acts on the intelligence and will, and at the same time, it is a conscious and free act of the human subject.

Faith, a gift of God to man, is also a theological virtue. At the same time, it is a stable disposition of the mind, that is, a habit or a lasting interior attitude. It requires that the believer cultivate it continually, by cooperating actively and consciously with the grace that God offers.

Living and active

Since the faith has its source in divine revelation, an essential aspect of collaboration with the grace of faith is provided by the constant and as far as possible systematic contact with Sacred Scripture, which transmits God's revealed truth to us in its most genuine form. This finds many expressions in the life of the Church, as we read also in the Constitution *Dei Verbum.*

"All the preaching of the Church must be nourished and regulated by Sacred Scripture. For in the sacred books, the Father who is in heaven meets his children with great love and speaks with them; and the force and power in the word of God is so great that it stands as the support and energy of the Church, the strength of faith for her sons, the food of the soul, the pure and everlasting source of spiritual life. Consequently these words are perfectly applicable to Sacred Scripture: 'For the word of God is living and active' (Heb 4:12) and 'it has power to build you up and give you your heritage among all those who are sanctified' (Acts 20:32; see 1 Thess 2:13)" *(DV 21).*

Supreme rule of faith

This is why the Constitution *Dei Verbum,* in referring to the teaching of the Fathers of the Church, does not hesitate to place together the "two tables," that is, the table of the Word of God and that of the Body of the Lord. It notes that the Church never ceases "particularly in the Sacred Liturgy, to partake of the Bread of Life" from both tables "and to offer it to the faithful" (cf. *DV* 21). The Church has always considered and continues to consider Sacred Scripture, together with sacred Tradition, "as the supreme rule of her faith" *(DV* 21) and as such she offers it to the faithful for their daily life.

Practical suggestions

From this flow some practical suggestions which have a great importance for consolidating the faith in the word of the living God. In a particular way they apply to bishops, "depositories of the apostolic doctrine" (St. Irenaeus, *Adv. Haer.* IV, 32, 1; PG 1071), "who have been placed by the Holy Spirit to feed the Church of God" (cf. Acts 20:28). But they apply respectively also to all the other members of the People of God: priests, especially parish priests, deacons, religious, the laity and families.

First of all "easy access to Sacred Scripture should be provided for all the Christian faithful" *(DV* 22). Here the question arises of the translation of the sacred books. "The Church from the very beginning accepted as her own that very ancient Greek translation of the Old Testament which is called the Septuagint; and she has always given a place of honor to other Eastern translations and Latin ones" *(DV* 22). The Church also works incessantly so that "suitable and correct translations are made into various languages, especially from the original texts of the sacred books" *(DV* 22).

The Church is not opposed to the initiative of translations made "in cooperation with the separated brethren" *(DV* 22)—the so-called ecumenical translations. With the opportune permission of the Church, Catholics can also use them.

Intellectus fidei

The subsequent task is connected with the correct understanding of the Word of divine revelation: *intellectus fidei* (the understanding of the faith) which culminates in theology. To this end the Council recommends "the study of the Holy Fathers of both East and West and of sacred liturgies" *(DV* 23), and attributes great importance to the work of exegetes and of theologians, always in close relationship with Sacred Scripture: "Sacred theology rests on the written word of God, together with sacred Tradition, as its primary and perpetual foundation. By scrutinizing in the light of faith all truth stored up in the mystery of Christ, theology is most powerfully strengthened and constantly rejuvenated by that word. For the Sacred Scriptures contain the word of God and since they are inspired, really are the word of God; and so the study of the sacred page is, as it were, the soul of sacred theology" *(DV 24)*.

The Council addresses an appeal to exegetes and to all theologians to offer the nourishment of the Scriptures for the people of God, to enlighten their minds, strengthen their wills, and set men's hearts on fire with the love of God" *(DV 23)*. In conformity with what was already said before on the rules of the transmission of revelation, exegetes and theologians should carry out their task "under the watchful care of the sacred Magisterium" *(DV 23)* and at the same time, with the use of the opportune helps and scientific methods (cf. *DV 23*).

Manifold ministry

The vast and manifold ministry of the word in the Church then opens up: "pastoral preaching, catechetics and all Christian instruction," (particularly liturgical homiletics)...all this ministry "is nourished by the word of Scripture" (cf. *DV 24*).

Therefore all those who exercise the ministry of the word are encouraged to "share the abundant wealth of the divine word with the faithful committed to them" *(DV 25)*. For this purpose, reading, study and meditation-prayer are indispensable so that one does not become "an empty preacher of the Word of God to others, not being a bearer of the word in his own heart" (St. Augustine, *Sermon 179,* 1: PL 3, 966).

Reading and prayer

The council addresses a similar exhortation to all the faithful, referring to the words of St. Jerome: "Ignorance of the Scriptures is ignorance of Christ" (St. Jerome, *Comm. in Is.,* Prol. PL 24, 17). To everyone, therefore, the Council recommends not only reading but also prayer which should accompany the reading of Sacred Scripture, that: "through the reading and study of the sacred books...the treasure of revelation, entrusted to the Church, may more and more fill the hearts of men" *(DV* 26). Such "filling of the heart" goes step by step with the consolidation of our Christian "credo" in the word of the living God.

General audience of June 19, 1985

Faith Is the Stimulus to Work for the Union of Christians

God's self-revelation reached its fullness in Jesus Christ. This revelation is the source of the Christian faith, of that "credo" which the Church expresses in the symbols of faith. However, in the matter of this Christian faith, various ruptures and divisions have occurred during the centuries. "All profess to be followers of the Lord, but (the Christian communions) differ in mind and go their different ways, as if Christ himself were divided (cf. 1 Cor 1:13). Christ the Lord founded one Church and one Church only. However, many Christian communions present themselves to men as the true inheritors of Jesus Christ" *(UR* 1), differing from the others and principally from the Roman Apostolic Catholic Church.

From earliest times

Even from apostolic times, there were complaints among the followers of Christ. St. Paul severely rebuked those responsible as worthy of condemnation (cf. 1 Cor 11:18-19; Gal 1:6-9; cf. 1 Jn 2:18-19) (cf. *UR* 3). Even in post-apostolic times divisions were not lacking. Those which took place in the East deserve special attention. They occurred "when the dogmatic formulas of the Councils of Ephesus and Chalcedon were challenged" *(UR* 13), concerning the relationship between the divine and human natures of Jesus Christ.

Major divisions

However, two major divisions should be mentioned here in particular, the first of which concerned Christianity especially in the East, the second in the West. The division in the East, the so-called Eastern Schism, linked to the year 1054, came about when "ecclesiastical communion between the Eastern patriarchates and the Roman See was dissolved" *(UR* 13). As a result of this rupture there are within the ambit of Christianity the Catholic Church (Roman Catholic) and the Orthodox Church or Churches whose historical center is at Constantinople.

"Other divisions arose more than four centuries later in the West, stemming from the events which are usually referred to as the Reformation. As a result, many communions, national or confessional were separated from the Roman See. Among those in which Catholic traditions and institutions in part continue to exist, the Anglican communion occupies a special place. These various divisions differ greatly from one another not only by reason of their origin, place and time, but especially in the nature and seriousness of questions bearing on faith and the structure of the Church" *(UR* 13).

Belief in Christ

So it is not merely a question of divisions concerning discipline. It is the very content of the Christian "credo" which is affected. A modern Protestant theologian, Karl Barth, has expressed this situation of division in the following terms: "We all believe in one Christ, but not all in the same way."

The Second Vatican Council stated as follows: "Such division openly contradicts the will of Christ, scandalizes the world, and damages the holy cause of preaching the Gospel to every creature" (UR 1).

Christians of today should recall and meditate with a particular sensitivity on the words of the prayer which Christ the Lord addressed to his Father on the evening on which he was betrayed: "that they may all be one; even as you, Father, are in me, and I in you, that they also may be in us, so that the world may believe that you have sent me" (Jn 17:31).

Christian "credo"

Especially in the present-day historical situation, the living echo of these words imbues us during the recitation of the Christian "credo" with an ardent desire for the union of Christians until full unity in the faith.

Let us read from the Council document: "But the Lord of Ages wisely and patiently follows out the plan of grace on our behalf, sinners that we are. In recent times more than ever before, he has been rousing divided Christians to remorse over their divisions and to a longing for unity. Everywhere large numbers have felt the impulse of this grace, and among our separated brethren also there increases from day to day the movement, fostered by the grace of the Holy Spirit, for the restoration of unity among all Christians. This movement toward unity is called 'ecumenical.' Those belong to it who invoke the Triune God and confess Jesus as Lord and Savior, doing this not merely as individuals but also as corporate bodies. For almost everyone regards the body in which he has heard the Gospel as his Church and indeed, God's Church. All however, though in different ways, long for the one visible Church of God, a Church truly universal and sent forth into the world that the world may be converted to the Gospel and so be saved, to the glory of God" *(UR 1)*.

Awaiting his grace

This long quotation is taken from the decree on ecumenism, *Unitatis Redintegratio.* In it, the Second Vatican Council has detailed the manner in which the desire for Christian unity should penetrate the faith of the Church, the manner in which it should be reflected in the concrete attitude of faith of every Catholic Christian and influence his actions, and the response which he should make to the words of Christ's priestly prayer.

Paul VI saw in the ecumenical commitment the first and nearest circle of that "dialogue of salvation," which the Church should carry on with all brothers in the faith, separated but always brothers! Many events of recent times, after the initiative of John XXIII, the work of the Council, and later the post-conciliar efforts, help us to understand and to experience that, notwithstanding everything, "there is more that unites us than divides us."

It is also with this disposition of spirit that in professing the "credo" we "abandon ourselves to God" (cf. *DV* 5), awaiting especially from him the grace of the gift of full union in this faith of all who witness to Christ. On our part we shall make our entire commitment of prayer and of work for unity, by seeking the ways of truth in charity.

General audience of June 26, 1985

THE EXISTENCE
AND NATURE OF GOD

The Right Attitude Before God

Today our catechesis arrives at the great mystery of faith, the first article of our Credo—I believe in God. To speak of God means to treat of a theme sublime, unlimited, mysterious and attractive. But here on the threshold, like one preparing for a long, fascinating journey of discovery—and such is always a genuine discourse about God—we feel the need first of all to take the right path by preparing our minds for the understanding of truths which are so noble and decisive.

For this purpose I think it necessary to respond at once to some questions, the first of which is: why speak about God today?

An irrepressible need

At the school of Job who humbly confessed: "Behold, I am of small account.... I lay my hands on my mouth" (40:4), we perceive rather forcibly that the source of our supreme certainties as believers, the mystery of God, is first of all the fruitful source of our deepest queries: Who is God? Can we know him in a truthful way in our human condition? Who are we, creatures, before God?

97

From these questions, great and sometimes tormenting difficulties have always arisen. If God exists, then why is there so much evil in the world? Why do the evil prosper and why are the just trampled under foot? Does not God's omnipotence end up by crushing our liberty and responsibility?

These questions and difficulties are intertwined with the expectations and aspirations of which the Bible characters, especially in the Psalms, have become the universal mouthpiece: "As a deer longs for flowing streams, so my soul longs for you, O God. My soul thirsts for God, for the living God: when shall I come and behold the face of God?" (Ps 42:2, 3). From God, the Psalmist expects health, freedom from evil, happiness, and also with a splendid thrust of confidence the possibility of staying with God—"to dwell in your house" (cf. Ps 84:2 ff.). We speak then of God because this is an irrepressible need for us.

How to speak of God

The second question is how to speak about God, how to speak about him correctly. Even many Christians have a deformed image of God. It is necessary to ask oneself if there has been a correct course of research, drawing the truth from genuine sources and in an adequate way. Here I think it right to recall above all, as a primary attitude, honesty of intelligence, namely, to remain open to those signs of truth which God himself has left of himself in the world and in our history.

There is certainly the path of right reason (and we will have time to consider what man of his own powers can know about God). But here I am bound to say that God himself offers to the reason, well beyond its natural resources, a splendid documentation of himself—what the language of faith calls "revelation." The believer, and every person of good will who is looking for the face of God, has at his disposition in the first place the immense treasure of Sacred Scripture. This is a real diary of God in his relationships with his people, which has at its center the supreme revealer of God, Jesus Christ: "He who sees me, sees the Father" (Jn 14:9). Jesus, on his part, has entrusted his testimony to the Church which has always with the help of the Spirit of God, made it the object of dedicated research, of progressive investigation and also of strenuous defense against error and deformation. God's genuine documentation, then, passes through the living Tradition of which all the Councils are fundamental witnesses—from Nicaea to that of Constantinople, from Trent to the First and Second Vatican Councils.

We will make it our duty to return to these genuine sources of truth.

Catechesis also draws its content about God from the twofold ecclesial experience: the faith as it is prayed—liturgy—whose formulations are a continual, untiring speaking of God by speaking to him; and also the faith lived by Christians, especially by the saints, who have had the grace of a profound communion with God. Therefore we are not destined merely to ask questions about God, thus losing ourselves in a forest of hypothetical or too abstract responses. God himself has come to meet us with an organic wealth of secure indications. The Church knows that it possesses, through the grace of God himself, in its patrimony of doctrine and of life, the correct direction to speak with respect and truth about him. Never as much as today does it feel the commitment to offer to men with fidelity and love the essential answer for which they are waiting.

Using Sacred Scripture

This is what I intend to do in these meetings. But how? There are different ways to impart catechesis and their legitimacy depends on fidelity in regard to the integral faith of the Church. I have deemed it opportune to choose the way which while calling directly upon the Sacred Scriptures, also refers to the symbols of the faith, in that deepened understanding received from twenty centuries of reflection in Christian thought.

It is my intention, in proclaiming the truth about God, to invite all of you to recognize the validity not only of the historico-positive way but also of that offered by the doctrinal reflection elaborated in the great Councils and in the ordinary Magisterium of the Church. In this way, without diminishing in the slightest the richness of the Biblical data, it will be possible to illustrate the truths of faith or those which are proximate to the faith, or in any event theologically well founded. By being expressed in dogmatic-speculative language, they run the risk of being less felt and appreciated by many people today with no little impoverishment of knowledge about him who is an unfathomable mystery of light.

Docile, grateful heart

I could not end this initial catechesis of our discourse on God without recalling a second fundamental attitude besides that of upright intelligence, mentioned above. This is the attitude of a docile and grateful heart. We speak of him whom Isaiah proposes to us as the three times holy (6:3). We must therefore speak of him with deepest and total respect, in adoration. At the same time, however, sustained by him "who is in the bosom of the Father and has made him known" (Jn 1:18), Jesus Christ our brother speaks of him with tenderest love. "For from him and through him and to him are all things. To him be glory for ever. Amen" (Rom 11:36).

General audience of July 3, 1985

The Proofs for God's Existence

When we ask ourselves "Why do we believe in God?" our faith provides the first response. God has revealed himself to humanity and has entered into contact with it. The supreme revelation of God has come to us through Jesus Christ, God incarnate. We believe in God because God has made himself known to us as the supreme Being, the great "Existent."

However, this faith in a God who reveals himself, also finds support in the reasoning of our intelligence. When we reflect, we observe that proofs of God's existence are not lacking. These have been elaborated by thinkers under the form of philosophical demonstrations in the sense of rigorously logical deductions. But they can also take on a simpler form. As such, they are accessible to everyone who seeks to understand the meaning of the world around him.

Scientific proofs

In speaking of the existence of God we should underline that we are not speaking of proofs in the sense implied by the experimental sciences. Scientific proofs in the modern sense of the word are valid only for things perceptible to the senses, since it is only on such things that scientific instruments of investigation can be used. To desire a scientific proof of God would be equivalent to lowering God to the level of the beings of our world, and we would therefore be mistaken methodologically in regard to what God is. Science must recognize its limits and its inability to reach the existence of God. It can neither affirm nor deny his existence.

From this, however, we must not draw the conclusion that scientists in their scientific studies are unable to find valid reasons for admitting the existence of God. If science as such cannot reach God, the scientist who has an intelligence, the object of which is not limited to things of sense perception, can discover in the world reasons for affirming a Being which surpasses it. Many scientists have made and are making this discovery.

Whoever reflects with an open mind on what is implied in the existence of the universe, cannot help but pose the question of the problem of the origin. Instinctively, when we witness certain happenings, we ask ourselves what caused them. How can we not but ask the same question in regard to the sum total of beings and phenomena which we discover in the world?

A supreme Cause

A scientific hypothesis such as that of the expansion of the universe makes the problem all the more clear. If the universe is in a state of continual expansion, should not one go back in time to that which could be called the "initial moment," the moment in which that expansion began? But, whatever the theory adopted concerning the origin of the universe, the most basic question cannot be avoided. This universe in constant movement postulates a Cause which, in giving it being, has communicated to it this movement, and continues to sustain it. Without such a supreme Cause, the world and every movement in it would remain "unexplained" and "inexplicable," and our intelligence would not be satisfied. The human mind can receive a response to its questions only by admitting a Being who has created the world with all its dynamism, and who continues to maintain it in existence.

The necessity to go back to a supreme Cause is all the greater if one considers the perfect organization which science has ceaselessly discovered in the structure of matter. When human intelligence is applied with so much effort to determine the constitution and modalities of action of material particles, is it not perhaps induced to seek their origin in a superior Intelligence which has conceived the whole? In face of the marvel of what can be called the immensely small world of the atom, and the immensely great world of the cosmos, the human mind feels itself completely surpassed in its possibilities of creation and even of imagination. It understands that a work of such quality and of such proportions demands a Creator whose wisdom is beyond all measure and whose power is infinite.

Impressive finality

All the observations concerning the development of life lead to a similar conclusion. The evolution of living beings, of which science seeks to determine the stages and to discern the mechanism, presents an internal finality which arouses admiration. This finality which directs beings in a direction for which they are not responsible or in charge, obliges one to suppose a Mind which is its inventor, its creator.

The history of humanity and the life of every human person manifest a still more impressive finality. Certainly, man cannot explain to himself the meaning of all that happens to him, and therefore he must recognize that he is not the master of his own destiny. Not only has he not made himself, but he has not even the power to dominate the course of events in the development of his existence. However, he is convinced that he has a destiny and he seeks to discover how he received it and how it is inscribed in his being. In certain moments he can more easily discern a secret finality which appears from a convergence of circumstances and events. Thus he is brought to affirm the sovereignty of him who has created and directs his present life.

Finally, among the qualities of this world which impel us to raise our gaze aloft, there is beauty.

"The heavens proclaim the glory of God;
Day to day pours forth speech
and night to night declares knowledge" (Ps 19:1, 2).

It is manifested in the various marvels of nature. It is expressed in the numberless works of art, literature, music, painting and the plastic arts. It is appreciated also in moral conduct—there are so many good sentiments, so many stupendous deeds.

Man is aware of "receiving" all this beauty, even though he cooperates by his action in its manifestation. He discovers and admires it fully only when he recognizes its source, the transcendent beauty of God.

Faith stimulates

To all these "indications" of the existence of God the Creator, some oppose the power of chance or of the proper mechanisms of matter. To speak of chance for a universe which presents such a complex organization in its elements, and such a marvelous finality in its life would be equivalent to giving up the search for an explanation of the world as it appears to us. In fact, this would be equivalent to admitting effects without a cause. It would be to abdicate human intelligence which would thus refuse to think, and to seek a solution for its problems.

In conclusion, a myriad of indications impels man, who tries to understand the universe in which he lives, to direct his gaze toward his Creator. The proofs for the existence of God are many and convergent. They contribute to show that faith does not humble human intelligence, but stimulates it to reflection and permits it to understand better all the "whys" posed by the observation of reality.

General audience of July 10, 1985

Scientists and God

A widespread notion exists that scientists are generally agnostics and that science leads one away from God. Is there any truth to this opinion?

The extraordinary advances of science, particularly over the last two centuries, have sometimes led to the belief that by itself it is capable of answering all our questions and of resolving all our problems. Some have concluded that by now there is no longer any need for God. For them, faith in science has supplanted faith in God.

It has been said that one must choose between faith and science—either one embraces one or believes in the other. Whoever proceeds with a commitment to scientific research no longer has need of God; vice versa, whoever wishes to believe in God cannot be a serious scientist, because between science and faith an irremediable conflict exists.

No conflict with faith

The Second Vatican Council expressed a very different conviction. The Constitution *Gaudium et Spes* affirms: "If methodical investigation within every branch of learning is carried out in accord with moral norms, it never truly conflicts with faith. For earthly matters and the concerns of the faith derive from the same God. Indeed whoever labors to penetrate the secrets of reality with a humble and steady mind, even though he is unaware of the fact, is nevertheless being led by the hand of God, who holds all things in existence, and gives them their identity" *(GS* 36).

There have always been, and still are today, scientists who in the context of their human scientific experience have positively and beneficially believed in God. Fifty years ago a survey was made of 398 of the most illustrious scientists in the world, in which only 16 declared themselves unbelievers, 15 agnostics and 367 believers (cf. A. Eymieu, *La Part des croyants dans les progrès de la science,* sixth ed., Perrin 1935, p. 274).

It is even more interesting and profitable to become aware of the reasons for which many scientists, past and present, see rigorously conducted scientific research as not only compatible, but even happily capable of integration with the sincere and joyous recognition of the existence of God.

From the considerations which often accompany their scientific endeavors in the manner of a spiritual diary, it is easy to see the intersection of two elements. The first is the way in which research itself, be it great or small, carried out with extreme rigor, always leaves an opening for further questions in an endless process which reveals in reality an immensity, a harmony, and a finality which cannot be explained in terms of causality or through scientific resources alone. To this is added the irrepressible question of meaning, of higher rationality—indeed, of something or of Someone capable of satisfying interior needs—which refined scientific progress itself, far from suppressing, intensifies.

Joyous recognition

It is true that the step to religious affirmation is not achieved *per se* by virtue of the experimental scientific method. It is rather by virtue of elementary philosophical principles such as causality, finality and sufficient reason, which a scientist, as a man, finds himself exercising in his daily contact with life and with the reality he studies. Indeed, the scientist's condition as a sentinel in the modern world, as one who is the first to glimpse the enormous complexity together with the marvelous harmony of reality, makes him a privileged witness of the plausibility of religion. The scientist can show how the admission of transcendence, far from harming the autonomy and the ends of research, rather stimulates it to continually surpass itself in an experience of self-transcendence which reveals the human mystery.

If we consider that today the broadened horizons of research, especially in what concerns the very origins of life, pose troubling questions regarding the right use of scientific conquests, we are not surprised by the increasingly frequent request on the part of scientists for sure moral criteria capable of freeing man from arbitrary willfulness. And who if not God is able to establish a moral order in which the dignity of every person is firmly cared for and promoted?

Certainly the Christian religion cannot consider certain professions of atheism or agnosticism in the name of science as rational. But it is equally firm in not accepting affirmations regarding God which arise from tendencies that are not rigorously attentive to rational processes.

Reasons for affirmation

At this point it would be very beautiful to make heard in some way the reasons for which many scientists positively affirm the existence of God, and to see by what personal relationship with God, with man, and with the great problems and supreme values of life they are sustained. How often silence, meditation, creative imagination, serene detachment from material things, the social significance of discovery, and purity of heart are factors which open to them a world of meaning which cannot be disregarded by anyone who proceeds with equal faithfulness and love toward the truth.

May a reference to an Italian scientist, Enrico Medi, a few years deceased, be sufficient. At the International Catechetical Congress of Rome in 1971 he affirmed: "When I tell a young person: Look, there is a new star, a galaxy, a neutron star 100 million light-years away, yet the protons, electrons, neutrons and mesons which are found there are identical with those which are found in this microphone.... Identity excludes probability. That which is identical is not probable.... Therefore there is a cause, outside of space, outside of time, the master of being, which made being to be in this way. And this is God....

"The being—I am speaking scientifically—which has caused things to be identical at a distance of billions of light-years, exists. And the number of identical particles in the universe is 10 raised to the 85th power.... Do we wish then to take in the song of the galaxies? If I were Francis of Assisi I would say: O galaxies of the immense heavens, give praise to my Lord, for he is omnipotent and good. O atoms, O protons, O electrons, O bird-songs, O blowing of the leaves and of the air, in the hands of man as a prayer, sing out the hymn which returns to God!" *(Acts of the Second International Catechetical Congress,* Rome, September 20-25, 1971; Rome, Studium, 1972, pp. 449-450).

General audience of July 17, 1985

The God of Our Faith

In the previous cycle of catechesis I sought to explain the meaning of the phrase: "I believe"; what it means to say: "to believe as Christians." In the cycle which we are now beginning I wish to concentrate on the first article of faith: "I believe in God" or, more fully: "I believe in God the Father almighty, Creator...." This is the first and fundamental truth of faith in the Apostles' Creed, and almost identically in the Nicene-Constantinopolitan Creed: "I believe in one God, the Father almighty, Creator." Thus the subject of our catechesis in this cycle will be God—the God of our faith. Since faith is the response to revelation, the theme of the catechesis which will follow will be about God who has made himself known to man, to whom "he has revealed himself and made known the hidden purpose of his will" (cf. *DV* 2).

The beginning and the end

The first article of the creed speaks of this God. All the subsequent articles of the creeds of faith speak of him indirectly. They are all united organically to the first and fundamental truth about God who is the source from which they derive. God is "the Alpha and the Omega" (Rev 1:8); he is also the beginning and the end of our faith. We can say that all the subsequent truths enunciated in the creed enable us to know ever more fully the God of our faith of whom the first article speaks. They enable us to know better who God is in himself and in his intimate life. Indeed, by knowing his works—the work of creation and of redemption—by knowing his whole plan of salvation in regard to the human race, we enter ever more deeply into the truth about God as he is revealed in the Old and New Covenants. It is the case of a progressive revelation whose contents are synthetically formulated in the creeds of faith. In being set out in the articles of the creeds, the truth expressed by the first words: "I believe in God," acquires a fullness of meaning—naturally, within the limits in which God's mystery is accessible to us through revelation.

The God of our faith, whom we profess in the Creed, is the God of Abraham, our father in faith (cf. Rom 4:12-16). He is "the God of Isaac and of Jacob," that is, of Israel (Mk 12:26 and parallel passages), the God of Moses—and finally and above all he is God, "the Father of Jesus Christ" (cf. Rom 15:6). We affirm this when we say: "I believe in God the Father...." He is the one and identical God of whom the Letter to the Hebrews tells us that having already "spoken in many and various ways of old to our fathers by the prophets, finally in these last days he has spoken to us by the Son..." (Heb 1:1-2). He, who is the source of the word which describes his progressive self-revelation in history, is fully revealed in the Incarnate Word, the eternal Son of the Father. In this Son—Jesus Christ—the God of our faith is definitively confirmed as Father. As such he is recognized and glorified by Jesus who prayed: "I thank you, Father, Lord of heaven and earth..." (Mt 11:25), clearly teaching us also to discover in this God, Lord of heaven and earth, "our" Father (Mt 6:9).

A personal God

Thus the God of revelation, "God, Father of Our Lord Jesus Christ" (Rom 15:6), is placed before our faith as a personal God, as an inscrutable divine "I" before our human "I," before each and all. He is indeed an inscrutable "I," in his profound mystery, but he has "opened" himself to us in revelation so that we can turn to him as the most holy divine "You." Each one of us is in a position to do so, because our God, who embraces in himself and surpasses and transcends in an infinite way everything that exists, is very close to all, and indeed intimate to our innermost being— *"interior intimo meo,"* as St. Augustine wrote *(Confessions,* bk. III, c. VI, 11; PL 32, 687).

This God, the God of our faith, the God and Father of Jesus Christ, God and our Father, is at the same time the "Lord of heaven and earth," as Jesus himself invoked him (Mt 11:25). He is the Creator.

When the Apostle Paul of Tarsus appeared before the Athenians in the Areopagus, he proclaimed: "Men of Athens...observing the objects of your worship, I found also an altar with this inscription, 'To an unknown god.' What you worship as unknown, I proclaim to you. The God who made the world and everything in it, being Lord of heaven and earth, does not live in shrines made by man, nor is he served by human hands, as though he needed anything, since he himself gives to all men life and breath and everything. He...determined allotted periods and the boundaries of their habitation, that they should seek God, in the hope that they might grope after him and find him. Yet he is not far from each one of us, for 'In him we live and move and have our being'" (Acts 17:23-28).

In these words Paul of Tarsus, the apostle of Jesus Christ, announced in the Areopagus of Athens the first and fundamental truth of the Christian faith. It is the truth which we too confess in the words: "I believe in God (in one God), the Father almighty, Creator of heaven and earth." This God—the God of revelation—today, as then, is for many "an unknown God." He is that God whom many today, as then, "seek," "groping after him" (Acts 17:27). He is the inscrutable and ineffable God. But he comprehends everything: "in him we live and move and have our being" (Acts 17:28). In our subsequent meetings we shall seek gradually to approach this God.

General audience of July 24, 1985

God Who Reveals Himself
Is He Who Exists

In pronouncing the words "I believe in God," we express first of all the conviction that God exists. This is a subject we have touched on in the catechesis of the preceding cycle, regarding the meaning of the words "I believe." According to the Church's teaching, the truth about the existence of God is accessible to mere human reason, if free from prejudice. The passages of the Book of Wisdom (13:1-9) and of the Letter to the Romans (cf. 1:19-20) which we have quoted previously, witness to this. They speak of the knowledge of God as Creator (or First Cause). This truth also recurs in other pages of Sacred Scripture. The invisible God becomes in a certain sense "visible" by means of his works.

"The heavens proclaim the glory of God,
and the firmament shows forth the work of his hand.
Day unto day takes up the story and night unto night
makes known the message" (Ps 19:2-3).

This cosmic hymn of exaltation of creatures is a song of praise to God as Creator. Here we have another text:

"O Lord, how manifold are your works!
In wisdom you have made them all;
the earth is full of your creatures" (Ps 104:24).

"He it is who made the earth by his power,
who established the world by his wisdom,
and by his understanding stretched out the heavens....
Every man is stupid and without knowledge"
(Jer 10:12,14).

"He has made everything beautiful in its time...
I know that whatever God does endures forever;
nothing can be added to it, nor anything taken from it"
(Eccl 3:11,14).

These are only some passages in which the inspired authors express the religious truth about God the Creator, by using the image of the world which was contemporary to them. It is certainly a pre-scientific image, but religiously true and poetically exquisite. The image available to the people of our time, thanks to the development of philosophical and scientific cosmology, is incomparably more meaningful and efficacious for those who act with an unprejudiced mind.

The marvels which the various specific sciences reveal to us about man and the world, about the microcosm and macrocosm, about the internal structure of matter and the depths of the human psyche, are such as to confirm the words of the sacred authors, leading us to recognize the existence of a supreme Intelligence which created the universe and gives it order.

The words "I believe in God" refer first of all to him who has revealed himself. God who reveals himself is he who exists. Only one who really exists can in fact reveal himself. In a certain sense, revelation concerns itself only marginally and indirectly with the problem of the existence of God. The creed does not present the existence of God as a problem in its own right. As we have already said, Sacred Scripture, Tradition, and the Magisterium affirm the possibility of a certain knowledge of God with the help of reason alone (cf. Wis 13:1-9; Rom

1:19-20; Vatican I, *DS* 3004; Vatican II, *DV* 6). Indirectly, such an affirmation includes the postulate that the knowledge of the existence of God through faith—which we express with the words "I believe in God"—has a rational character which reason can investigate. "I believe, that I may understand," as also "I understand, that I may believe"—this is the path from faith to theology.

When we say "I believe in God," our words have a precise character of "profession." By our profession we respond to God who has revealed himself. By professing we become sharers in the truth which God has revealed, and we express it as the content of our conviction. He who reveals himself not only makes it possible for us to know that he exists, but he also enables us to know Who he is, and also how he is. Thus God's self-revelation leads us to the question about God's essence: Who is God?

Here we may refer to the biblical event narrated in the Book of Exodus (3:1-14). Moses, who was pasturing the flock near the mountain of Horeb, noted an extraordinary phenomenon. "He looked, and lo, the bush was burning, yet it was not consumed" (Ex 3:2). He approached and "God called to him out of the bush, 'Moses, Moses!' And he said, 'Here am I.' Then God said, 'Do not come near; put off your shoes from your feet, for the place on which you are standing is holy ground.' And God said, 'I am the God of your fathers, the God of Abraham, the God of Isaac, and the God of Jacob.' And Moses hid his face, for he was afraid to look at God" (Ex 3:4-6).

The event described by the Book of Exodus is defined as a "theophany," a manifestation of God in an extraordinary sign. Among all the theophanies of the Old Testament, this one is particularly striking as a sign of the presence of God. A theophany is not a direct revelation of God, but only the manifestation of his special presence. In this case, God's presence was made known both by means of the words spoken from within the burning bush, and also by means of the bush itself which was burning but was not consumed.

God revealed to Moses the mission he intended to entrust to him. Moses was to withdraw the Israelites from the slavery of Egypt and lead them into the promised land. God promised Moses his powerful help to carry out his mission: "I will be with you." Then Moses said to God, "If I come to the people of Israel and say to them, 'The God of your fathers has sent me to you,' and they ask me, 'What is his name?' what shall I say to them? God said to Moses, 'I am who I am.' And he said, 'Say this to the people of Israel: I am has sent me to you'" (Ex 3:12-14).

Thus the God of our faith—the God of Abraham, of Isaac and of Jacob—revealed his name. It is "I am who I am." According to the tradition of Israel, the name expresses the essence.

The Sacred Scriptures give different names of God, such as "Lord" (e.g., Wis 1:1), "Love" (1 Jn 4:16), "Compassionate One" (e.g., Ps 86:15), "Faithful One" (1 Cor 1:9), "Holy One" (Is 6:3). But the name which Moses heard from the midst of the burning bush is as it were the root of all the others. *He who is* expresses the very essence of God, which is self-existence, subsistent Being, as the theologians and philosophers say. In his presence we cannot but prostrate ourselves and adore.

General audience of July 31, 1985

The God of Infinite Majesty

"We believe that this unique God is absolutely one in his infinitely holy essence as in all of his perfections, in his omnipotence, in his infinite love, in his providence, in his will and in his love. *He* is *he who is,* as he himself revealed to Moses. He is Love, as the apostle John teaches us. These two names, Being and Love, ineffably express the divine reality of him who wished to make himself known to us, and who inhabiting inaccessible light is in himself above every name, above all things and above every created intelligence" *(Insegnamenti di Paolo VI,* VI; 1968; 302).

Pope Paul VI spoke these words on the 1900th anniversary of the martyrdom of the holy Apostles Peter and Paul, June 30, 1968, during the profession of faith called the *Credo of the People of God.* They express in a more extended way than the ancient creeds, but still concisely and synthetically, that truth about God which the Church professes from the beginning of the creed: "I believe in God." He is the God who has revealed himself, the God of our faith. His name, "I am who I am," revealed to Moses from within the burning bush at the foot of Mount Horeb, re-echoes still in the creed of today.

Paul VI united this name—the name "Being"—with the name "Love" (according to the expression of the First Letter of St. John). These two names express the truth about God in the most essential way. We must still have recourse to them when, asking ourselves about the essence of God, we seek to answer the question: who is God?

Paul VI made reference to the name of God, "I am who I am," which is found in the Book of Exodus. Following the doctrinal and theological tradition of many centuries, he saw in it the revelation of God as "Being"—subsisting Being, which expresses, in the language of the philosophy of being (ontology or metaphysics) used by St. Thomas Aquinas, the essence of God. One must add that the strictly linguistic interpretation of the words "I am who I am" reveals other possible meanings to which we shall refer later. Paul VI's words make sufficiently evident that the Church, in replying to the question "Who is God?" continues to take as a starting point "being" *(esse),* in line with the centuries-old theological and patristic tradition. Nor can it be seen in what other way one could formulate a tenable and understandable reply.

The word with which God reveals himself by expressing himself in "the terminology of being," indicates a special coming together between the language of revelation and the language of that human knowledge of reality which from antiquity was called "first philosophy." The language of this philosophy enables one to approach, in some way, the name of God as "Being." However—as one of the most distinguished representatives of the Thomistic school of our time observes, echoing St. Thomas Aquinas himself (cf. *Contra Gentes,* 1, cc. 14, 30)—even making use of this language we can at most "mouth" this revealed name which expresses the essence of God (cf. E. Gilson, *Le Thomisme,* Paris 1944, ed. Vrin, pp. 33, 35, 41, 155-156). Human language does not suffice to express adequately and exhaustively the "Who is" of God! Our concepts and our words in regard to God serve only to say what he is not, rather than what he is (cf. *Summa Theologica* 1, q. 12, a. 12).

"I am who I am." The God who replied to Moses with these words is also "the Creator of heaven and of earth." Anticipating here for a moment what we shall say in successive catecheses in regard to the revealed truth about creation, it is opportune to note that according to the common interpretation, the word "create" means "to call into being from non-being," that is, from "nothingness." To be created means not to possess in oneself the source, the reason of one's being, but to receive it "from another." This is synthetically expressed in the Latin phrase *ens ab alio*. He who creates—the Creator—possesses existence in himself and from himself *(ens a se)*.

To be pertains to his substance: his essence is *to be*. He is subsisting being *(esse subsistens)*. Precisely for this reason he cannot not be, he is "necessary" being. Differing from God who is "necessary being," the things which receive existence from him, that is, creatures, are able not to be. *Being* does not constitute their essence; they are "contingent" beings.

These considerations regarding the revealed truth about the creation of the world help us to understand God as "Being." They help also to link this Being with the reply received by Moses to the question about the name of God: "I am who I am." In the light of these reflections the solemn words heard by St. Catherine of Siena acquire full clarity: "You are who are not, I am who am" (S. Catherine, *Legenda major,* 1, 10). This is the essence of God, the name of God, read in depth in the faith inspired by his self-revelation, confirmed in the light of the radical truth contained in the concept of creation.

When we refer to God it would be fitting to write that "I Am" and that "He Is" in capitals, reserving the lower case for creatures. This would also signify a correct way of reflecting on God according to the categories of "being."

Inasmuch as he is *"ipsum Esse Subsistens"*—that is the absolute fullness of Being and therefore of every perfection—God is completely transcendent in regard to the world. By his essence, by his divinity, he "goes beyond" and infinitely "surpasses" everything created—both every single creature, however perfect, and the ensemble of creation, the visible and invisible beings.

It is clear then that the God of our faith, *he who is* is the God of infinite majesty. This majesty is the glory of the divine Being, the glory of the name of God, many times celebrated in Sacred Scripture.

"O Lord, our God,

how majestic is your name in all the earth!" (Ps 8:2)

"For you are great and do wondrous things,

you alone are God" (Ps 86:10).

"There is none like you, O Lord..." (Jer 10:6).

Before the God of immense glory we cannot but bend the knee in an attitude of humble and joyous adoration, repeating with the liturgy in the song of the *Te Deum: "Pleni sunt caeli et terra maiestatis gloriae tuae.... Te per orbem terrarum sancta confitetur Ecclesia: Patrem immensae maiestati."* "The heavens and the earth are filled with your majesty and glory...and to the ends of the earth your holy Church proclaims her faith in you—Father, whose majesty is boundless."

General audience of August 7, 1985

Man Contacts God
in the Obscurity of Faith

The God of our faith, the One who in a mysterious way revealed his name to Moses at the foot of Mount Horeb by stating "I am who I am" is, as regards the world, completely transcendent. He "is really and essentially distinct from the world..., and ineffably raised above all things which are outside of himself or which can be conceived as being so" *(DS* 3002): *"est re et essentia a mundo distinctus, et super omnia quae praeter ipsum sunt aut concipi possunt ineffabiliter excelsus"* (Const. *Dei Filius,* Vatican I, cap. I, ca 1-4). This is what the First Vatican Council taught, professing the perennial faith of the Church.

Even if the existence of God can be known and demonstrated, and even if his essence is in some manner knowable in the mirror of creation, as the same Council has taught, no sign, no created image can reveal the essence of God, as such, to the human mind. It exceeds all that exists in the created world and all that could be thought in the human mind. God is the *"ineffabiliter excelsus."*

To the question "Who is God?" if it refers to the essence of God, we cannot answer with a definition in the strict sense of the term. The essence of God—which is the divinity—is found to be outside every category of genus and species which we use in our definitions. So the essence of God cannot be enclosed in any definition. If, in our thought about God, with the category of "being," we use the analogy of being, with this we bring out the "non-resemblance" much more than the resemblance. We bring out the incomparability much more than the comparability of God with the creature (as the Fourth Council of the Lateran also recorded in 1215). This affirmation holds true for all creatures, for those of the visible world as well as for those of the spiritual order, and also for man, inasmuch as he is created "in the image and likeness of God" (cf. Gen 1:26).

In this way, the fact that God can be known through creatures does not take away his essential "incomprehensibility." God is "incomprehensible," as the First Vatican Council has declared. The human intellect, inasmuch as it possesses a certain idea of God, and although it has been elevated significantly, through the revelation of the Old and of the New Covenant, to a deeper and more complete knowledge of his mystery, is unable to comprehend God adequately and exhaustively. He remains ineffable and inscrutable to the created mind. "No one has ever been able to comprehend the thoughts of God except the Spirit of God," proclaimed the Apostle Paul (1 Cor 2:11).

In the modern world, scientific thought is above all oriented toward that which is "visible" and in some way "measurable" in the light of sense experience and with the instruments of observation and investigation now available. In a world of positivist methodologies and of technological applications, this "incomprehensibility" of God becomes still more realized by many, particularly in the sphere of Western culture. Thus particular conditions have arisen for the expansion of agnostic or directly atheistic attitudes, due to the thought premises common to many people today. Some consider that this intellectual situation can, in its own way, favor the conviction—which pertains also to the universal religious tradition, if one may so speak, and which Christianity has, under certain aspects, emphasized—that God is incomprehensible. It would be a tribute to the infinite, real transcendence of God, which cannot be catalogued among the things of our common experience and knowledge.

Yes, truly, the God who has revealed himself, has manifested himself as the One who is incomprehensible, inscrutable, ineffable. The Book of Job says: "Can you find out the deep things of God? Can you find out the limit of the Almighty? It is higher than heaven; what can you do? It is deeper than Sheol; what can you know?" (Job 11:7-8).

We read in the Book of Exodus of a happening which in a significant way sets this truth in relief. Moses asked God: "Show me your glory." The Lord replied: "I will make all my goodness pass before you, and will proclaim my name before you [which had already happened in the theophany at the foot of Mount Horeb], but you will not be able to see my face, for man shall not see me and live" (Ex 33:18-20).

For his part, the prophet Isaiah confessed:

"Truly you are a God who hides yourself.
O God of Israel, the Savior" (Is 45:15).

This God, who revealed himself by means of the prophets and finally by means of his Son, remains a "hidden God." The Apostle John wrote at the beginning of his Gospel: "No one has ever seen God; the only One, who is in the bosom of the Father, has made him known" (Jn 1:18). Through the Son, the God of revelation has, in a unique way, approached the human race. The idea of God which man acquires through faith reaches its peak in this approach. Nevertheless, even though God made himself still closer to man through the Incarnation, he continues in his essence to remain the "hidden God." "Not that anyone has seen the Father" we read in that same Gospel of John, "except him who is from God; he has seen the Father" (Jn 6:46).

In this way, therefore, God, who has revealed himself, remains an inscrutable mystery in this life. This is the mystery of faith. The first article of the creed, "I believe in God," expresses the first and fundamental truth of faith, which, at the same time, is the first and fundamental mystery of the faith. God, who has revealed himself, remains for the human intellect a Something which is at the same time known and incomprehensible. In the course of earthly life, man enters into contact with the God of revelation in the "obscurity of faith." This has been elaborated in a whole vein of classical and modern theology which insists on the ineffability of God and finds a particularly deep, and at times sad, confirmation in the experience of the great mystics. But properly this "obscurity of faith"—as St. John of the Cross affirmed—is the light which infallibly leads to God (cf. *The Ascent of Mount Carmel,* 2 S 9, 3).

According to the words of St. Paul, this God is "the King of kings and Lord of lords, who alone has immortality and dwells in unapproachable light, whom no man has ever seen or can see" (1 Tim 6:15-16).

The obscurity of faith inevitably accompanies the earthly pilgrimage of the human spirit toward God, in the attempt to open itself to the light of the glory that is found only in the future life, in eternity. "Now we see in a mirror, but then face to face" (1 Cor 13:12).

"In lumine tuo videbimus lumen."
"In your light we see light" (Ps 36:9).

General audience of August 28, 1985

The Living God Has Revealed Himself As Eternity Itself

The Church incessantly professes the faith expressed in the most ancient Christian creeds: "I believe in one only God, the Father almighty, creator of heaven and earth." These words mirror in a concise and synthetic way, the witness which the God of our faith, the living and true God of revelation, has given about himself, according to the Letter to the Hebrews, speaking "by the prophets," and ultimately "by the Son" (Heb 1:1-2). The Church comes forward to meet the changing needs of the times and it probes the truth about God, as the various Councils witness. I refer to the First Vatican Council whose teaching was dictated by the need to withstand both the errors of nineteenth century pantheism and those of materialism, which had begun to assert themselves at that time.

The First Vatican Council taught: "Holy Church believes and confesses that there is one only living and true God, creator and Lord of heaven and earth, omnipotent, eternal, immense, incomprehensible, infinite in intellect, will, and in every perfection; who being one single spiritual substance, absolutely simple and immutable, must be proclaimed as really and essentially distinct from the world, in himself and of himself most blessed, and ineffably supreme over all things that are outside of himself or that are conceivable" (Const. *Dei Filius,* can. 1-4, *DS* 3001).

It is easily seen that the conciliar text starts off from these same ancient symbols of faith which we too recite: "I believe in God...almighty...creator of heaven and earth." But it develops this fundamental formulation in accordance with the doctrine contained in Sacred Scripture, Tradition and the Magisterium of the Church. Vatican I lists the "attributes" of God in a more complete form than those of the ancient symbols.

By "attributes" we mean the properties of the divine "Being" which are manifested by revelation, as well as the best philosophical consideration (cf. e.g. *Summa Theol.,* I, qq. 3 ff.). Sacred Scripture describes God by using various adjectives. They are expressions of human language, which shows itself to be so limited, especially when it seeks to express that totally transcendent reality which is God in himself.

The passage from the First Vatican Council, quoted above, confirms the impossibility of adequately expressing God. He is incomprehensible and ineffable. The faith of the Church and its teaching about God maintains this "incomprehensibility" and "ineffability." But they do not content themselves with a negative kind of recognition, as does the so-called apophatic theology. This view maintains that human language, and so theology, can express only or almost only what God is not, since it lacks adequate expressions to explain what he is.

Thus Vatican I does not limit itself to statements which speak of God in a "negative way," but it expresses itself also in an "affirmative way." Thus, for example, it teaches that this God who is essentially distinct from the world *(a mundo distinctus re et essentia),* is an eternal God. Sacred Scripture expresses this truth in various passages and in different ways. For example, we read in the Book of Sirach: "He who lives forever created the whole universe" (Sir 18:1), and in the Book of the Prophet Daniel: "He is the living God, enduring forever" (6:27).

The words of Psalm 102, echoed by the Letter to the Hebrews, are similar. The Psalm says: "Of old you did lay the foundation of the earth, and the heavens are the work of your hands. They will perish, but you endure; they will all wear out like a garment. You change them like raiment, and they pass away; but you are the same, and your years have no end" (Ps 102:25-27). Some centuries later, the author of the Letter to the Hebrews will take up the words of the psalm just quoted: "You, Lord, did found the earth in the beginning, and the heavens are the work of your hands; they will perish, but you remain; they will all grow old like a garment; like a mantle you will roll them up, and they will be changed like a garment; but you are the same, and your years will never end" (Heb 1:1-12).

Eternity is here the element which essentially distinguishes God from the world. While the latter is subject to change and passes away, God remains beyond the passing of the world. He is necessary and immutable: "you are the same...."

St. Paul wrote, conscious of faith in the eternal God: "To the king of ages, immortal, invisible, the only God, be honor and glory for ever and ever. Amen" (1 Tim 1:17). The Book of Revelation again expresses the same truth: "'I am the Alpha and the Omega,' says the Lord God, 'who is and who was and who is to come, the Almighty'" (Rv 1:8).

These facts of revelation also express the rational conviction to which one comes when one considers that God is the subsisting Being, and therefore necessary, and therefore eternal. Because he cannot not be, he cannot have beginning or end nor a succession of moments in the only and infinite act of his existence. Right reason and revelation wonderfully converge on this point. Being God, absolute fullness of being, *(ipsum Esse subsistens)*, his eternity "inscribed in the terminology of being" must be understood as the "indivisible, perfect, and simultaneous possession of an unending life," and therefore as the attribute of being absolutely "beyond time."

God's eternity does not go by with the time of the created world. "It does not coincide with the present." It does not precede it or "prolong" it into infinity. It is beyond and above "being." Eternity, with all that mystery of God, includes in some way the "beyond" and the "above," all that "from within" is subject to time, to change, to the contingent. The words of St. Paul at the Areopagus of Athens come to mind: "In him...we live and move and have our being" (Acts 17:28). Let us say "from the outside" in order, by this metaphorical expression, to affirm God's transcendence over things, and of eternity over time. We realize and reaffirm that God is the Being that is intrinsic to the very being of things, and therefore also to time which passes as a succession of moments, none of which is outside his eternal embrace.

The witness of Vatican I expresses the Church's faith in the living, true, and eternal God. He is eternal because he is the absolute fullness of being which cannot be understood as a sum of fragments or of "particles" of being which change with time. The texts quoted from the Bible clearly indicate this. The absolute fullness of being can come to be understood only as eternity, which is, as the total and indivisible possession of that being, God's own life. In this sense God is eternal: a "Now," a "Present," subsisting and unchanging. This mode of being is essentially distinguished from that of creatures, which are "contingent" beings.

Thus the living God, who has revealed himself, is the eternal God. More correctly let us say that God is eternity itself. The perfect simplicity of the divine Being *(omnino simplex)* demands such a form of expression.

When with our human language we say: "God is eternal," we indicate an attribute of the divine Being. Since no attribute of God is distinguished in the concrete from the very essence of God (while human attributes are distinguished from the person who possesses them), in saying: "God is eternal" we wish to affirm: "God is eternity."

For us who are subject to space and to time, this eternity is incomprehensible, just like the divine essence. However, it makes us perceive the infinite greatness and majesty of God, also under this aspect. We are filled with joy at the thought of this Being-Eternity which includes all that is created and contingent, including also our little being, our every act, every moment of our life.

"In him we live and move and have our being."

General audience of September 4, 1985

God, the Fullness of Life, Is Spirit, Immense and Invisible

"God is spirit." Our Lord Jesus Christ pronounced these words during the conversation with the Samaritan woman near Jacob's well, in Sychar.

In the light of such words, let us continue to comment in this catechesis on the first truth of the symbol of faith: "I believe in God." Let us refer in particular to the teaching of the First Vatican Council in the Constitution *Dei Filius,* in the first chapter: "God creator of all things." "This God who has revealed himself, speaking 'through the prophets, and ultimately...through the Son' (Heb 1:1), being creator of the world is distinguished essentially from the world, which he has created." He is Eternity, as the preceding catechesis explained, while all that is created is contingent and subject to time.

Since the God of our faith is Eternity, he is the fullness of life. As such, he is distinguished from all that lives in the visible world. It is a question of a "life" which is to be understood in the highest sense of the word when it refers to the God who is spirit, pure spirit. So he is immense and invisible, as Vatican I teaches. We do not find in him anything that can be measured according to the criteria of the created and visible world and of the time which marks the passage of man's life.

God is above matter, he is absolutely "immaterial." Nevertheless, the "spirituality" of the divine Being is not limited to that which we can reach according to the negative way—namely, only to immateriality. We come to know by the affirmative way that spirituality is an attribute of the divine Being, when Jesus of Nazareth replied to the Samaritan woman by saying: "God is spirit" (Jn 4:24).

The conciliar text of Vatican I to which we refer, affirms the doctrine on God. The Church professes and proclaims it with two fundamental assertions: "God is a unique spiritual substance, utterly simply and immutable"; and again: "God is infinite in intellect, will, and in every perfection."

The doctrine on the spirituality of the divine Being, passed on by revelation, is clearly written in this text in the "terminology of being." This is displayed in the formulation: "spiritual substance." The word "substance" pertains to the language of the philosophy of being.

The conciliar text intends to state by this phrase that God, who by his essence is distinguished from the whole created world, is not only subsisting Being, but that, as such, he is also subsisting Spirit. The divine Being is by its own essence absolutely spiritual.

Spirituality signifies intellect and free will. God is Intelligence, Will and Liberty in an infinite degree, just as he is also all perfection in an infinite degree.

The facts of revelation which we find in Sacred Scripture and in Tradition often confirm these truths about God. For the present we will refer only to some citations from the Bible which emphasize the infinitely perfect intelligence of the divine Being. We shall devote the subsequent catecheses to the infinitely perfect liberty and will of God.

First of all, St. Paul's magnificent exclamation in the Letter to the Romans comes to mind: "O the depth of the riches and wisdom and knowledge of God! How unsearchable are his judgments and how inscrutable his ways! Indeed, who has ever known the mind of the Lord?" (Rom 11:33 ff.).

The words of the Apostle resound as a powerful echo of the teaching in the sapiential books of the Old Testament: "His (referring to God) wisdom is beyond measure," Psalm 147:5 proclaims. God's majesty is united to his wisdom: "Great is the Lord and greatly to be praised, and his greatness is immeasurable" (Ps 145:3). "It is not possible to diminish or increase them, nor is it possible to trace the wonders of the Lord. When a man has finished, he is just beginning, and when he stops he will be at a loss" (Sir 18:5-7). The sage then states: "He is greater than all his works" (Sir 43:28), and concludes: "He is the all" (Sir 43:27).

The prophet Isaiah passes to the first person, "I," while the "sapiential" authors speak of God in the third person, "he." Isaiah makes God, who inspires him, say: "As the heavens are higher than the earth, so are my ways higher than your ways, and my thoughts higher than your thoughts" (Is 55:9).

The "thoughts" of God and his "knowledge and wisdom" express the infinite perfection of his Being. God superlatively surpasses through his unlimited intellect all that exists outside of him. No creature can deny this perfection, in particular no man. "Who are you, O man, to answer back to God? Will what is molded say to its molder, 'Why have you made me thus?' Is not the potter master of the clay?" asks St. Paul (Rom 9:20). This way of thinking and of expressing oneself is inherited from the Old Testament. Similar questions and replies are found in Isaiah (cf. Is 29:15; 45:9-11) and in the Book of Job (cf. 2:9-10; 1:21). The Book of Deuteronomy proclaims in its turn: "Give glory to our God! He is the rock, his work is perfect; for all his ways are justice. A God of faithfulness and without iniquity, just and right is he" (Dt 32:3-4). The praise of the infinite perfection of God is not only confession of his wisdom, but also of his justice and integrity, that is, of his moral perfection.

In the Sermon on the Mount, Jesus Christ urged: "Be you then perfect as your heavenly Father is perfect"(Mt 5:48). This call is an invitation to confess that God is perfect! He is "infinitely perfect" (Vatican I, *DS* 3001).

The infinite perfection of God is constantly present in the teaching of Jesus Christ. He said to the Samaritan woman: "God is spirit...true worshippers must worship him in spirit and truth..." (Jn 4:23-24). He expressed himself in a significant way when he replied to the young man—who had turned to him with the words: "Good Teacher..." by saying: "Why do you call me good? No one is good but God alone..." (Mk 10:17-18).

Only God is good, and he possesses the infinite perfection of goodness. God is the fullness of every good. Just as he "is" all the fullness of being, similarly he "is Good" with all the fullness of good. This fullness of good corresponds to the infinite perfection of his will. In the same way, the absolute fullness of truth corresponds to the infinite perfection of his intellect and of his intelligence. The fullness of truth subsists in it inasmuch as it is known by his intellect as identical with his knowing and his being. God is infinitely perfect spirit, through whom those who have known him become his true adorers. They adore him in spirit and truth.

God, this infinite Good which is the absolute fullness of truth, *"est diffusivum sui" (Summa Theol.,* I, q. 5, a. 4, ad 2). God has revealed himself by this also. Revelation is the same good which communicates itself as Truth.

This God who has revealed himself, desires to communicate himself in an ineffable and superlative way, to give himself! This is the God of the covenant and of grace.

General audience of September 11, 1985

God the Almighty Father

"I believe in God, the Father Almighty, creator of heaven and earth...."

God who has revealed himself, the God of our faith, is an infinitely perfect spirit. We spoke of this in the previous catechesis. As an infinitely perfect spirit he is the absolute fullness of Truth and Goodness, and he desires to give himself. Goodness extends itself: *bonum est diffusivum sui (Summa Theol.*, I, q. 5, a. 4, ad 2).

The creeds express in a certain sense this truth about God viewed as the infinite fullness of goodness. They do this by affirming that God is the creator of heaven and earth, of all things visible and invisible. It is fitting to examine here in the light of revelation that which in God corresponds to the mystery of creation, even though we shall deal with the truth about creation somewhat later.

The Church professes that God is omnipotent ("I believe in God, the Father Almighty") inasmuch as he is an infinitely perfect spirit. God is also omniscient, that is, his knowledge penetrates everything.

This omnipotent and omniscient God has the power to create, to call into being from non-being, from nothingness.

We read in the Book of Genesis 18:14: "Is anything impossible for the Lord?"

The Book of Wisdom (11:21) states: "For it is always in your power to show great strength, and who can withstand the might of your arm?" The Book of Esther professes the same faith in the words: "Lord, King who rules over the universe, all things are in your power and there is no one who can oppose you" (Esther 4:17b). The Archangel Gabriel will say to Mary of Nazareth at the Annunciation: "With God nothing is impossible" (Lk 1:37).

God, who reveals himself by the mouth of the prophets, is omnipotent. These truths run deeply through the whole of revelation, beginning with the first words of the Book of Genesis: "God said: 'Let there be...'" (Gen 1:3). The creative act is manifested as the all-powerful word of God: "For he spoke, and it came to be..." (Ps 33:9). By creating everything from nothing, being from non-being, God reveals himself as the infinite fullness of goodness which extends itself. *He who is,* Subsisting Being, infinitely perfect Being, in a certain sense gives himself in that "is," by calling into existence outside of himself the visible and invisible cosmos—the created beings. By creating things he begins the history of the universe. By creating man as male and female he begins the history of humanity. As Creator he is the Lord of history. "There are varieties of working, but it is the same God who inspires them all in every one" (1 Cor 12:6).

The God who reveals himself as Creator, and so as Lord of the history of the world and of humanity, is the omnipotent God, the living God.... According to the First Vatican Council: "The Church believes and acknowledges that there exists one only living and true God, creator and Lord of heaven and earth, omnipotent" *(DS* 3001). This God, a spirit infinitely perfect and omniscient, is absolutely free and sovereign even in regard to the very act of creation. He is first of all Lord of his own will in the work of creation if he is the Lord of all that he creates. He creates because he wills to create. He creates because this is in accordance with his infinite wisdom. In creating he acts with the inscrutable fullness of his liberty, under the impulse of eternal love.

The text of the First Vatican Council's Constitution *Dei Filius,* already quoted on several occasions, emphasizes God's absolute liberty in creation and in his every action. God is "most happy in himself and of himself." He possesses the complete fullness of goodness and happiness in himself and of himself. He does not call the world into existence in order to complete or integrate the goodness which he is. He creates solely and exclusively for the purpose of bestowing the goodness of a manifold existence on the world of invisible and visible creatures. It is a multiple and varied participation of the unique, infinite, eternal good, which is identical with the very Being of God.

God is absolutely free and sovereign in the work of creation. He remains fundamentally independent of the created universe. This does not in any way imply that he is indifferent in regard to creatures. Rather, he guides them as Eternal Wisdom, Love and Omnipotent Providence.

Sacred Scripture sets out the fact that in this work God is alone. The prophet Isaiah declares "I am the Lord, who made all things, who stretched out the heavens alone, who spread out the earth—who was with me?" (Is 44:24). God's sovereign liberty and his paternal omnipotence stand out in his "solitude" in the work of creation.

"The God who formed and created the earth and established it, did not create it as a chaos, but formed it to be inhabited" (Is 45:18).

The Church professes from the very beginning her faith in the "Almighty Father," creator of heaven and earth, of all things visible and invisible. She does so in the light of the self-revelation of God who "spoke by the prophets and in these last days...by his Son" (Heb 1:1-2). This omnipotent God is also omniscient and omnipresent. Or better, one could say that, as an infinitely perfect spirit, God is simultaneously Omnipotence, Omniscience and Omnipresence.

God is first of all present to himself—in his One and Triune Divinity. He is also present in the universe which he has created. His presence is a consequence of the work of creation by means of his creative power *(per potentiam),* which makes present his transcendental Essence itself *(per essentiam).* This presence surpasses the world, penetrates it and keeps it in existence. The same can be repeated of God's presence through his knowledge, as the infinite glance which sees, penetrates and scrutinizes everything *(per visionem or per scientiam).* Finally, God is present in a special way in human history, which is also the history of salvation. This is (if one may say so) the most "personal" presence of God—his presence through grace, which humanity received in its fullness in Jesus Christ (cf. Jn 1:16-17). We shall speak of this last mystery of the faith in a proximate catechesis.

"O Lord, you search me and you know me..." (Ps 139:1).

Let us profess together with the entire People of God present in every part of the world, while we repeat the inspired words of this Psalm, our faith in the omnipotence, omniscience and omnipresence of God who is our Creator, Father and Providence! "In him...we live, and move and have our being" (Acts 17:28).

General audience of September 18, 1985

The God of the Covenant

We seek to reply progressively in our catechetical talks to the question: Who is God? It concerns an authentic reply, because it is based on the word of God's self-revelation. The certainty of faith as well as the intellect's conviction enlightened by faith characterizes this response.

Let us return again to the foot of Mount Horeb. Moses was pasturing the flock there. He heard from the midst of the burning bush the voice which said: "Put off your shoes from your feet, for the place on which you are standing is holy ground" (Ex 3:5). The voice continued: "I am the God of your fathers, the God of Abraham, the God of Isaac, and the God of Jacob." He is the God of the fathers who sent Moses to free his people from the Egyptian bondage.

We know that after having received this mission, Moses asked God his name. He received the reply: "I am who I am." The exegetical, theological and magisterial tradition of the Church has interpreted this reply as the revelation of God as "Being." Paul VI repeated this in the *Credo of the People of God* (1968).

One can attain a richer and more precise idea of God in the light of the history of salvation in the reply given by God—

"I am who I am." God—Yahweh—reveals himself above all as the God of the covenant by sending Moses in virtue of this name: "I am who I am for you; I am here as the God who desires the covenant and salvation," as the God who loves you and saves you.

God is thus presented as a Being who is a Person. He reveals himself to persons, whom he treats as such. God has gone forth in a certain sense, from his "solitude" to communicate himself, already in creating the world, by his opening to the world and especially to men created in his image and likeness (cf. Gen 1:26). The revelation of the name "I am who I am" (Yahweh) seems to especially set out in relief the truth that God is the Being-Person who knows, loves and draws all people to himself, the God of the covenant.

New stage of the covenant

God prepares a new stage of the covenant, a new stage of the history of salvation in this conversation with Moses. God's initiative of the covenant marks the history of salvation through numerous events, as the fourth Eucharistic Prayer shows in the words: "Again and again you offered a covenant to man."

God-Yahweh is presented as "the God of Abraham, the God of Isaac, the God of Jacob," in conversing with Moses at the foot of Mount Horeb. He is the God who had drawn up a covenant with Abraham (cf. Gen 17:1-14) and with his descendants, the patriarchs, the founders of the family of the chosen people, which has become the People of God.

However, the initiatives of the God of the covenant go back even before Abraham. The Book of Genesis mentions the covenant with Noah after the flood (cf. Gen 9:1-17). One can even speak of the primeval covenant before original sin (cf. Gen 2:15-17). We can say that, in the perspective of salvation,

God desired to establish a covenant with his people from the beginning of human history.

Salvation is the communion of endless life with God. The "tree of life" (cf. Gen 2:9) in the earthly paradise symbolized it. All the covenants which God has sealed with the human race after the sin of Adam confirm the truth that God wills man's salvation. The God of the covenant is the God "who gives himself" in a mysterious way—the God of revelation and the God of grace. He not only makes himself known to man, but he makes him a sharer in the divine nature (2 Pet 1:4).

The covenant reaches its definitive stage in Jesus Christ—the "new" and "eternal covenant" (Heb 12:24; 13:20). It witnesses to the complete originality of that truth about God which we profess in the Christian creed. In pagan antiquity, the divinity was the object of human aspiration. The revelation of the Old and still more of the New Testament shows God who is seeking man, who draws near to him. It is God who wishes to make a covenant: "I shall be your God and you shall be my people" (Lev 26:12); "I shall be their God and they shall be my people" (2 Cor 6:16).

Meaning of creation

The covenant is a completely free and sovereign divine initiative, just as creation is. It reveals in a still more eminent way the importance and the meaning of creation in the depths of divine liberty. The wisdom and love which guide the transcendent liberty of the God-Creator stand out still more in the transcendent liberty of the God of the covenant.

Through the covenant, especially that full and definitive covenant in Jesus Christ, God becomes in a certain way immanent in regard to the world. Yet he completely preserves his own transcendence. The incarnate God, and still more the crucified God, remains an incomprehensible and ineffable God.

But he becomes for us still more incomprehensible and ineffable precisely in so far as he is manifested as a God of an infinite, inscrutable love.

Monotheistic creed

We do not wish to anticipate the themes of future catecheses. Let's go back again to Moses. The revelation of God's name at the foot of Mount Horeb prepared that stage of the covenant which the God of the fathers would have wished to make with his people on Sinai. It sets out in relief the monotheistic sense of the creed based on the covenant in a strong and expressive way: "I believe in one God!" God is one, he is unique. The Book of Exodus states: "I am the Lord your God, who brought you out of the land of Egypt, out of the house of bondage. You shall have no other gods before me" (Ex 20:2-3). We find the basic formula of the Old Testament creed expressed in the words of Deuteronomy: "Hear O Israel: the Lord our God is one Lord" (Dt 6:4; cf. Dt 4:39-40).

Isaiah will give to this monotheistic creed of the Old Testament a magnificent prophetic expression: "You are my witnesses—says the Lord—my servants whom I have chosen, that you may know and believe me and understand that I am he. Before me no God was formed, nor shall there be any after me. I, I am the Lord, and besides me there is no savior.... You are my witnesses—says the Lord—and I am God, always the same from eternity" (Is 43:10-13). "Turn to me and be saved, all the ends of the earth, for I am God, and there is no other" (Is 45:22).

Pagan polytheism

This truth about the one God constitutes the fundamental deposit of the two Testaments. St. Paul expresses it in the New

Covenant in the words: "One God and Father of all who is above all and through all and in all" (Eph 4:6). The same Paul combated pagan polytheism (cf. Rom 1:23; Gal 3:8) with an ardor no less than that of the Old Testament. He proclaims with equal firmness that this one true God "is God of all, both of the circumcised and the uncircumcised, of both Jews and Gentiles" (cf. Rom 3:29-30). The revelation of a one true God given in the old covenant to the chosen people of Israel, was destined for the whole human race. Humanity would have found in monotheism the expression of the conviction at which man can arrive even with the light of reason. If God is perfect, infinite, subsistent Being, he must be One. The truth revealed in the Old Testament has become the faith of the universal Church in the new covenant, by means of Jesus Christ. The Church confesses: "I believe in one God."

General audience of September 25, 1985

Faith Culminates in
the Truth That God Is Love

"God is love...." These words are contained in one of the last books of the New Testament, the First Letter of St. John (4:16). They are the keystone of the truth about God. That truth is revealed through numerous words and many events until it reaches the full certainty of faith with the coming of Christ, and especially with his cross and resurrection. These words faithfully echo Christ's own statement: "God so loved the world that he gave his only Son, that whoever believes in him may not die but may have eternal life" (Jn 3:16).

The Church's faith reaches its peak in this supreme truth: God is love! In Christ's cross and resurrection he revealed himself definitively as love. "So we know and believe the love God has for us. God is love, and he who abides in love abides in God, and God abides in him" (1 Jn 4:16).

The truth that God is love constitutes the apex of all that has been revealed "by the prophets and in these days by the Son..." as the Letter to the Hebrews states (1:1). This truth illumines the whole content of divine revelation, and particularly the revealed reality of the creation and of the covenant. Creation manifests the omnipotence of God the Creator. But the exercise of omnipotence is definitively explained by means

144

of love. God created because he could do so, because he is omnipotent. But his omnipotence was guided by wisdom and moved by love. This is the work of creation. The work of redemption has a more powerful eloquence and offers us a more radical demonstration. Love remains as the expression of omnipotence in the face of evil, in the face of the sin of creatures. Only omnipotent love can draw forth good from evil and new life from sin and death.

Love giving life

Love as power gives life and animates. It is present in the whole of revelation. The living God, the God who gives life to all living beings, is he of whom the Psalms speak: "These all look to you, to give them their food in due season. When you give to them, they gather it up; when you open your hand, they are filled with good things. When you hide your face, they are dismayed; when you take away their breath, they die and return to the dust" (Ps 104:27-29). The image is drawn from the heart of creation. This picture has anthropomorphic features (like many texts of Sacred Scripture). But this anthropomorphism has its own biblical motivation. Seeing that man is created in the image and likeness of God, there is a reason for speaking of God "in the image and likeness" of man. However, this anthropomorphism does not obscure God's transcendence. It does not reduce God to human dimensions. It observes all the rules of analogy and of analogical language, as well as those of the analogy of faith.

God makes himself known in the covenant, first of all to his chosen people. The God of the covenant manifests the properties of his Being, following a pedagogic progression. Those properties are usually called his attributes. They are attributes of the moral order above all, in which the God who is love gradually reveals himself. God reveals himself—

especially in the covenant of Sinai—as the lawgiver, the supreme source of law. This legislative authority finds its full expression and confirmation in the attributes of the divine action which Sacred Scripture makes known to us.

The inspired books of the Old Testament manifest them to us. For example, we read in the Book of Wisdom: "For your strength is the source of righteousness, and your sovereignty over all causes you to spare all.... You who are sovereign in strength judge with mildness, and with great forbearance you govern us; for you have power to act whenever you choose" (Wis 12:16-18).

And again: "Who can measure his majestic power? And who can fully recount his mercies?" (Sir 18:5).

The writings of the Old Testament emphasize God's justice, but also his clemency and mercy.

They underline especially God's faithfulness to the covenant, which is an aspect of his "immutability" (cf. e.g., Ps 111:7-9; Is 65:1-2, 16-19).

They speak of God's anger, but this is always the just anger of a God who is "slow to anger and abounding in steadfast love" (Ps 145:8). They always set out in relief, in the above-mentioned anthropomorphic concept, God's "jealousy" of his covenant with his people. But they always present it as an attribute of love: "the zeal of the Lord of hosts" (Is 9:7).

We have already said that God's attributes are not distinguished from his essence. So it would be more exact to speak, not so much of a just, faithful, clement God, but rather of God who is justice, faithfulness, clemency, mercy—just as St. John has written that "God is love" (1 Jn 4:16).

The Old Testament prepared for the definitive revelation of God as love with an abundance of inspired texts. In one of these we read: "You are merciful to all, for you can do all things.... For you love all things that exist and loathe none of the things which you have made, for you would not have made

anything if you had hated it. How would anything have endured if you had not willed it?... You spare all things, for they
are yours, O Lord who loves the living" (Wis 11:23-26).

Can it not be said that these words of the Book of Wisdom already shown forth clearly the God who is love
(Amor-Caritas) by means of the creator "Being" of God?

But we see other texts, such as that of the Book of Jonah:
"For I knew that you are a gracious God and merciful, slow to
anger, and abounding in steadfast love, and who repents of
evil" (Jon 4:2).

Or also Psalm 145: "The Lord is gracious and merciful,
slow to anger and abounding in steadfast love. The Lord is
good to all, and his compassion is over all that he has made"
(Ps 145:8-9).

Definitive fulfillment in Christ

The more we read the writings of the major prophets, the
more the countenance of the God of love is revealed to us. The
Lord speaks to Israel by the mouth of Jeremiah: "I have loved
you with an everlasting love; therefore I have continued my
faithfulness to you" (in Hebrew *hesed)* (Jer 31:3).

To quote the words of Isaiah: "But Zion said: 'The Lord
has forsaken me, my Lord has forgotten me.' 'Can a woman
forget her child, that she should have no compassion on the
child of her womb? Even though she may forget, yet I will not
forget you'" (Is 49:14-15).

How significant in God's words is this reference to ma-
ternal love. God's mercy is made known by the unequaled
tenderness of motherhood, besides being made known to us by
fatherhood. Again Isaiah says: "For the mountains may depart
and the hills be removed, but my steadfast love shall not depart
from you, and my covenant of peace shall not be removed,
says the Lord who has compassion on you" (Is 54:10).

This marvelous preparation carried out by God in the history of the Old Covenant, especially by means of the prophets, awaited its definitive fulfillment. The definitive word of God-Love came with Christ. It was not merely pronounced, but lived in the paschal mystery of the cross and of the resurrection. Paul announces it in the Letter to the Ephesians: "God, who is rich in mercy, out of the great love with which he loved us, even when we were dead through our trespasses, made us alive together with Christ (by grace you have been saved)" (2:4-5).

Indeed we can give fullness to our profession of faith in "God the Father Almighty, Creator of heaven and earth" with St. John's stupendous definition: "God is love" (1 Jn 4:16).

General audience of October 2, 1985

THE BLESSED TRINITY

God Is the Blessed Trinity, Father, Son and Holy Spirit

The Church professes her faith in the one God, who is at the same time the Most Holy and ineffable Trinity of Persons: Father, Son and Holy Spirit. The Church lives by this truth contained in the most ancient symbols of faith. Paul VI recalled it in our times on the occasion of the 1900th anniversary of the martyrdom of the holy Apostles Peter and Paul (1968), in the symbol he presented which is universally known as the *Credo of the People of God.*

Only "he who has wished to make himself known to us, and who 'dwelling in light inaccessible' (1 Tim 6:16) is in himself above every name, above every thing and above every created intellect...can give us right and full knowledge of this reality by revealing himself as Father, Son and Holy Spirit, in whose eternal life we are by grace called to share, here below in the obscurity of faith and after death in eternal light..." *(L'Osservatore Romano,* English edition, July 11, 1968, p. 4).

God is incomprehensible to us. He wished to reveal himself, not only as the one creator and Almighty Father, but also as Father, Son, and Holy Spirit. This revelation reveals in its essential source the truth about God, who is love: God is love

in the interior life itself of the one divinity. This love is revealed as an ineffable communion of persons.

This mystery—the most profound, the mystery of the
intimate life of God himself—has been revealed to us by Jesus
Christ: "He who is in the bosom of the Father, he has made
him known" (Jn 1:18). The last words with which Christ concluded his earthly mission after the resurrection were
addressed to the apostles, according to St. Matthew's Gospel:
"Go therefore and make disciples of all the nations. Baptize
them in the name of the Father and of the Son and of the Holy
Spirit" (Mt 28:19). These words began the Church's mission
and indicated her fundamental and constitutive task. The
Church's first task is to teach and baptize—to baptize means
"to immerse" (therefore one baptizes with water)—so that all
may come to share God's trinitarian life.

Trinity in New Testament

Jesus Christ expressed in these final words all that he had
previously taught about God, the Father, Son and Holy Spirit. He
had announced from the beginning the truth about the one God,
in conformity with the tradition of Israel. Jesus answered the
question: "Which commandment is the first of all?" by stating:
"The first is, 'Hear, O Israel: the Lord our God is one Lord,'"
(Mk 12:29). At the same time Jesus had constantly addressed
God as "his Father," to the point of asserting: "I and the Father
are one" (Jn 10:30). He had revealed in the same way the "Spirit
of truth who proceeds from the Father" and whom—as he
assured us—"I will send to you from the Father" (Jn 15:26).

The words of baptism "in the name of the Father and of
the Son and of the Holy Spirit," entrusted by Jesus to the
apostles at the end of his earthly mission, have a special significance. They have consolidated the truth about the Most
Holy Trinity, by placing it at the basis of the Church's sacra-

mental life. The life of faith of all Christians begins in baptism, with immersion in the mystery of the living God. The letters of the apostles prove this, especially those of Paul. Among the trinitarian formulas which they contain, the best known and the one constantly used in the liturgy is that in the Second Letter to the Corinthians: "The grace of the Lord Jesus Christ and the love of God (the Father) and the fellowship of the Holy Spirit be with you all" (2 Cor 13:14). We find others in the First Letter to the Corinthians, in the Letter to the Ephesians and also in the First Letter of St. Peter, at the beginning of the first chapter (1 Pet 1:1-2).

Indirectly the whole development of the Church's life of prayer has taken on a trinitarian awareness and orientation—in the Spirit, through Christ, to the Father.

Thus faith in the Triune God has entered from the beginning into the tradition of the life of the Church and of Christians. Consequently the whole liturgy has been—and is—essentially trinitarian, inasmuch as it expresses the divine economy. One must emphasize that faith in the redemption, that is, faith in Christ's work of salvation, has contributed to understanding this supreme mystery of the Blessed Trinity. It manifests the mission of the Son and of the Holy Spirit who in the bosom of the eternal Trinity proceed "from the Father." It reveals the "trinitarian economy" present in the redemption and in sanctification. The Holy Trinity is announced first of all through soteriology, that is, through the knowledge of the "economy of salvation," which Christ announced and put into effect in his messianic mission. The path to the knowledge of the "immanent" Trinity, of the mystery of God's inner life, begins from this knowledge.

In this sense the New Testament contains the fullness of trinitarian revelation. God reveals both who God is for us, and who God is in himself, namely, in his inner life, by the revelation of himself in Jesus Christ. The truth that "God is love" (1 Jn 4:16), expressed in the First Letter of John, is a keystone here. This truth reveals who God is for us. It also reveals who God is in himself, (as far as is possible for the human mind to understand it and for human language to express it). He is a Unity, that is, a Communion of the Father, the Son and the Holy Spirit.

The Old Testament has not revealed this truth explicitly. It prepared the way for it by showing God's Fatherhood in the covenant with his people, and by manifesting his activity in the world with Wisdom, the Word and the Spirit (cf. e. g., Wis 7:22-30; Prov 8:22-30; Ps 33:4-6; Ps 147:15; Is 55:11; Wis 12:1; Is 11:2; Sir 48:12). The Old Testament has principally consolidated the truth about the one God, the hinge of the monotheistic religion, first of all in Israel and then outside of it. One must then conclude that the New Testament has brought the fullness of revelation about the Blessed Trinity. The trinitarian truth has been from the beginning at the root of the living faith of the Christian community by means of baptism and the liturgy. The rules of faith, which we meet frequently both in the letters of the apostles and in the testimony of the kerygma, kept pace with the Church's catechesis and prayer.

The formation of the trinitarian dogma in the context of the defense against the heresies of the early centuries is a separate subject. The truth about the Triune God is the most profound mystery of the faith and also the most difficult to understand. The possibility of erroneous interpretations existed, especially when Christianity came into contact with Greek culture and philosophy. It was a case of correctly "inscribing" the mystery of the Triune God "into the terminology of being." That is, it was to express in a precise form in the philosophical language of the age the concepts which unequivocally defined both the unity and trinity of the God of our revelation.

This happened first of all in the two great ecumenical councils of Nicaea (325) and Constantinople (381). The magisterium of these councils bore fruit in the Nicene-Constantinopolitan Creed. The Church has expressed in it from those times her faith in the Triune God—Father, Son and Holy Spirit. Recalling the work of the councils one must mention some particularly outstanding theologians, especially among the Fathers of the Church. For the pre-Nicene period we may mention Tertullian, Cyprian, Origen, Irenaeus; for the Nicene period, Athanasius and Ephraim the Syrian; for the period preceding the Council of Constantinople we recall Basil the Great, Gregory Nazianzen and Gregory of Nyssa, Hilary, down to Ambrose, Augustine and Leo the Great.

From the fifth century we have the so-called Athanasian Creed which begins with the word *Quicumque*. It is like a kind of comment on the Nicene-Constantinopolitan Creed.

Paul VI's *Credo of the People of God* confirms the faith of the primitive Church when it proclaims: "The mutual bonds which eternally constitute the three Persons who are each one and the same Divine Being, are the blessed inmost life of God thrice holy, infinitely beyond all that we can conceive in human measure" (cf. *DS* 804) *(L'Osservatore Romano,* English edition, July 11, 1968, p. 4)—truly, the ineffable and Most Holy Trinity—the One God.

General audience of October 9, 1985

God Is the Father of All Humanity

"You are my son, today I have begotten you" (Ps 2:7).

The author of the Letter to the Hebrews went back to the Old Testament for the purpose of making intelligible the full truth of the fatherhood of God which has been revealed in Jesus Christ (cf. Heb 1:4-14). He quoted, among others, the passage just read from the second Psalm, and also a similar phrase from the Book of Samuel: "I will be his father, and he shall be my son" (2 Sam 7:14).

They are prophetic words. God is speaking to David about his descendant. While in the Old Testament context these words seem to refer only to adoptive sonship, by analogy with human fatherhood and sonship, the New Testament reveals their authentic and definitive significance. They speak of the Son who is of the same substance of the Father, of the Son who is truly generated from the Father. They speak also of the real fatherhood of God, of a fatherhood to which belongs the generation of the Son consubstantial with the Father. They speak of God who is Father in the highest and most authentic meaning of the word. They speak of God who eternally generates the eternal Word, the Word consubstantial with the

Father. God is Father in the ineffable mystery of his divinity, in regard to the Word.

"You are my son, today I have begotten you."

The adverb "today" speaks of eternity. It is the "today" of the intimate life of God. It is the "today" of eternity, the "today" of the Most Holy and ineffable Trinity—Father, Son and Holy Spirit, who is eternal love and eternally consubstantial with the Father and the Son.

The mystery of the divine paternity within the Trinity was not yet explicitly revealed in the Old Testament. However, the whole context of the Old Covenant was rich with allusions to God's fatherhood in a moral and analogical sense. Thus God is revealed as Father of his people, Israel, when he commands Moses to ask for their liberation from Egypt: "The Lord says: Israel is my first-born son, and I say to you 'Let my son go...'" (Ex 4:22-23).

This is a fatherhood of choice, on the basis of the covenant, and is rooted in the mystery of creation. Isaiah wrote: "Yet, Lord, you are our Father; we are clay, and you are our potter; we are all the work of your hand" (Is 64:8; 63:16).

This fatherhood does not regard only the chosen people. It reaches every person and surpasses the bond existing with earthly parents. Here are some texts: "For my father and mother have forsaken me, but the Lord will take me up" (Ps 27:10). "As a father pities his children, so the Lord pities those who fear him" (Ps 103:13). "The Lord reproves him whom he loves, as a father the son in whom he delights" (Prov 3:12). The analogical character of the fatherhood of God is evident in the texts just quoted. It is the Lord to whom the prayer is directed: "O Lord, Father and Ruler of my life, do not abandon me to their counsel, and let me not fall because of them.... O Lord, Father and God of my life, do not leave me at the mercy of brazen looks" (Sir 23:1-4). He again says in the same light: "If the righteous man is God's son, he will help him, and will deliver him from the hand of his adversaries" (Wis 2:18).

God's fatherhood is manifested in merciful love, both in regard to Israel and to individuals. We read, for example, in Jeremiah: "With weeping they had departed, and with consolations I will lead them back...for I am a father to Israel, and Ephraim is my first-born" (Jer 31:9).

Numerous passages in the Old Testament present the merciful love of the God of the covenant. Here are some of them:

"But you are merciful to all, for you can do all things, and you overlook men's sin, that they may repent....
You spare all things, for they are yours,
O Lord who loves the living" (Wis 11:23-26).

"I have loved you with an everlasting love;
therefore I have continued my faithfulness to you" (Jer 31:3).

In Isaiah we meet moving testimonies of care and affection:

"But Zion said, 'The Lord has forsaken me,
my Lord has forgotten me.'
Can a woman forget her child...?
Even if she forget, yet I will not forget you"
(Is 49:14-15; cf. also 54:10).

It is significant that in the passages of the prophet Isaiah God's fatherhood is enriched with allusions inspired by motherhood (cf. *Dives in Misericordia,* note 52).

Jesus frequently announced, in the fullness of the Messianic times, God's fatherhood in regard to humanity by linking it with the numerous expressions contained in the Old Testament. Thus it expresses divine providence in regard to creatures, especially man: "Your heavenly Father feeds them..." (Mt 6:26; cf. Lk 12:24); "Your heavenly Father knows that you need them all" (Mt 6:32; cf. Lk 12:30). Jesus sought to make the divine mercy understood by presenting as proper to God the welcoming reception of the father for the prodigal son (cf. Lk 15:11-32). He exhorted those who heard his word: "Be merciful, even as your Father is merciful" (Lk 6:36).

To conclude, we can say that, through Jesus, God is not only "the father of Israel, the Father of mankind," but "our Father." We shall speak more about this in the next catechesis.

General audience of October 16, 1985

Christ Reveals
the Father's Countenance to Us

In the previous catechesis we had a quick look at some of the Old Testament testimonies which paved the way for the reception of the full revelation of the mystery of the fatherhood of God. This truth was announced by Jesus Christ, who spoke about his Father many times, presenting in various ways his providence and merciful love.

But his teaching goes further. Let us listen again to the particularly solemn words, recorded by the evangelist Matthew (and in the parallel passage of Luke): "I thank you, Father, Lord of heaven and earth, that you have hidden these things from the wise and understanding and revealed them to babes..." and later, "All things have been delivered to me by my Father, and no one knows the Father except the Son and any one to whom the Son chooses to reveal him" (Mt 11:25, 27; cf. Lk 10:21-22).

Therefore, for Jesus, God is not merely "the Father of Israel, the Father of mankind," but "my Father!" "My"—precisely for this reason the Jews wished to kill Jesus, because "he called God his Father" (Jn 5:18). "His" in a very literal sense—he whom only the Son knows as Father, and by whom alone he is reciprocally known. We are already on the same ground on which the prologue of John's Gospel shall later arise.

The "my Father" is the Father of Jesus Christ; he who is the origin of his being, of his messianic mission, of his teaching.

The evangelist John has abundantly recorded the messianic teaching which enables us to plumb the depths of the mystery of God the Father and of Jesus Christ, his only begotten Son.

Jesus said: "He who believes in me, believes not in me, but in him who sent me" (Jn 12:44). "I have not spoken on my own authority; the Father who sent me has himself commanded me what to say and what to speak" (Jn 12:49). "Truly, truly I say to you, the Son can do nothing of his own accord, but only what he sees the Father doing; for whatever he does, the Son does likewise" (Jn 5:19). "For as the Father has life in himself, so he has granted the Son also to have life in himself" (Jn 5:26). And finally, "As the living Father sent me, and I live because of the Father..." (Jn 6:57).

The Son lives by the Father first of all because he has been generated by him. There is a strict co-relationship between paternity and sonship precisely in virtue of generation: "You are my Son, today I have begotten you" (Heb 1:5).

At Caesarea Philippi when Simon Peter professed: "You are the Christ, the Son of the living God," Jesus answered him: "Blessed are you...because flesh and blood has not revealed this to you, but my Father..." (Mt 16:16-17). Only "the Father knows the Son" just as only the "Son knows the Father" (Mt 11:27). Only the Son makes the Father known—the visible Son makes us see the Father who is invisible. "He who has seen me has seen the Father" (Jn 14:9).

We learn from an attentive reading of the Gospels that Jesus lived and worked in constant and fundamental reference to the Father. He frequently addressed him with the word full of filial love—"Abba." Even during the prayer in Gethsemane this same word was again on his lips (cf. Mk 14:36 and parallel passages). When the disciples asked him to teach them to pray, he taught them the "Our Father" (cf. Mt 6:9-13). After the resurrection, at the moment of his departure from earth, he seemed once again to refer to this prayer when he said: "I am ascending to my Father and your Father, to my God and your God" (Jn 20:17).

Thus God is revealed in the fullness of the mystery of his paternity by means of the Son (cf. Heb 1:2). Only the Son could reveal this fullness of the mystery, because only "the Son knows the Father" (Mt 11:27). "No one has ever seen God; the only Son, who is in the bosom of the Father, he has made him known" (Jn 1:18).

Who is the Father? In the light of the definitive testimony which we have received through the Son, Jesus Christ, we have faith's awareness that God's fatherhood pertains first of all to the fundamental mystery of God's inner life, to the trinitarian mystery. The Father is he who eternally generates the Word, the Son who is consubstantial with him. The Father, in union with the Son, is eternally the principle of the "spiration" of the Holy Spirit, who is the love in which the Father and Son reciprocally remain united (cf. Jn 14:10).

The Father is the "Beginning-without-beginning," in the trinitarian mystery. The Father is "not made, nor created nor generated by anyone" (Symbol *Quicumque*). He is of himself the principle of the life which God has in himself. This life— that is, the divinity itself—is possessed in absolute communion with the Son and the Holy Spirit, who are consubstantial with him.

Paul, the apostle of the mystery of Christ, fell down in adoration and prayer "before the Father from whom all paternity in heaven and on earth is named" (Eph 3:15), the beginning and model. There is "one God and Father of us all, who is above all and through all and in all" (Eph 4:6).

General audience of October 23, 1985

Christic Is the Son of the Living God

"I believe in one God, the Father Almighty...I believe in...Jesus Christ, the only Son of God, eternally begotten of the Father, God from God, Light from Light, true God from true God, begotten, not made, one in Being with the Father...."

These words of the Nicene-Constantinopolitan Creed are a synthetic expression of the Councils of Nicaea and Constantinople. They make explicit the trinitarian doctrine of the Church, and with them we profess our faith in the Son of God.

Thus, we approach the mystery of Jesus Christ. Today as in ages past, Jesus challenges and questions mankind with his words and actions. Christians, animated by the faith, show him love and devotion. But even some non-Christians sincerely admire him.

What then is the secret of the attraction which Jesus of Nazareth exercises? The search for the full identity of Jesus Christ has from the very beginning engaged the heart and intelligence of the Church, which proclaims him Son of God, Second Person of the Most Holy Trinity.

Divine paternity and sonship strictly correlated

God has repeatedly spoken "by the prophets and in these last days...by a Son," as the Letter to the Hebrews states (1:1-2). God has revealed himself as the Father of an eternal and consubstantial Son. In his turn Jesus has also made known his own divine sonship by revealing the fatherhood of God. The divine paternity and sonship are strictly correlated within the mystery of the Triune God. "The Person of the Father is one, another is the Person of the Son, another is the Person of the Holy Spirit; but the divinity of the Father, of the Son and of the Holy Spirit is one, equal in glory, co-eternal in majesty.... The Son is not made, not created, but generated by the Father alone" (Symbol *Quicumque*).

The Father's testimony

Jesus of Nazareth who exclaimed: "I thank you, Father, Lord of heaven and earth, that you have hidden these things from the wise and understanding and revealed them to babes..." also solemnly affirmed: "All things have been delivered to me by my Father; and no one knows the Son except the Father, and no one knows the Father except the Son and anyone to whom the Son chooses to reveal him" (Mt 11:25, 27).

The Son, come into the world to "reveal the Father" as only he knew him, has at the same time revealed himself as Son as he was known only by the Father. This revelation has been sustained by the awareness wherewith, already in his youth, Jesus had made known to Mary and Joseph that "he must be concerned about his Father's business" (cf. Lk 2:49). His word of revelation was moreover strengthened by the Father's testimony, especially on decisive occasions, such as during the baptism in the Jordan. Those present heard the mysterious voice: "This is my beloved Son, with whom I am

well pleased" (Mt 3:17), or during the transfiguration on the
mountain (cf. Mk 9:7 and parallel passages).

Clear and unequivocal

Jesus Christ's mission to reveal the Father by manifesting
himself as Son was not devoid of difficulty. He had to overcome the obstacles deriving from the strictly monotheistic
mentality of his hearers. They were formed according to the
Old Testament teaching, in fidelity to the tradition going back
to Abraham and Moses, and in the struggle against polytheism.
We find many traces of this difficulty in the Gospels, and
especially in that of John. Jesus was able to overcome it with
wisdom, by placing with supreme pedagogic acumen those
signs of revelation by which well-disposed disciples let themselves be persuaded.

Jesus spoke to his hearers in a clear and unequivocal
way: "The Father who sent me bears witness to me." To the
question "Where is your Father?" he replied: "You know neither me nor my Father; if you knew me, you would know my
Father also...." "I speak of what I have seen with my Father...."
To his hearers who objected: "We have one Father, God..." he
retorted: "If God were your Father, you would love me, for I
proceeded and came forth from God...he sent me...." "Truly,
truly I say to you, before Abraham was, I am" (cf. Jn 8:12-59).

"I and the Father are one"

Christ said: "I am," just as centuries earlier at the foot of
Mount Horeb, when Moses asked the divine name, God replied, "I am who I am" (cf. Ex 3:14). Christ's words: "Before
Abraham was, I am" provoked the violent reaction of his hearers who "sought to kill him, because he called God his Father,
making himself equal with God" (Jn 5:18).

Jesus did not limit himself to saying: "My Father is working still, and I am working" (Jn 5:17), but he even proclaimed: "I and the Father are one" (Jn 10:30).

Jesus was dragged before the tribunal of the Sanhedrin in the dramatic moments at the close of his life. The High Priest himself addressed to Jesus the question which was also an accusation: "I adjure you by the living God, tell us if you are the Christ, the Son of God" (Mt 26:63). Jesus replied: "You have said so" (Mt 26:64).

The tragedy was consummated and the sentence of death was pronounced against Jesus.

Christ was revealer of the Father and revealer of himself as Son of the Father. Christ died because he bore witness to the truth of his divine sonship until the very end.

With a heart full of love we wish to repeat to him also today with the Apostle Peter the attestation of our faith: "You are the Christ, the Son of the living God" (Mt 16:16).

General audience of October 30, 1985

The Church Professes
Her Faith in God the Son

In last Wednesday's catechesis we considered how Jesus Christ, in revealing the Father, manifested himself in a special way as the consubstantial Son of the Father.

Basing herself on Christ's testimony, the Church professes and proclaims her faith in God the Son with the words of the Nicene-Constantinopolitan Creed: "God from God, Light from Light, true God from true God, begotten, not made, one in Being with the Father...."

This is a truth of faith announced by the very word of Christ, sealed with his blood shed on the cross, ratified by his resurrection, attested by the teaching of the apostles and transmitted by the New Testament writings.

Christ stated: "Before Abraham was, I am" (Jn 8:58). He did not say: "I was," but "I am," that is, from always, in an eternal present. The Apostle John wrote in the prologue to his Gospel: "In the beginning was the Word, and the Word was with God, and the Word was God. He was in the beginning with God; all things were made through him, and without him nothing was made" (Jn 1:1-3). Therefore, those words, "before Abraham," in the context of Jesus' controversy with the heirs of the tradition of Israel who appealed to Abraham, mean "well before Abraham." They are illumined by the words of the prologue to the fourth Gospel: "In the beginning he was with God," that is, in the eternity proper to God alone—in the eternity common to the Father and the Holy Spirit. The *Quicumque* Creed states: "In this Trinity none is before or after, none greater or less, but all three Persons are among themselves coeternal and coequal."

Incomprehensible mystery of the Triune God

According to John's Gospel, the Son who is the Word was in the beginning with God (cf. Jn 1:1-2). We find the same concept in the apostolic teaching. We read in the Letter to the Hebrews that God appointed the Son "heir of all things, through whom also he created the world. He reflects the glory of God and bears that very stamp of his nature, upholding the universe by his word of power" (Heb 1:2-3). Paul in his Letter to the Colossians wrote: "He is the image of the invisible God, the first-born of all creation" (1:15).

Therefore, according to the apostolic teaching, the Son is of the same substance as the Father since the Son is the God-Word. Everything has been made, the universe has been created, in this Word and through him. Before creation, before the beginning of "all things visible and invisible," the Word has eternal Being and divine life in common with the Father, since he "reflects the glory of God and bears the very stamp of his nature" (Heb 1:3). In this principle without beginning the Word is the Son, since he is eternally begotten by the Father. The New Testament reveals this mystery, incomprehensible to us, of a God who is One and Three. So, in the ontologically absolute unity of his essence, God is eternally and without beginning the Father who begets the Word, and he is the Son, begotten as the Word of the Father.

This eternal generation of the Son is a truth of faith proclaimed and defined by the Church many times (not only at Nicaea and Constantinople, but also in other Councils, for example in the Fourth Lateran Council in 1215). It was examined and explained by the Fathers and theologians, naturally in so far as the inscrutable reality of God can be expressed by our human concepts, which are always so inadequate. This explanation is summarized by the Catechism of the Council of Trent, which states very exactly: "God's infinite fecundity is so great that in knowing himself he begets the Son equal and the same."

Identity precludes plurality

It is certain that this eternal generation in God is of an absolutely spiritual nature, for "God is Spirit." In the cognitive process of the human mind, man, in knowing himself, produces an image of himself, an idea, a "concept," that is, a "conceived idea," which from the Latin *verbum* (word) is frequently called the interior word. By analogy with this process, we dare to think of the generation of the Son, or the eternal "concept" and interior Word of God. God, in knowing himself, begets the Word, the Son, who is God just as the Father. In this begetting, God is at the same time Father, as he who begets, and Son, as he who is begotten, in the supreme identity of the divinity which excludes a plurality of "Gods." The Word is the Son of the same substance of the Father, and with him he is the one God of the Old and New Testament revelation.

The whole Christian tradition contains this exposition of the mystery of God's inner life, which is inscrutable to us. If the divine generation is a truth of faith contained directly in revelation and defined by the Church, we can say that the explanation given of it by the Fathers and Doctors of the Church is a well-founded and certain theological doctrine.

But we cannot thereby pretend to eliminate the obscurity which envelops, before our mind's eye, him who "dwells in unapproachable light" (1 Tim 6:16). Precisely because the human intellect is not at a level to comprehend the divine essence it cannot penetrate the mystery of God's inner life. The saying: "If you comprehend it, it is not God," is particularly applicable here.

However, revelation unfolds for us the essential terms of the mystery. It expresses it for us and enables us to savor it in a way well beyond all intellectual understanding, while we await and prepare for the beatific vision in heaven. We believe then, that the "Word was God" (Jn 1:1), "he became flesh and dwelt among us" (Jn 1:14), and "to all who received him...he gave power to become children of God" (Jn 1:12). We believe in "the only Son who is in the bosom of the Father" (Jn 1:18), and who on leaving the earth promised "to prepare a place for us" (Jn 14:2) in the glory of God, as adopted children and his brothers (cf. Rom 8:15-23; Gal 4:5; and Eph 1:5).

General audience of November 6, 1985

Through Christ, the Spirit Guides Us to the Father

"I believe in the Holy Spirit, the Lord, the giver of life, who proceeds from the Father and the Son. With the Father and the Son he is worshipped and glorified. He has spoken through the prophets."

Today we begin our catechesis on the Holy Spirit. As we did when speaking of the Father and of the Son, we make use of the Nicene-Constantinopolitan Creed according to the usage established in the Latin liturgy.

The Councils of Nicaea (325) and Constantinople (381) in the fourth century contributed to the clarification of the concepts generally employed to present the doctrine of the Most Holy Trinity—one God who is, in the unity of the divinity, Father, Son and Holy Spirit. The formulation of the doctrine on the Holy Spirit comes particularly from the above-mentioned Council of Constantinople.

Faith is response to God's self-revelation

The Church confesses her faith in the Holy Spirit in the words quoted above. Faith is the response to God's self-revelation. He has made himself known "by the prophets, and in these last days...by a Son" (Heb 1:1). The Son, who has revealed the Father to us, has also made known the Holy Spirit. The *Quicumque* Creed of the fifth century proclaims: "Such as the Father is, such likewise is the Son, and such also is the Holy Spirit." That "such" is explained by the words of the *Quicumque* which follow, and is taken as meaning: "uncreated, immense, eternal, omnipotent...not three omnipotents, but only one omnipotent: thus God the Father, God the Son, God the Holy Spirit.... There do not exist three Gods, but only one God."

Etymology helps to explain the meaning of dogma

It is well to begin with an explanation of the name Spirit-Holy Spirit. The word "spirit" appears in the very first pages of the Bible. We read in the description of creation: "And the Spirit of God was moving over the face of the waters" (Gen 1:2). Spirit is the translation of the Hebrew word, *"ruah,"* which is equivalent to breath, puff of air, wind. It is translated in Greek as *"pneuma"* from *"pneo,"* and in Latin as *"spiritus"* from *"spiro,"* (and also in Polish as *"duch," tchnac, tchienie).* Etymology is important because as we shall see, it helps to explain the meaning of dogma and suggests the way in which it is to be understood.

Spirituality is an essential attribute of the divinity. Christ said in his conversation with the Samaritan woman: "God is Spirit..." (Jn 4:24). In one of the previous catecheses we spoke of God as an infinitely perfect spirit. In God "spirituality" implies not only supreme and absolute immateriality, but also a pure and eternal act of knowledge and love.

The Bible, and especially the New Testament, in speaking of the Holy Spirit, does not refer to God's Being itself, but to One who is in a special relationship with the Father and the Son. Many texts, especially in St. John's Gospel, make this

fact evident, especially the passages of Christ's farewell discourse on the Thursday before the Pasch, during the Last
Supper.

In the perspective of his leave-taking of the apostles,
Jesus announced to them the coming of "another Counselor."
He said: "I will pray the Father, and he will give you another
Counselor, to be with you forever, the Spirit of Truth..." (Jn
14:16). "But the Counselor, the Holy Spirit, whom the Father
will send in my name, will teach you all things" (Jn 14:26).
The Holy Spirit, whom Jesus here calls the Counselor, will be
sent by the Father in the name of the Son. This sending is
gradually made more explicit by Jesus himself: "When the
Counselor comes, whom I shall send to you from the Father,
the Spirit of truth, who proceeds from the Father, he will bear
witness to me..." (Jn 15:26).

The Holy Spirit, then, who proceeds from the Father, will
be sent to the apostles and to the Church both by the Father in
the name of the Son, and by the Son himself once he has
returned to the Father.

Jesus also said: "He (the Spirit of truth) will glorify me
for he will take what is mine and declare it to you. All that the
Father has is mine; therefore I said that he will take what is
mine and declare it to you" (Jn 16:14-15).

Decisive for whole economy of salvation

All these words are extremely important for understanding the economy of salvation, as are the other texts we find in
the New Testament. They tell us who the Holy Spirit is in
relation to the Father and the Son. They have a trinitarian
significance. They tell us not only that the Holy Spirit is "sent"
by the Father and the Son, but also that he "proceeds" from the
Father.

Here we touch questions which have a key importance in

the Church's teaching on the Most Holy Trinity. The Holy Spirit is sent by the Father and the Son after the Son, on the completion of his redemptive mission, has entered into his glory (cf. Jn 7:39; 16:7). These missions *(missiones)* are decisive for the whole economy of salvation in the history of humanity.

These "missions" involve and reveal the "processions" in God himself. The Son proceeds eternally from the Father as begotten from him and has assumed in time a human nature for our salvation. The Holy Spirit, who proceeds from the Father and the Son, is manifested first of all in the baptism and Transfiguration of Jesus, and then on the day of Pentecost in his disciples. He dwells in the hearts of the faithful through the gift of charity.

Let us hearken then to the warning of the Apostle Paul: "Do not grieve the Holy Spirit of God, in whom you were sealed for the day of redemption" (Eph 4:30). Let us be guided by him. He guides us on the "way" which is Christ to the blissful meeting with the Father.

General audience of November 13, 1985

The Holy Spirit Proceeds
from the Father and the Son

In the last catechesis we concentrated our attention on the Holy Spirit, reflecting on the words of the Nicene-Constantinopolitan Creed according to the form in use in the Latin liturgy: "I believe in the Holy Spirit, the Lord, the giver of life, who proceeds from the Father and the Son. With the Father and the Son he is worshipped and glorified. He has spoken through the prophets."

The Holy Spirit is "sent" by the Father and Son, as he also "proceeds" from them. For this reason he is called "the Spirit of the Father" (e.g., Mt. 10:20; 1 Cor 2:11; also Jn 15:26), but also "the Spirit of the Son" (Gal 4:6), or "the Spirit of Jesus" (Acts 16:7), since it is Jesus himself that sends him (cf. Jn 15:26). Therefore the Latin Church professes that the Holy Spirit proceeds from the Father and the Son *(qui a Patre Filioque procedit)* while the Orthodox Churches profess from the Father through the Son. He proceeds "by way of will," "in the manner of love" *(per modum amoris)*. This is a *sententia certa,* that is, a theological doctrine commonly accepted in the Church's teaching and therefore sure and binding.

This conviction is confirmed by the etymology of the name "Holy Spirit," to which I alluded in the previous catechesis—Spirit, *spiritus, pneuma, ruah.* Starting from this etymology "the procession" of the Spirit from the Father and the Son is described as "spiration"—*spiramen*—a breath of Love.

This spiration is not generation. Only the Word, the Son, "proceeds" from the Father by eternal generation. God, who eternally knows himself and everything in himself, begets the Word. In this eternal begetting, which takes place by way of intellect *(per modum intelligibilis actionis),* God, in the absolute unity of his nature, that is, of his divinity, is Father and Son. "He is," and not "he becomes," "he is" so eternally. "He is" from the beginning and without beginning. Under this aspect the word "procession" must be understood correctly. There is no connotation proper to a temporal "becoming." The same is true of the "procession" of the Holy Spirit.

The Spirit is the source of every gift from God

Therefore, by means of generation, in the absolute unity of the divinity, God is eternally Father and Son. The Father who begets loves the Son who is begotten. The Son loves the Father with a love which is identical with that of the Father. In the unity of the divinity, love is on one side paternal and on the other, filial. At the same time the Father and the Son are not only united by that mutual love as two Persons infinitely perfect. But their mutual gratification, their reciprocal love, proceeds in them and from them as a person. The Father and the Son "spirate" the Spirit of Love consubstantial with them. In this way God, in the absolute unity of the divinity, is from all eternity Father, Son and Holy Spirit.

The *Quicumque* Creed proclaims: "The Holy Spirit is not made, nor created, nor begotten, but he proceeds from the Father and the Son." The "procession" is *per modum amoris,* as already said. Because of this the Fathers of the Church call the Holy Spirit "Love, Charity, Spiritual Love, Bond of Love, Kiss of Love." All these expressions testify to the way in which the Holy Spirit "proceeds" from the Father and the Son.

It can be said that God in his innermost life is "love" which is personalized in the Holy Spirit, the Spirit of the Father and the Son. The Spirit is also called Gift.

The Spirit who is Love, is the source of every gift having its origin in God in regard to creatures—the gift of existence by means of creation, the gift of grace through the economy of salvation.

We understand better the words of the Acts of the Apostles in the light of this theology of the trinitarian Gift: "You will receive the gift of the Holy Spirit" (Acts 2:38). With these words Christ takes his final leave of his dear ones when going to the Father. We also understand the words of the Apostle in this light: "God's love has been poured into our hearts through the Holy Spirit who has been given to us" (Rom 5:5).

Let us conclude our reflection by invoking with the liturgy, *Veni, Sancte Spiritus.* "Come, O Holy Spirit, fill the hearts of your faithful and enkindle within them the fire of your love."

General audience of November 20, 1985

Unity and Distinction in the Eternal Communion of the Trinity

One God the Trinity....

The Synod of Toledo (675) expressed the faith of the Church in the Triune God with this concise formula, in the wake of the great fourth century councils of Nicaea and Constantinople.

In our own times, Paul VI in the *Credo of the People of God* expressed the same faith in the words already quoted in previous catecheses: "The mutual bonds which eternally constitute the Three Persons who are each one and the same Divine Being, are the blessed inmost life of God thrice holy, infinitely beyond all that we can conceive in human measure" *(L'Osservatore Romano,* English edition, July 11, 1968, p. 4).

God is ineffable and incomprehensible. In his essence God is an inscrutable mystery, whose truth we have sought to illustrate in the previous catecheses. Before the Most Holy Trinity, in which is expressed the inmost life of the God of our faith, one must repeat and admit it with a still greater force of conviction. The unity of the divinity in the Trinity of Persons is indeed an ineffable and inscrutable mystery! "If you comprehend it, it is not God."

179

Paul VI continues in the text cited above: "We give thanks, however, to the divine goodness that very many believers can testify with us before men to the unity of God, even though they know not the mystery of the Most Holy Trinity."

Holy Church in her trinitarian faith feels united to all those who confess the one God. Faith in the Trinity does not affect the truth of the one God. Rather, it makes evident its richness, its mysterious content—God's inmost life.

This faith has its source—its only source—in the New Testament revelation. It is possible to know the truth about the Triune God only by means of this revelation. This is one of those "mysteries hidden in God which can never be known unless they are revealed by God,"—according to the First Vatican Council (Const. *Dei Filius,* IV).

The dogma of the Most Holy Trinity has always been considered in Christianity as a mystery—the most fundamental and inscrutable mystery. Jesus Christ himself said: "No one knows the Son except the Father, and no one knows the Father except the Son and any one to whom the Son chooses to reveal him" (Mt 11:27).

The First Vatican Council taught: "The divine mysteries by their nature transcend the created intellect in such a way that, while made known by revelation and accepted by faith, they remain however covered by the veil of the same faith and wrapped in a kind of obscurity as long as in this mortal life 'we are away from the Lord, for we walk by faith, not by sight' (2 Cor 5:6)" (Const. *Dei Filius,* IV).

This statement is especially valid for the mystery of the Most Holy Trinity. Even after being revealed, it remains the most profound mystery of faith. The intellect by itself can neither comprehend nor penetrate it. But in a certain way the intellect enlightened by faith can grasp and explain the meaning of the dogma. Thus it can bring the mystery of the inmost life of the Triune God close to man.

The concept of "person" as distinct from that of "nature" (or essence) is shown to be particularly important and fundamental in the accomplishment of this sublime work—whether by means of the work of many theologians and first of all that of the Fathers of the Church, or by the definitions of the Councils. A person is he or she who exists as a concrete human being, as an individual possessing humanity, that is, human nature. Nature (essence) is all that whereby that which concretely exists is what it is. For example, when we speak of "human nature," we indicate what makes a human being a human being, with his essential components and properties.

Applying this distinction to God, we recognize the unity of nature, the unity of the divinity, which belongs in an absolute and exclusive way to him who exists as God. At the same time—both by the light of the intellect alone, and still more by the light of revelation—we cultivate the conviction that he is a personal God. God the Creator should appear as a personal Being, even to those who have not received the revelation of the existence of God in three Persons. The person is what is most perfect in the world *(id quod est perfectissimum in tota natura*: St. Thomas, *Summa Theol.*, I, q. 29, a. 3). One cannot but attribute this qualification to the Creator, even in regard to his infinite transcendence (cf. St. Thomas, *Summa Theol.*, I, q. 29, a. 3). Precisely for this reason the non-Christian monotheistic religions understand God as a person infinitely perfect and absolutely transcendent as regards the world.

Uniting our voices with that of every other believer, let us also lift up our hearts to the living and personal God, the one God who created the world and who is the origin of all that is good, beautiful and holy. To him be praise and glory forever.

General audience of November 27, 1985

Distinction of Relations in the Trinity

One God the Trinity....

The definitions of the Councils set out the results of a long period of reflection by the Fathers of the Church. The Church speaks of the Father, Son and Holy Spirit as three "Persons," who subsist in the unity of the identical divine substance.

"Person" refers to a single being of rational nature, as Boethius made clear in his famous definition *("Persona proprie dicitur rationalis naturae individua substantia,"* in: *De duabus naturis et una persona Christi,* PL 64, 1343 D). But the ancient Church immediately clarified that the intellectual nature in God is not multiplied with the Persons. It remains one, so that the believer can proclaim with the *Quicumque* Creed: "Not three Gods, but only one God."

Here the mystery deepens—three distinct Persons and only one God. How is this possible? Reason understands that there is no contradiction, because it is a trinity of Persons and a unity of divine Nature. But the difficulty remains. Each of the Persons is the same God. How can they be really distinct?

Councils' teaching

The reply which our reason stammers is based on the concept of "relation." The three divine persons are distinguished among themselves solely by the relations which they have with one another—precisely by the relation of the Father to the Son, of the Son to the Father; of the Father and the Son to the Spirit, of the Spirit to the Father and the Son. In God, therefore, the Father is pure Paternity, the Son is pure Sonship, and the Holy Spirit is pure "Nexus of Love" of the two, so that the personal distinctions do not divide the same and unique divine nature of the three.

The Eleventh Council of Toledo (675) made it clear with great exactitude: "For the Father is Father not with respect to himself but to the Son, and the Son is Son not to himself but in relation to the Father; and likewise the Holy Spirit is not referred to himself but is related to the Father and the Son, inasmuch as he is called the Spirit of the Father and the Son" *(DS* 528).

The Council of Florence (1442) could therefore state: "These three persons are one God...because the three are one substance, one essence, one nature, one divinity, one immensity, one eternity; in God everything is one and the same where there is no opposition of relation" *(DS* 1330).

"Subsisting" relations

The relations which distinguish the Father, Son and Holy Spirit, and which really relate them to one another in their same being, possess in themselves all the richness of light and life of the divine nature, with which they are totally identified. They are "subsisting" relations, which by virtue of their vital impulse go out to meet one another in a communion in which each is completely open to the other. This loving communion is a supreme model of the sincerity and spiritual liberty which should characterize human interpersonal relations, which are always so far removed from this transcendent model.

In this regard the Second Vatican Council observed: "The Lord Jesus, when he prayed to the Father, 'that all may be one...as we are one' (Jn 17:21-22) opened up vistas closed to human reason, for he implied a certain likeness between the union of the divine Persons, and the unity of God's sons in truth and charity. This likeness reveals that man, who is the only creature on earth which God willed for itself, cannot fully find himself except through a sincere gift of himself" *(GS* 24).

Before the mystery our puny mind is lost

The most perfect unity of the three Persons is the transcendent summit which illuminates every form of authentic communion between us human beings. It is right that our thoughts should frequently return to the contemplation of this mystery to which the Gospel so often refers. Suffice it to recall Jesus' words: "I and the Father are one" (Jn 10:30); and again: "Believe at least the works, that you may know and understand that the Father is in me and I am in the Father" (Jn 10:38). We read in another context: "The words that I say to you I do not speak on my own authority. The Father who dwells in me does his works. Believe me that I am in the Father and the Father is in me" (Jn 14:10-11).

The ancient ecclesiastical writers frequently treat of this reciprocal compenetration of the divine Persons. The Greeks define it as *perichóresis*, the West (especially from the eleventh century) as *circumincessio* (reciprocal compenetration) or *circuminsessio* (mutual indwelling). The Council of Florence expressed this trinitarian truth in the following words: "Through this unity...the Father is completely in the Son and completely in the Holy Spirit; the Son is completely in the

Father and completely in the Holy Spirit; the Holy Spirit is completely in the Father and completely in the Son" *(DS* 1331). The three distinct divine Persons, even though reciprocal relations, are the same Being, the same Life, the same God.

Our puny mind is lost before this dazzling mystery of communion. The acclamation of the liturgy comes spontaneously to our lips:

"Gloria Tibi Trinitas, aequalis, una Deitas et ante omnia saecula, et nunc et in perpetuum."

"Glory to you, Holy Trinity, equal in Persons, one God, before all ages, now and forever" (First Vespers of the Solemnity of the Most Holy Trinity, first Antiphon).

General audience of December 4, 1985

The Thrice Holy God

"Holy, holy, holy Lord, God of power and might, heaven and earth are full of your glory" (Eucharistic Liturgy).

Every day the Church proclaims God's holiness. It does so especially during the liturgy of the Mass, after the preface, at the beginning of the Eucharistic prayer. The People of God addresses its praise to the Triune God and professes his supreme transcendence and inaccessible perfection by repeating three times the word "holy."

The words of the Eucharistic Liturgy are taken from the Book of Isaiah, which describes the manifestation of the deity which the prophet was permitted to contemplate. He saw the majesty of God's glory, to announce it to the people:

"I saw the Lord sitting upon a throne, high and lifted up...above him stood the seraphim...and one called to another and said: 'Holy, holy, holy is the Lord of hosts; the whole earth is full of his glory" (Is 6:13).

God's holiness also connotes his glory *(kabod Yahweh),* which inhabits the intimate mystery of his divinity and, at the same time, irradiates the whole of creation.

The last book of the New Testament, the Book of Revela-

186

tion, takes many elements from the Old Testament. It repro-
poses the "Thrice Holy" of Isaiah, together with elements
taken from another theophany, found in the prophet Ezekiel
(Ez 1:26). In this context we hear proclaimed anew:

"Holy, holy, holy, is the Lord God Almighty,

who was and is and is to come!" (Rev 4:8).

In the Old Testament the term "holy" corresponds to the
Hebrew word "*gados.*" Its etymology contains the idea of
light—"to be illuminated, to be luminous." The Old Testament
theophanies contain the element of fire, like the manifestation
of the deity to Moses (Ex 3:2), and that of Sinai (Dt 4:12).
They also reflect the idea of a blinding light, like the vision of
Ezekiel (Ez 1:27-28), the above-mentioned vision of Isaiah (Is
6:1-3), and that of Habakkuk (Hab 3:4). In the Greek of the
New Testament, the word "*hagios*" corresponds to the term
"holy."

The Old Testament etymology also clarifies the following phrase from the Letter to the Hebrews: "Our God is a
consuming fire" (Heb 12:29; cf. Dt 4:24), as well as the words
of St. John at the Jordan concerning the Messiah: "He will
baptize you with the Holy Spirit and with fire" (Mt 3:11). We
also know that in the descent of the Holy Spirit upon the
apostles, which took place in the Cenacle in Jerusalem,
"tongues as of fire" appeared (Acts 2:3).

Modern scholars of the philosophy of religion (e.g.,
Rudolph Otto) see in man's experience of God's holiness the
elements of the "fascinating" and of the "awe-inspiring." This
is confirmed by both the etymology of the Old Testament term,
already mentioned, and by the biblical theophanies in which
the element of fire appears. Fire symbolizes the splendor, the
irradiation of God's glory *(fascinosum).* It also symbolizes the
heat that burns and, in a certain sense, drives away the fear
which his holiness (awe-inspiring) arouses. The "*gados*" of the
Old Testament includes both the "fascination" which attracts

and the "fearful" which repels by indicating "the separation," and therefore the inaccessibility.

Several times already in this cycle of catechesis, we have referred to the theophany of the Book of Exodus. In the desert, at the foot of Mount Horeb, Moses saw a bush which burned but was not consumed (cf. Ex 3:2). When he drew near to the bush he heard the voice: "Do not draw near; take off your shoes from your feet, for the place on which you are standing is holy ground" (Ex 3:5). These words emphasize the holiness of God. From the burning bush, God revealed his name to Moses: "I am who I am." In this name, God sent Moses to liberate Israel from the land of Egypt. In this manifestation there is the element of the "fearful." God's holiness remains inaccessible to man—"do not come near." Moreover, the entire description of the covenant made on Mount Sinai (Ex 19-20) has similar characteristics.

Later, especially in the teaching of the prophets, this trait of God's holiness, inaccessible to man, gives way to God's "drawing near," to his accessibility, to his condescension.

We read in Isaiah:

"For thus says the high and lofty one,
who inhabits eternity, whose name is Holy:
'I dwell in the high and holy place,
and also with whoever has a contrite and humble spirit,
to revive the spirit of the humble,
and to revive the heart of the contrite'" (Is 57:15).

Likewise in Hosea:

"I am God and not man, the Holy One in your midst,
and I will not come to destroy" (Hos 11:9).

God has given the greatest testimony of his nearness by sending his Word to earth. The second person of the Most Holy Trinity took a body like ours and came to live among us.

With gratitude for this condescension of God who desired

to draw near to us, not merely by speaking to us through the prophets, but by addressing us in the person of his only-begotten Son, we repeat with humble and joyous faith: *"Tu solus Sanctus...."* "You alone are the Holy One, you alone are the Lord, you alone are the Most High Jesus Christ, with the Holy Spirit, in the glory of God the Father. Amen."

General audience of December 11, 1985

The Moral Law Is Identified with the Will of God

In the previous catechesis we reflected on God's holiness and on the two characteristics which distinguish it—inaccessibility and condescension. Now we wish to listen to God's exhortation to the entire community of the children of Israel through the various phases of the old covenant:

"You shall be holy; for I the Lord your God am holy" (Lev 19:2).

"I am the Lord who sanctifies you" (Lev 20:8).

In the New Testament, God thoroughly reveals the meaning of his holiness. It fully takes up this exhortation, conferring on it its own characteristics, in harmony with the "new fact" of Christ's cross. God, who "is Love," has fully revealed himself in a gift without reserve on Calvary. Yet even in this new context the apostolic teaching again proposes forcefully the exhortation inherited from the old covenant. For instance, St. Peter wrote: "As he who called you is holy, be holy yourselves in all your conduct; since it is written, 'You shall be holy, for I am holy'" (1 Pet 1:15).

What is God's holiness? It is absolute "separation" from all moral evil, and the exclusion and radical rejection of sin and, at the same time, it is absolute goodness. In virtue of that,

God, infinitely good in himself, is likewise good in regard to creatures *(bonum diffusivum sui),* naturally according to the measure of their ontological "capacity." It is in this sense that Christ's reply to the young man in the Gospel is to be understood: "Why do you call me good? No one is good but God alone" (Mk 10:18).

In the previous catecheses we already recalled the words of the Gospel: "You, therefore, must be perfect, as your heavenly Father is perfect" (Mt 5:48). This exhortation refers to God's perfection in the moral sense, that is, to his holiness. It expresses the same concept contained in the words of the Old Testament quoted above, and taken up again in the First Letter of Peter. Moral perfection consists in the exclusion of sin and in the absolute affirmation of moral good. For human beings, for rational creatures, such an affirmation is translated into conformity of the will with the moral law. God is holy in himself, he is substantial holiness, because his will is identified with the moral law. This law exists in God himself as in its eternal source, and therefore it is called Eternal Law *(Lex Aeterna)* (cf. *Summa Theol.,* I-II, q. 93, a. 1).

God made himself known as the source of the moral law and, in this sense, as holiness itself. He did this both before original sin as regards our first parents (Gen 2:16), and later as regards the chosen People, especially in the covenant of Sinai (cf. Ex 20:1-20). The moral law revealed by God in the old covenant and, above all, in the Gospel teaching of Christ, aims to show gradually but clearly the substantial superiority and importance of love. The commandment: "You shall love" (Dt 6:5; Lev 19:18; Mk 12:30-31 and parallel places) reveals that God's holiness also consists in love. All that was said in the catechesis entitled "God is Love," refers to the holiness of the God of revelation.

God is holiness because he is love (cf. 1 Jn 4:16). Through love he is absolutely separated from moral evil, from sin. He is essentially, absolutely and transcendentally identified with moral good in its source, which is himself. Love means precisely this—to will the good, to adhere to the good. From this eternal will of the Good there gushes forth the infinite goodness of God in regard to creatures and, in particular, in regard to man. Love is the origin of God's clemency, of his readiness to give freely and to pardon. Luke relates Jesus' parable of the prodigal son, which magnificently expresses this mercy (cf. Lk 15:11-32). Love is expressed in providence by which God continues and sustains the work of creation.

In a particular way love is expressed in the work of the redemption and justification of man to whom God offers his own justice in the mystery of Christ's cross, as St. Paul clearly stated (cf. Letters to the Romans and Galatians). Love is the essential and decisive element of God's holiness. Through redemption and justification, it guides man to his own sanctification by the power of the Holy Spirit.

In this way, in the economy of salvation God himself, as trinitarian holiness (thrice holy), undertakes in a certain sense the initiative of accomplishing for us and in us what he expressed in the words: "You shall be holy; for I the Lord your God am holy" (Lev 19:2).

To this God, who is holiness because he is love, man turns with the deepest confidence. To God he entrusts the whole intimate mystery of his humanity, the entire mystery of his human "heart."

"I love you, O Lord, my strength.
The Lord is my rock, and my fortress, and my deliverer, my God, my rock, in whom I take refuge,
my shield, and the horn of my salvation, my stronghold" (Ps 18:1-3).

Man's salvation is most closely linked to God's holiness, since salvation depends on God's eternal, infinite love.

General audience of December 18, 1985

GOD THE CREATOR

The Mystery of Creation

In the inevitable and necessary reflection which people of every age have made about their lives, two questions forcefully emerge, almost as an echo of the voice of God: "Where do we come from? Where are we going?" If the second question regards the final end, the definitive goal, the first refers to the origin of the world and of the human race, and is equally fundamental. For this reason we are rightly impressed by the extraordinary interest devoted to the problem of origins. It is not merely a question of knowing when and how the cosmos began and man appeared. It involves discovering the meaning of such an origin, and whether it was presided over by chance, by blind destiny, or by a transcendent Being, intelligent and good, called God. In fact, evil exists in the world and those who experience it are drawn to ask what its origin is and who is responsible for it, and whether there is any hope of deliverance from it. "What is man that you are mindful of him?" asked the Psalmist, lost in admiration before the event of creation (Ps 8:5).

The question about creation surfaces in everyone's mind, the simple and learned alike. The roots of modern science are closely linked to the biblical truth about creation, even though the relationship between the two has not always been harmonious. In our own day the mutual relationship between scientific and religious truth is better understood. Many scientists have assumed an attitude of increasing respect for the Christian view of creation, while legitimately raising serious problems. These problems concern the evolution of living forms, and of human beings in particular, as well as the immanent finality of the cosmos itself in coming into being. This field allows for the possibility of fruitful dialogue concerning the different ways of approaching the reality of the world and of the human person. These ways are sincerely recognized as different, though they converge at the deepest level in favor of man who is unique. Man was created in the "image of God" and therefore as the intelligent and wise master of the world, as the first page of the Bible states (cf. Gen 1:27-28).

Creation, rebellion and promise

We Christians recognize with deep amazement, though with due critical approach, that all religions, from the most ancient which have now disappeared to those existing today, seek an "answer to the unsolved riddles of the human condition.... What is man? What is the meaning, the aim of our life? What is moral good, what sin? Whence suffering and what purpose does it serve?... Whence do we come, and where are we going?" *(NA* 1). Following the Second Vatican Council in its *Declaration on the Relation of the Church to Non-Christian Religions,* we reaffirm that "the Catholic Church rejects nothing of what is true and holy in these religions," for "they often reflect a ray of that truth which enlightens all men" *(NA* 2). But the Biblical-Christian view of the origins of the cosmos and of history, and of humanity in particular has had an important influence on the spiritual, moral and cultural formation of entire peoples for more than twenty centuries. This view is so undeniably outstanding, inspiring and original, that to speak of it explicitly, even if synthetically, is a duty which no pastor or catechist can omit.

The Christian revelation manifests an extraordinary richness concerning the mystery of creation. This is a moving and by no means indifferent sign of the affection of God. This revelation provides a continuous and consistent explanation of the knotty problems of human existence, such as man's origin and his future destiny, though it does so in accordance with the variety of cultural expressions.

Thus the Bible begins absolutely with a first, and then with a second account of creation. The origin of everything from God, of things, of life, of man (Gen 1-2), is interwoven with the other sad chapter about the origin of man, not without the temptation of the devil, of sin and of evil (Gen 3). But God does not abandon his creatures. So a tiny flame of hope is lit toward a future of a new creation freed from evil (the so-called *proto-evangelium,* Gen 3:15; cf. 9:13). These three threads— God's creative and positive action, man's rebellion, and, already from the beginning, God's promise of a new world— form the texture of the history of salvation. They determine the global content of the Christian faith in creation.

While in the forthcoming catecheses on creation due place will be given to Scripture as an essential source, it will be my task to recall the great tradition of the Church. This will be done first with texts of the Councils and of the ordinary Magisterium, and also in the interesting and penetrating reflections of so many theologians and Christian thinkers.

As a journey comprising many stages, the catechesis on creation will deal especially with this marvelous fact as we profess it at the beginning of the Apostles' Creed: "I believe in God, Creator of heaven and earth." We shall reflect on the calling forth from nothingness of all created reality. At the same time we shall admire God's omnipotence and the joyous surprise of a contingent world which exists by virtue of such omnipotence. We shall recognize that creation is the loving work of the Blessed Trinity, and it reveals its glory. This does not deny but rather affirms the legitimate autonomy of created things. We shall focus a profound attention on man, as the center of the cosmos, in his reality as the "image of God," of a spiritual and corporeal being, subject of knowledge and freedom. Other themes will help us later on to explore this formidable creative event, especially God's government of the world, his omniscience and providence, and how in the light of God's faithful love the enigma of evil and suffering finds its satisfactory solution.

After God spoke about his divine creative power to Job, (Job 38-41), Job replied to the Lord and said: "I know that you can do all things, and that no purpose of yours can be thwarted.... I had heard of you by the ear, but now my eyes see you" (Job 42:2-5). May our reflection on creation lead us to the discovery that, in the act of creating the world and man, God has provided the first universal testimony of his powerful love, the first prophecy of the history of our salvation.

General audience of January 8, 1986

God the Creator
of Heaven and Earth

The truth about creation is the object and content of the Christian faith. This truth is present in an explicit manner only in revelation. It is only vaguely found in the mythological cosmogonies outside the Bible. It is absent from the speculations of the ancient philosophers, even the greatest, such as Plato and Aristotle, although they had reached a rather elevated concept of God as a totally perfect Being, the Absolute. Unaided human intelligence can arrive at the formulation of the truth that the world and contingent beings (i.e., those not existing of necessity) depend on the Absolute. However, the formulation of this dependence as "creation"—therefore on the basis of the truth about creation—pertains originally to divine revelation and in this sense it is a truth of faith.

It is proclaimed at the beginning of the professions of faith, beginning with those most ancient, such as the Apostles' Creed: "I believe in God...Creator of heaven and earth." Likewise the Nicene-Constantinopolitan Creed states: "I believe in God...Creator of heaven and earth, of all things visible and invisible." Finally, the *Credo of the People of God* proclaimed by Pope Paul VI declares: "We believe in one only God...Creator of things visible such as this world in which our transient life passes, of things invisible such as the pure spirits which are also called angels, and creator in each man of his spiritual and immortal soul" *(L'Osservatore Romano,* English edition, July 11, 1968, p. 4).

Because of the richness of its content, the truth about the creation of the world and of man by God occupies a fundamental place in the Christian creed. It not only refers to the origin of the world as the result of God's creative act, but it also reveals God as the Creator. God has spoken by the prophets, and in these last days by the Son (cf. Heb 1:1). He has made known to all those who accept his revelation not merely that it is precisely he who created the world, but above all, what it means to be Creator.

Sacred Scripture (Old and New Testament) is full of the truth about creation and about God the Creator. The first book of the Bible, the Book of Genesis, begins by asserting this truth: "In the beginning God created the heavens and the earth" (Gen 1:1). Many other biblical passages repeat this truth, showing how deeply it had penetrated the faith of Israel. Let us recall at least a few. We read in the Psalms: "The earth is the Lord's and its fullness, the world and those who dwell in it; for he has founded it upon the seas" (24:1-2). "The heavens are yours, the earth is also yours; the world and all that is in it, for you have founded them" (89:11). "The sea is his, for he made it; for his hands formed the dry land" (95:5).

"The earth is full of the steadfast love of the Lord. By the word of the Lord the heavens were made...for he spoke, and it came to be; he commanded and it stood forth" (33:5-6, 9). "May you be blessed by the Lord, who made heaven and earth" (114:15). The same truth is professed by the author of the Book of Wisdom: "O God of my fathers and Lord of mercy, who has made all things by your word..." (9:1). The prophet Isaiah, speaking in the first person, quotes the word of God the Creator: "I am the Lord who made all things" (44:24).

God is in the creature and the creature is in God

The testimonies in the New Testament are no less clear. For example, the Prologue of John's Gospel states: "In the beginning was the Word...all things were made through him, and without him nothing was made" (1:1, 3). The Letter to the Hebrews states: "By faith we understand that the world was created by the word of God, so that what is seen was made out of things which do not appear" (11:3).

The truth of creation expresses the thought that everything existing outside of God has been called into existence by him. In Sacred Scripture we find texts which speak clearly of this.

The Book of Maccabees records the case of the mother of the seven sons. In the presence of the threat of death, she encouraged the youngest of them to profess the faith of Israel, saying to him: "Look at the heavens and the earth...God did not make them out of things that existed. So also mankind came into being" (2 Macc 7:28). We read in the Letter to the Romans: "Abraham believed in God who gives life to the dead and calls into existence the things that do not exist" (4:17).

"Creation" therefore means: to make from nothing, to call into existence, that is, to form a being from nothing. Biblical language gives us a glimpse of this significance in the opening words of the Book of Genesis: "In the beginning God created the heavens and the earth." The word "created" is a translation of the Hebrew *bara,* which describes an action of extraordinary power whose subject is God alone. Reflection after the exile resulted in a better understanding of the significance of the initial divine intervention. The Second Book of Maccabees finally presents it as a production "not out of things that existed" (7:28). The Fathers of the Church and theologians further clarified the meaning of the divine action by speaking of creation "from nothing" *(Creatio ex nihilo;* more precisely *ex nihilo sui et subjecti).*

In the act of creation, God is the exclusive and direct principle of the new being, to the exclusion of any pre-existing matter.

As Creator, God is in a certain sense "outside" of created being and what is created is "outside" of God. At the same time the creature fully and completely owes to God its own existence (its being what it is), because the creature has its origin fully and completely from the power of God.

Through this creative power (omnipotence) God is in the creature and the creature is in him. However, this divine immanence in no way diminishes God's transcendence in regard to everything to which he gives existence.

When the Apostle Paul set foot in the Areopagus of Athens he spoke as follows to those assembled there: "As I passed along and observed the objects of your worship, I also found an altar with this inscription, 'To an unknown God.' What you worship as unknown, I proclaim to you. The God who made the world and everything in it, is Lord of heaven and earth..." (Acts 17:23-24).

It is interesting that the Athenians, who recognized many gods (pagan polytheism), should have heard these words about the one God, the Creator, without raising objections. This seems to confirm that the truth about creation constitutes a meeting-point between those who profess different religions. Perhaps the truth about creation is rooted in an innate and fundamental way in diverse religions, even if they do not have sufficiently clear concepts, such as those contained in Sacred Scripture.

General audience of January 15, 1986

In Creation God Calls the World into Existence from Nothingness

The truth that states that God has created—that he has drawn forth from nothingness all that exists outside himself, both the world and man—is already expressed on the first page of Sacred Scripture, even though its full exposition is found only in the later development of revelation.

The beginning of the Book of Genesis has two accounts of creation. Biblical scholars judge that the second account is more ancient. It has a more figurative and concrete character; it addresses God by the name of "Yahweh," and for this reason it is known as the "Yahwistic source."

The first account, later in time of composition, is more systematic and theological. It uses the term *"Elohim"* to designate God. It distributes the work of creation over a series of six days. Scholars have concluded that this text had its origin in the priestly and cultic circles, since the seventh day is presented as the day on which God rests. It proposes to man the worker the example of God the Creator. The author of the first chapter of Genesis wished to confirm the teaching contained in the Decalogue by inculcating the obligation to keep holy the seventh day.

The account of the work of creation deserves to be read

and meditated upon frequently in the liturgy and outside of it. As regards the individual days, one detects between one account and the other a strict continuity and a clear analogy. The account begins with the words: "In the beginning God created the heavens and the earth," that is, the entire visible world. Then, in the description of the individual days, the expression recurs: "God said: Let there be...." Through the power of this word of the Creator—"*fiat,* let there be," the visible world gradually arises. In the beginning the earth is "without form and void." Later, under the action of God's creative word, it becomes suitable for life and is filled with living beings, with plants and animals, in the midst of which God finally created man "in his own image" (Gen 1:27).

Above all, this text has a religious and theological importance. It doesn't contain significant elements from the point of view of the natural sciences. Research on the origin and development of the individual species in nature does not find in this description any definitive norm or positive contributions of substantial interest. Indeed, the theory of natural evolution, understood in a sense that does not exclude divine causality, is not in principle opposed to the truth about the creation of the visible world, as presented in the Book of Genesis.

Taken as a whole, the image of the world is delineated by the pen of the inspired author with the characteristics of the cosmogonies of the time. In them, he inserts with absolute originality the truth about the creation of everything by the one God—this is the revealed truth. The biblical text affirms the total dependence of the visible world on God, who as Creator has full power over every creature (the so-called *dominium altum).* It sets out in relief the value of all creatures in God's eyes. At the end of each day the phrase recurs: "God saw that it was good." On the sixth day, after the creation of man, the center of the cosmos, we read: "God saw everything that he had made and behold, it was very good" (Gen 1:31).

The biblical description of creation has an ontological character, that is, it speaks of being. At the same time it has an axiological character because it bears witness to value. By creating the world as the manifestation of his infinite goodness, God created it good. Such is the essential teaching we draw from the biblical cosmogony, and in particular from the introductory description of the Book of Genesis.

Together with all that Sacred Scripture says in different places about the work of creation and about God the Creator, this description enables us to set out certain elements in relief:

1) God created the world by himself. The creative power is not transmissible—*incommunicabilis.*

2) God freely created the world, without any exterior compulsion or interior obligation. He could create or not create; he could create this world or another one.

3) The world was created by God in time, therefore, it is not eternal. It has a beginning in time.

4) The world created by God is constantly maintained in existence by the Creator. This "maintenance" is, in a certain sense, a continual creation *(conservatio est continua creatio).*

For almost two thousand years the Church has consistently professed and proclaimed the truth that the creation of the visible and invisible world is the work of God. It has done this in continuity with the faith professed and proclaimed by Israel, the People of God of the old covenant. The Church explains and thoroughly examines this truth by making use of the philosophy of being, and she defends it from the distortions that arise from time to time in the history of human thought. In the First Vatican Council, in reply to the trends of the pantheistic and materialistic thought of the time, the Church's Magisterium has confirmed with particular solemnity and force the truth that the creation of the world is the work of God. Those same tendencies are present also in our century in certain developments of the exact sciences and of the atheistic ideologies.

In the Constitution *Dei Filius* of the First Vatican Council we read: "This one true God, in his goodness and 'omnipotent power,' not to increase his own happiness, nor to acquire, but to manifest his perfection through the gifts he distributes to creatures, by a supremely free decision, 'simultaneously from the beginning of time drew forth from nothingness both the one creature and the other, the spiritual and the corporeal, that is, the angelic and the material, and then the human creature, who as it were shares in both orders, being composed of spirit and body' (Conc. Lat. IV)" *(DS* 3002).

According to the "canons" added to this doctrinal text, the First Vatican Council confirmed the following truths:

1) The one, true God is Creator and Lord "of visible and invisible things" *(DS* 3021).

2) It is contrary to faith to affirm that only matter exists (materialism) *(DS* 3022).

3) It is contrary to faith to assert that God is essentially identified with the world (pantheism) *(DS* 3023).

4) It is contrary to faith to maintain that creatures, even spiritual ones, are an emanation of the divine substance, or to affirm that the divine Being by its manifestation or evolution becomes everything *(DS* 3024).

5) Also contrary to faith is the idea that God is the universal or indefinite being which in becoming determinate constitutes the universe divided into genera, species and individuals *(DS* 3024).

6) It is likewise contrary to faith to deny that the world and all things contained in it, whether spiritual or material, in their entire substance have been created by God out of nothing *(DS* 3025).

It will be necessary to treat separately of the finality of the work of creation. This aspect takes up much space in revelation, in the Magisterium of the Church and in theology.

For the present, to conclude our reflection let it suffice to refer to a beautiful text of the Book of Wisdom which sings the praises of God for the love with which he created the universe and keeps it in being:

"For you love all things that exist,
and loathe none of the things
which you have made,
for you would not have made anything
if you had hated it.
How would anything have endured
if you had not willed it?
Or how would anything not called forth
by you have been preserved?
You spare all things, for they are yours,
O Lord who loves the living"
(Wis 11:24-26).

General audience of January 29, 1986

Creation Is the Work of the Trinity

The reflection on the truth of creation, whereby God calls the world into existence from nothingness, urges the eye of our faith to contemplate God the Creator, who reveals in creation his omnipotence, wisdom and love. The Creator's omnipotence is shown both in calling creatures into existence from nothingness and also in maintaining them in existence. "How would anything have endured if you had not willed it? Or how would anything not called forth by you have been preserved?" asked the author of the Book of Wisdom (11:25).

Omnipotence reveals also the love of God who, in creating, gives existence to beings different from himself, and at the same time different among themselves. The reality of his gift permeates the whole being and existence of creation. To create means to give, and especially to give existence. And he who gives, loves. The author of the Book of Wisdom stated this when he exclaimed: "You love all things that exist, and loathe none of the things which you have made, for you would not have made anything if you had hated it" (11:24); and he added: "You spare all things, for they are yours, O Lord who loves the living" (11:26).

God's love is a disinterested love. It aims solely at this:

that the good comes into existence, endures and develops according to its own dynamism. God the Creator is he "who accomplishes all things according to the counsel of his will" (Eph 1:11). The whole work of creation belongs to the plan of salvation, "the mystery hidden for ages in God who created all things" (Eph 3:9). Through the act of the creation of the world, and especially of man, the plan of salvation begins to be realized. Creation is the work of a loving Wisdom, as Sacred Scripture mentions on several occasions (cf. e.g., Prov 8:22-36).

It is clear that the truth of faith about creation is radically opposed to the theories of materialistic philosophy. These view the cosmos as the result of an evolution of matter reducible to pure chance and necessity.

Active role of Son and Spirit

St. Augustine wrote: "It is necessary that we, viewing the Creator through the works of his hands, raise up our minds to the contemplation of the Trinity, of which creation bears the mark in a certain and due proportion" *(De Trinitate,* VI, 10, 12). It is a truth of faith that the world has its beginning in the creator, who is the Triune God. Although the work of creation is attributed especially to God the Father—this we profess in the creeds of the faith ("I believe in God the Father Almighty, Creator of heaven and earth")—it is also a truth of faith that the Father, the Son and the Holy Spirit are the unique and indivisible "principle" of creation.

Sacred Scripture confirms this truth in different ways— first of all as regards the Son, the Word consubstantial with the Father. Some significant references are already present in the Old Testament, such as this eloquent verse of the Psalm: "By the word of the Lord the heavens were made" (Ps 33:6). This statement becomes fully explicit in the New Testament, as in the Prologue of John: "In the beginning was the Word, and the

Word was God...all things were made through him, and without him nothing was made...and the world was made through him" (Jn 1:1-2, 10). Paul's letters proclaim that everything was made "in Jesus Christ." St. Paul speaks of "one Lord, Jesus Christ, through whom are all things and through whom we exist" (1 Cor 8:6). In the Letter to the Colossians we read: "He (Christ) is the image of the invisible God, the first-born of all creation; for in him all things were created, in heaven and on earth, visible and invisible...all things were created through him and for him. He is before all things, and in him all things hold together" (Col 1:15-17).

The Apostle emphasizes the active presence of Christ both as the cause of creation ("through him") and as its final cause ("for him"). It is a subject to which we shall have to return. Meanwhile we also note that the Letter to the Hebrews states that God through the Son "also created the world" (1:2), and that the "Son...upholds the universe by his word of power" (1:3).

Especially in the writings of St. Paul and St. John, the New Testament deepens and enriches the creative Word already present in the Old Testament: "By the word of the Lord the heavens were made" (Ps 33:6). It makes clear that that creative Word was not only "with God," but it "was God." Precisely as the Son consubstantial with the Father, the Word created the world in union with the Father—"And the world was made through him" (Jn 1:10).

Not only that, the world was created also in reference to the person *(hypostasis)* of the Word. "The image of the invisible God" (Col 1:15), the Word, who is the Eternal Son "reflecting the glory of God and bearing the very stamp of his nature" (cf. Heb 1:3), is also he who is the "first-born of all creation" (Col 1:15), in the sense that all things have been created in the Word-Son, to become, in time, the world of creatures called from nothingness into existence "outside of God." In this sense "all things were made through him, and without him nothing was made" (Jn 1:3).

Revelation presents a "logical" (from *Logos*—Word) structure of the universe and also an "iconic" (from *Eikon*— image, image of the Father) structure. From the times of the Fathers of the Church, that teaching has been consolidated according to which the created world bears within itself the "vestiges of the Trinity" *(vestigia Trinitatis).* It is the work of the Father through the Son in the Holy Spirit. Creation reveals the Wisdom of God. In creation, the above-mentioned twofold "logical-iconic" structure of creatures is intimately joined to the structure of the gift.

The individual creatures are not only "words" of the Word, whereby the Creator is manifested to our intelligence, but they are also "gifts" of the Gift. They bear within themselves the imprint of the Holy Spirit, the creator Spirit.

The first verses of Genesis already stated: "In the beginning God created the heavens and the earth (the universe)...and the Spirit of God was moving over the face of the waters" (Gen 1:1-2). Evocative even though vague, that reference to the action of the Spirit in that first "beginning" of the universe, appears significant for us who read it in the light of the full New Testament revelation.

Creation is the work of the Triune God. The world "created" in the Word-Son, is "restored" together with the Son to the Father, through that Uncreated Gift, the Holy Spirit, consubstantial with both. In this way the world is created in that Love, which is the Spirit of the Father and of the Son. This universe embraced by eternal Love begins to exist in the instant chosen by the Trinity as the beginning of time.

In this way the creation of the world is the work of Love. A created gift, the universe springs from the Uncreated Gift, from the reciprocal Love of the Father and Son, from the Most Holy Trinity.

General audience of March 5, 1986

Creation Reveals God's Glory

In previous catecheses we have dwelt on the truth of faith about creation from nothing *(ex nihilo)*. This truth introduces us into the depths of the mystery of God, Creator "of heaven and earth." Creation is attributed principally to the Father, according to the expression of the Apostles' Creed: "I believe in God the Father Almighty, Creator...." It is the work of the three Persons of the Trinity, according to the teaching which was already present in a certain way in the Old Testament, and fully revealed in the New, particularly in the texts of Paul and John.

In the light of these apostolic texts we can affirm that the creation of the world finds its model in the eternal generation of the Word, of the Son, who is of the same substance of the Father. Creation finds its source in the Love which is the Holy Spirit. This Love-Person, consubstantial with the Father and the Son, together with the Father and the Son, is the source of the creation of the world from nothing, that is, of the gift of existence to every being. The whole multiplicity of beings participate in this gratuitous gift—the "visible and the invisible," so varied as to appear almost unlimited, and all that the language of cosmology indicates as the "macrocosm" and "microcosm."

The truth of faith about the creation of the world leads us to penetrate the depths of the trinitarian mystery. It reveals to us what the Bible calls the "Glory of God" *(Kabod Yahweh, doxa tou Theou)*. The Glory of God is first of all in himself. It is the "interior" glory, which fills the unlimited depth and infinite perfection of the one divinity in the Trinity of Persons. Inasmuch as it is the absolute fullness of being and holiness, this infinite perfection is also the fullness of truth and of love in the mutual contemplation and giving (and hence in the communion) of Father, Son and Holy Spirit.

God's interior glory springs from the mystery of the divinity. Through the work of creation, it is in a certain sense transferred "outside"—in the creatures of the visible and invisible world, in proportion to their degree of perfection.

A new dimension of God's glory begins with the creation of the visible and invisible world. This glory is called "exterior" to distinguish it from the previous one. Sacred Scripture speaks of it in many passages and in different ways. Some examples will suffice.

Psalm 19 proclaims: "The heavens declare the glory of God; and the firmament proclaims his handiwork.... There is no speech, nor are there words whose sound is not heard. Their voice goes out through all the earth, and their words to the end of the world" (Ps 19:1, 2, 4). The Book of Sirach states: "The sun looks down on everything with its light, and the work of the Lord is full of his glory" (42:16). The Book of Baruch has a very singular and evocative expression: "The stars shone in their watches and were glad; he called them, and they said, 'Here we are!' They shone with gladness for him who made them" (3:34).

Elsewhere the biblical text sounds like an appeal addressed to creatures to proclaim the glory of God the Creator. For example, the Book of Daniel states: "O all you works of the Lord, bless the Lord, to him be highest glory and praise forever" (3:57). Or Psalm 66: "Make a joyful noise to God, all the earth; sing the glory of his name: give to him glorious praise! Say to God, 'How glorious are your deeds! So great is your power that your enemies cringe before you. All the earth worships you; they sing praises to you, sing praises to your name'" (1-4).

Sacred Scripture is full of similar expressions: "O Lord, how manifold are your works! In wisdom you have made them all; the earth is full of your creatures" (Ps 104:24). The whole created universe is a multiple, powerful and incessant appeal to proclaim the glory of the Creator. "All the earth shall be filled with the glory of the Lord" (Num 14:21); for "both riches and honor come from you" (1 Chr 29:12).

This hymn of glory, inscribed in creation, awaits a being capable of giving it adequate conceptual and verbal expression, a being who will praise the holy name of God and narrate the greatness of his works (cf. Sir 17:8). This being in the visible world is man. The appeal which goes up from the universe is addressed to him as the spokesman of creatures and their interpreter before God.

Let us return again for a moment to the words in which the First Vatican Council expressed the truth about creation and about the Creator of the world. "This one true God, in his goodness and 'omnipotent power,' not to increase his own happiness, nor to acquire, but to manifest his perfection through the gifts he distributes to creatures, by a supremely free decision, 'simultaneously from the beginning of time drew forth from nothingness both the one creature and the other, the spiritual and the corporeal...'" *(DS* 3002).

This text makes explicit with a language all its own the same truth about creation and about its finality, which we find in the biblical texts. The Creator does not seek any "completion" of himself in the work of creation. Such reasoning would be a direct antithesis of what God is in himself. He is the Being totally and infinitely perfect. Consequently he has no need of the world. Creatures, both visible and invisible, cannot "add" anything to the divinity of the Triune God.

But, God creates! God calls creatures into existence by a fully free and sovereign decision. In a real, though limited and partial way, they participate in the perfection of God's absolute fullness. They differ from one another according to the degree of perfection they have received, beginning with inanimate beings, then up to animate beings, and finally to human beings; or rather, higher still, to the creatures of a purely spiritual nature. The ensemble of creatures constitutes the universe. In its totality as well as its parts, the visible and invisible cosmos reflects eternal Wisdom and expresses the inexhaustible love of the Creator.

The revelation of the wisdom and love of God is the first and principal end of creation. The mystery of God's glory is realized in creation, according to the words of Scripture. "O all you works of the Lord, bless the Lord" (Dan 3:57). All creatures acquire their transcendental meaning in the mystery of that glory. "They reach out beyond" themselves to be open to him in whom they have their beginning...and their end.

Let us admire with faith the work of the Creator and praise his greatness:

"O Lord, how manifold are your works!
In wisdom you have made them all;
the earth is full of your creatures.
May the glory of the Lord endure forever,
may the Lord rejoice in his works.
I will sing to the Lord as long as I live;
I will sing to my God all my life" (Ps 104:24, 31, 33).

General audience of March 12, 1986

Created Things Have a Legitimate Autonomy

In the previous catechesis we dwelt on the finality of creation from the viewpoint of the transcendent dimension. Creation also demands reflection from the point of view of the immanent dimension. Today this is particularly necessary because of the progress of science and technology, which has introduced important changes in the mentality of many people of our time. We read in the *Pastoral Constitution on the Church in the Modern World* of the Second Vatican Council: "Now many of our contemporaries seem to fear that a closer bond between human activity and religion will work against the independence of men, of societies, or of the sciences" *(GS* 36).

The Council faced this problem, which is closely connected with the truth of faith concerning creation and its finality, by giving a clear and convincing explanation of it. Let us listen to what the Council said.

"If by the autonomy of earthly affairs we mean that created things and societies themselves enjoy their own laws and values which must be gradually deciphered, put to use, and regulated by men, then it is entirely right to demand that autonomy. Such is not merely required by modern man, but harmonizes also with the will of the Creator. For by the very circumstance of their having been created, all things are endowed with their own stability, truth, goodness, proper laws, and order. Man must respect these as he isolates them by the appropriate methods of the individual sciences or arts. Therefore, if methodical investigation within every branch of learning is carried out in a genuinely scientific manner and in accord with moral norms, it never truly conflicts with faith. For earthly matters and the concerns of faith derive from the same God.

"Indeed, whoever labors to penetrate the secrets of reality with a humble and steady mind, is, even though he is unaware of the fact, nevertheless being led by the hand of God, who holds all things in existence, and gives them their identity. Consequently, we cannot but deplore certain habits of mind, sometimes found too among Christians, which do not sufficiently attend to the rightful independence of science, and which, from the arguments and controversies they spark, lead many minds to conclude that faith and science are mutually opposed.

"But if the expression, the independence of temporal affairs, is taken to mean that created things do not depend on God, and that man can use them without any reference to their Creator, anyone who acknowledges God will see how false such a meaning is. For without the Creator the creature would disappear. For their part, however, all believers of whatever religion always hear his revealing voice in the discourse of creatures. When God is forgotten, however, the creature itself grows unintelligible" *(GS* 36).

These words of the Council constitute a development of the teaching offered by faith on the subject of creation. They provide an illuminating comparison between this truth of faith and the mentality of our contemporaries, strongly influenced by the development of the natural sciences and by technological progress.

Let us endeavor to bring together in an organic synthesis the principal thoughts contained in paragraph 36 of the Constitution *Gaudium et Spes*.

A) In the light of the doctrine of the Second Vatican Council, the truth about creation is not merely a truth of faith based on the revelation of the Old and New Testaments. It is also a truth common to all believers "no matter what their religion," that is to say, all those "who recognize the voice and the revelation of the Creator in the language of creatures."

B) This truth is fully manifested in revelation. But it is *per se* accessible to human reason. We can deduce this from the overall reasoning of the Council text and in particular from the phrase: "Without the Creator the creature would disappear.... When God is forgotten, however, the creature itself grows unintelligible." These expressions (at least indirectly) indicate that the created world postulates an Ultimate Reason, a First Cause. By virtue of their very nature, contingent beings, in order to exist, require the support of the Absolute (of Necessary Being), which is Existence *per se* (Subsisting Being). The fleeting and contingent world "cannot exist without the Creator."

C) In relation to the truth about creation, understood in this way, the Council makes a fundamental distinction between the "legitimate" and "illegitimate" autonomy of earthly things. That autonomy would be illegitimate (that is, not in conformity with the truth of revelation) which proclaims the independence of created things from God the Creator, and which maintains "that created things do not depend on God, and that man can use them without any reference to their Creator." Such a way of understanding and behaving denies and rejects the truth about creation. In most cases, if not indeed in principle, this position is maintained precisely in the name of the "autonomy" of the world, and of man in the world, and of human knowledge and action.

However, one should add immediately that in the context

of an "autonomy" understood in this way, man is deprived of his autonomy in regard to the world. In the end he finds himself subjected to it. We shall return to this subject.

D) The "autonomy of earthly things" understood in this way is not only illegitimate but also useless, according to the text quoted from the Constitution *Gaudium et Spes.* Indeed, created things enjoy an autonomy proper to them "by will of the Creator." It is rooted in their nature, and pertains to the finality of creation (in its immanent dimension). "For by the very circumstance of their having been created, all things are endowed with their own stability, truth, goodness, proper laws and order." If this statement refers to all creatures of the visible world, it refers eminently to man. To the extent that he seeks to "discover, exploit and order" in a consistent way the laws and values of the cosmos, man not only participates creatively in the legitimate autonomy of created things, but fulfills correctly the autonomy proper to them. Thus one meets with the immanent finality of creation, and also indirectly with the Creator: "He is being led by the hand of God, who holds all things in existence, and gives them their identity" *(GS* 36).

One must add that the problem of the "legitimate autonomy of earthly things" is also linked with today's deeply felt problem of "ecology," that is, the concern for the protection and preservation of the natural environment.

Ecological destruction always presupposes a form of selfishness opposed to the well-being of the community. It arises from an arbitrary—and in the last analysis harmful—use of creatures, whose laws and natural order are violated by ignoring or disregarding the finality immanent in the work of creation. This mode of behavior derives from a false interpretation of the autonomy of earthly things. When man uses these things "without reference to the Creator," to quote once again the words of the Council, he also does incalculable harm to himself. The solution of the problem of the ecological threat is strictly related to the principles of the "legitimate autonomy of earthly things"—in the final analysis, with the truth about creation and about the Creator of the world.

General audience of April 2, 1986

Man Is Created in the Image of God

The creed speaks of God, "Creator of heaven and earth, of all things visible and invisible"; it does not speak directly of the creation of man. In the soteriological context of the creed, man appears in reference to the Incarnation. This is particularly evident in the Nicene-Constantinopolitan Creed, which professes faith in Jesus Christ, Son of God, who "for us men and for our salvation came down from heaven...and became man."

However, we should recall that the order of salvation not only presupposes creation, but indeed originates from it.

In its conciseness, the creed refers us back to the ensemble of revealed truth about creation, to discover the truly singular and eminent position granted to man.

The Book of Genesis contains two accounts of man's creation, as we have already recalled in previous catecheses. From the chronological point of view, the description contained in the second chapter of Genesis is earlier, while that in the first chapter is later.

Taken together, the two descriptions complete each other. They both contain elements which are theologically rich and precious.

In Genesis 1:26 we read that on the sixth day God said: "Let us make man in our image, after our likeness; and let them have dominion over the fish of the sea, and over the birds of the air, and over the cattle, and over all the earth, and over every creeping thing that creeps upon the earth."

It is significant that the creation of man is preceded by this kind of statement in which God expresses the intention to create man in his image, rather "in our image," in the plural (in harmony with the verb "let us make"). According to some interpretations, the plural would indicate the divine "we" of the one Creator. This would be, in some way, a first distant trinitarian indication. In any event, according to the description of Genesis 1, man's creation is preceded by the Creator's "addressing" himself, *ad intra*, in this particular way.

Then follows the act of creation. "God created man in his own image, in the image of God he created him; male and female he created them" (Gen 1:27). In this phrase, the triple use of the verb "created" *(barà),* is striking. It seems to give a particular importance and "intensity" to the creative act. It would appear that this same conclusion should also be drawn from the fact that, while each day of creation concludes with the observation: "God saw that is was good" (cf. Gen 1:3, 10, 12, 18, 21, 25), after the creation of man on the sixth day, it is said that "God saw everything that he had made and behold, it was very good" (Gen 1:31).

The "Yahwist" account of Genesis 2 is the more ancient description. It does not use the expression "image of God." This pertains exclusively to the later text which is more "theological."

Nonetheless, the Yahwist description presents the same truth, even though indirectly. It states that the man, created by God-Yahweh, while he had power to "name the animals" (cf. Gen 2:19-20), did not find among all the creatures of the visible world "a helper fit for him." This recognizes his uniqueness. Although the account of Genesis 2 does not speak directly of the "image" of God, it presents some of its essential elements—the capacity of self-knowledge, the experience of man's own being in the world, the need to fill his solitude, his dependence on God.

Share in dominion

These elements also indicate that man and woman are equal as regards nature and dignity. While man could not find in any creature "a helper fit for him," he finds such a "helper" in the woman created by God-Yahweh. According to Genesis 2:21-22, God calls the woman into being, by drawing her from the body of the man, from "one of his ribs." This indicates their identity in humanity, and their essential similarity although they are distinct. Both have the same dignity as persons, since both share the same nature.

The truth about man created "in the image of God" is found also in other passages of Sacred Scripture, both in Genesis itself ("God made man in his own image," 9:6), and in the Wisdom Books.

The Book of Wisdom says: "God created man for incorruption, and made him in the image of his own nature" (2:23). In the Book of Sirach we read: "God created man out of earth, and turned him back to it again...he endowed them with strength like his own, and made them in his own image."

Man is created for immortality. He does not cease to be the image of God after sin, even though he is subjected to death. He bears in himself the reflection of God's power, which is manifested especially in the faculty of intelligence and free will. Man is an autonomous subject. He is the source of his own actions, while maintaining the characteristics of dependence on God, the Creator (ontological contingency).

After the creation of man, male and female, the Creator

"blessed them and said to them, 'Be fruitful and multiply, and fill the earth and subdue it; and have dominion over the fish of the sea and over the birds...and over every living thing'" (Gen 1:28). Creation in the image of God is the basis of the dominion over the other creatures in the visible world, which are called into being in view of man and "for him."

The people deriving their origin from the first man and woman share in the dominion spoken of in Genesis 1:2. The Yahwist account also alludes to it (Gen 2:24). We shall have occasion to return to this narrative later. In transmitting life to their children, man and woman convey to them the inheritance of that "image of God" conferred on the first man in the moment of his creation.

In this way man becomes a particular expression of the glory of the Creator. "Living man is the glory of God, but the vision of God is man's life," as St. Irenaeus wrote *(Adv. Haer.* IV, 20, 7). He is the glory of the Creator inasmuch as he was created in God's image and especially inasmuch as he has access to the true knowledge of the living God.

This is the basis of the special value of human life, and also of all human rights, which are so much emphasized today.

Through creation in the image of God man is called to become, among the creatures of the visible world, a mouthpiece of the glory of God, and in a certain sense, a word of his glory.

The teaching about man contained in the first pages of the Bible (Gen 1), links with the New Testament revelation about the truth of Christ. As the eternal Word, Christ is "the image of the invisible God," and at the same time "the firstborn of all creation" (Col 1:15).

In God's plan, man created in the image of God acquires a special relationship with the Word, the Father's Eternal Image, who in the fullness of time will become flesh. St. Paul wrote: "Adam is the type of the one who was to come" (Rom

5:14). "Those whom (God the Creator) foreknew he also predestined to be conformed to the image of his Son, in order that he might be the first-born among many brethren" (Rom 8:29).

Thus, the truth about man created in the image of God does not merely determine man's place in the whole order of creation, but it already speaks even of his link with the order of salvation in Christ, who is the eternal and consubstantial "image of God" (2 Cor 4:4)—the image of the Father. Man's creation in the image of God, from the very beginning of the Book of Genesis, bears witness to his call. This call is fully revealed with the coming of Christ.

Thanks to the action of the "Spirit of the Lord," there opens up the perspective of the full transformation in the consubstantial image of God, which is Christ (cf. 2 Cor 3:18). Thus the "image" of the Book of Genesis (1:27) reaches the fullness of its revealed significance.

General audience of April 9, 1986

Man Is a Spiritual
and Corporeal Being

Created in the image of God, man is both a corporeal and spiritual being. Bound to the external world, he also transcends it. Besides being a bodily creature, as a spirit he is a person. This truth about man is an object of our faith, as is the biblical truth about his being constituted in the "image and likeness" of God. It is a truth constantly presented by the Church's Magisterium during the course of the centuries.

In the course of history, this truth has not ceased to be the object of intellectual analysis, both in the sphere of philosophy and of many other human sciences. In a word, it is the object of anthropology.

Man is an incarnate spirit, or if you wish, a body informed by an immortal spirit. This truth can already be inferred in some way from the description of creation contained in the Book of Genesis and in particular from the "Yahwist" account. This account uses a stage setting and anthropomorphic images. We read that "the Lord God formed man of dust from the ground, and breathed into his nostrils the breath of life; and man became a living being" (Gen 2:7). The continuation of the biblical text helps us clearly understand that created in this way, man is distinguished from the entire visible world, and in particular from the animal world. The "breath of life" has made him capable of knowing these beings, of naming them, and of recognizing that he was different from them (cf. Gen 2:18-20). The "Yahwist" account does not speak of the "soul." Nevertheless we can easily deduce from it that the life given to man in the act of creation transcends the mere corporeal dimension (that which is proper to animals). Beyond the material, it reaches the dimension of the spirit, which contains the essential foundation of that "image of God," which Genesis 1:27 sees in man.

Unity and duality

Man is a unit. He is one in himself. But this unity contains a duality. Sacred Scripture presents both the unity (the person) and the duality (body and soul). One thinks of the Book of Sirach which says: "The Lord created man out of earth, and turned him back to it again"; and further on: "He forms men's tongues and eyes and ears, and imparts to them an understanding heart. With wisdom and knowledge he fills them; good and evil he shows them" (17:1, 5-6).

From this point of view, Psalm 8 is particularly significant. Exalting man, it addresses God in the following words: "What is man that you should be mindful of him, or the son of man that you should care for him? You have made him little less than the angels, and crowned him with glory and honor. You have given him rule over the works of your hands, putting all things under his feet" (Ps 8:5-7).

It is frequently emphasized that biblical tradition stresses especially the personal unity of the human being, by using the term "body" to designate the whole man (cf. Ps 145:21, Joel 3:1; Is 66:23; Jn 1:14). The observation is exact. But notwithstanding this, the duality of man is also present in biblical tradition, sometimes very clearly. Christ's words reflect this tradition: "Do not fear those who deprive the body of life but cannot destroy the soul. Rather, fear him who can destroy both body and soul in Gehenna" (Mt 10:28).

Biblical sources authorize us to view man as a personal unity and at the same time as a duality of soul and body. This concept has found expression in the Church's entire Tradition and teaching. This teaching has assimilated not only the biblical sources, but also their theological interpretations, which have been given by developing the analyses conducted by certain schools of Greek philosophy (such as that of Aristotle). It has been a slow, constant work of reflection. Under the influence of St. Thomas Aquinas, it culminated principally in the pronouncements of the Council of Vienne (1312), which calls the soul the "form" of the body: *forma corporis humani per se et essentialiter (DS* 902). As a factor determining the substance of the being "man," the "form" is of a spiritual nature. This spiritual "form," the soul, is immortal. Later, the Fifth Lateran Council (1513) authoritatively stated this—the soul is immortal, in contrast with the body which is subject to death (cf. *DS* 1440). The Thomistic school emphasizes at the same time that, by virtue of the substantial union of body and soul, the soul, even after death, does not cease to "aspire" to be reunited with the body. This is confirmed by the revealed truth about the resurrection of the body.

The philosophical terminology used to express the unity and complexity (duality) of man is sometimes criticized. But it is beyond doubt that the doctrine on the unity of the human person and at the same time on the spiritual-corporeal duality of man is fully rooted in Sacred Scripture and Tradition. The conviction that man is the "image of God" because of the soul, has frequently been expressed. But traditional doctrine does not lack the conviction that the body also participates in the dignity of the "image of God" in its own way, just as it participates in the dignity of the person.

In modern times the theory of evolution has raised a special difficulty against the revealed doctrine about the creation of man as a being composed of soul and body. With their own methods, many natural scientists study the problem of the origin of human life on earth. Some maintain, contrary to other colleagues of theirs, not only the existence of a link between man and the ensemble of nature, but also his derivation from the higher animal species. This problem has occupied scientists since the last century and involves vast layers of public opinion.

The reply of the Magisterium was offered in the encyclical *Humani Generis* of Pius XII in 1950. In it we read: "The magisterium of the Church is not opposed to the theory of evolution being the object of investigation and discussion among experts. Here the theory of evolution is understood as an investigation of the origin of the human body from pre-existing living matter, for the Catholic faith obliges us to hold firmly that souls are created immediately by God..." (*DS* 3896).

It can therefore be said that, from the viewpoint of the doctrine of the faith, there are no difficulties in explaining the origin of man in regard to the body, by means of the theory of evolution. But it must be added that this hypothesis proposes only a probability, not a scientific certainty. However, the doctrine of faith invariably affirms that man's spiritual soul is created directly by God. According to the hypothesis mentioned, it is possible that the human body, following the order impressed by the Creator on the energies of life, could have been gradually prepared in the forms of antecedent living beings. However, the human soul, on which man's humanity definitively depends, cannot emerge from matter, since the soul is of a spiritual nature.

A fine synthesis of creation as set out above is found in the Second Vatican Council: "Though made of body and soul, man is one. Through his bodily composition he gathers to himself the elements of the material world; thus they reach their crown through him..." *(GS* 14). And further on: "Man is not wrong when he regards himself as superior to bodily concerns, and as more than a speck of nature or a nameless constituent of the city of man. For by his interior qualities he outstrips the whole sum of mere things" *(GS* 14).

In this way, then, the same truth about the unity and duality (the complexity) of human nature can be expressed in a language closer to the modern mentality.

General audience of April 16, 1986

Man Is a Subject
of Knowledge and Freedom

"God created man in his own image, in the image of God he created him; male and female he created them" (Gen 1:27). The man and the woman were created with equal dignity as persons, as units of spirit and body. They are differentiated by their psycho-physical structures. The human being bears the mark of masculinity or femininity.

While it is a sign of diversity, it is also an indication of complementarity. That can be deduced from a reading of the "Yahwist" text, where the man exclaimed upon seeing the woman just created: "This at last is bone of my bone and flesh of my flesh" (Gen 2:23). They are words of gladness and also of enthusiastic rapture of the man on seeing a being essentially like himself. The diversity and, at the same time, the psycho-spiritual complementarity are at the origin of the particular richness of humanity, which is proper to the descendants of Adam through their entire history. From this, marriage takes its origin, instituted by the Creator from the beginning: "Therefore a man leaves his father and his mother and cleaves to his wife, and they become one flesh" (Gen 2:24).

To this text of Genesis corresponds the blessing of fruitfulness mentioned in Genesis 1:28: "Be fruitful and multiply and fill the earth and subdue it...." Contained in the mystery of man's creation, the institution of marriage and the family seems to be linked with the command to "subdue" the earth, entrusted by the Creator to the first human couple.

Man is called to "subdue the earth." But note well—to "subdue" it, not to devastate it, because creation is a gift of God and, as such, it must be respected. Man is the image of God not only as male and female, but also because of the reciprocal relation of the two sexes. This reciprocal relation constitutes the soul of the "communion of persons" which is established in marriage and presents a certain likeness with the union of the three Divine Persons.

In this regard the Second Vatican Council tells us: "God did not create man a solitary being. From the beginning 'male and female he created them' (Gen 1:27). This partnership of man and woman constitutes the first form of communion between persons. For by his innermost nature man is a social being, and unless he relates himself to others he can neither live nor develop his potential" *(GS* 12).

Thus creation implies for man both a relationship with the world, and a relationship with the other human being (the man-woman relationship), as well as with others like them. "Subduing the earth" delineates the "relational" character of human existence. The dimensions "with others," "among others" and "for others" are proper to the human person as the "image of God." They establish from the beginning man's place among creatures. To this end man is called into existence as the subject (as the concrete "I"), endowed with intellectual consciousness and freedom.

Knowledge of truth
permeates sphere of relationship

Man's capacity of intellectual knowledge radically distinguishes him from the entire animal world, where the cognitive capacity is limited to the senses. Intellectual knowledge makes man capable of discernment, of distinguishing between truth and non-truth. It does this by opening before him the fields of science, of critical thought, of the methodical search for truth about reality. Man has within himself an essential relation to truth which determines his character as a transcendent being. The knowledge of the truth permeates the whole sphere of the relationship of man with the world and with other human beings. It is the indispensable premise of every form of culture.

Bound by an intrinsic relation to the good, the freedom of the human will is joined to intellectual knowledge and to the relation to truth. Human acts bear within themselves the sign of self-determination of the will and of choice. The whole sphere of morality derives from this. Man is capable of choosing between good and evil, sustained in this by the voice of conscience, which impels him to good and restrains him from evil.

Like the knowledge of truth, the capacity of choice—that is, free will—permeates the whole sphere of the relationship of man with the world, especially with other humans, and ventures even beyond.

Thanks to his spiritual nature and to his capacity for intellectual knowledge and freedom of choice and action, man is, from the very beginning, in a special relationship with God. The description of creation (cf. Gen 1-3) permits us to observe that the "image of God" is manifested above all in the relation of the human "I" to the divine "You." Man knows God, and his heart and will are capable of uniting themselves with God *(homo est capax Dei)*. Man can say "yes" to God, but he can also say "no." He has the capacity to accept God and his holy will, but also the capacity to oppose it.

All this is contained in the meaning of the "image of God" presented to us by the Book of Sirach, among others: "The Lord created human beings out of the earth, and turned them back to it again.... He endowed them with strength like his own, and made them in his own image. He placed the fear of them in all living beings, and granted them dominion over beasts and birds. He made for them tongue and eyes; he gave them ears and a mind for thinking. He filled them with knowledge and understanding, and showed them good and evil.... He set his eye upon their hearts [note the expression!] to show them the majesty of his works.... He has set before them knowledge, a law of life as their inheritance. An everlasting covenant he has made with them, his commandments he has revealed to them" (Sir 17:1, 3-7, 9-10). These words contain a wealth of richness and depth which make us reflect.

The Second Vatican Council expressed the same truth about man in language which is both perennial and contemporary. "Only in freedom can man direct himself toward goodness...man's dignity demands that he act according to a knowing and free choice..." *(GS* 17). "For by his interior qualities he outstrips the whole sum of mere things. He plunges into the depths of reality whenever he enters into his own heart; God, who probes the heart, awaits him there; there he discerns his proper destiny beneath the eyes of God" *(GS* 14). "Authentic freedom is an exceptional sign of the divine image within man" *(GS* 17). True freedom is freedom in truth, inscribed from the beginning in the reality of the "divine image."

By virtue of this "image" man, as the subject of knowledge and freedom, is not only called to transform the world according to the measure of his rightful needs. He is not only called to the communion of persons proper to marriage *(communio personarum)* from which the family begins. He is also called to the covenant with God. He is not merely a creature of the Creator, but also the image of God. He is creature as image of God, and he is image of God as creature. The description of creation in Genesis 1-3 is joined with that of the first covenant of God with man. This covenant (just like creation) is a competely sovereign initiative of God the Creator. It will remain unchanged throughout the history of salvation, until the definitive and eternal covenant which God will make with humanity in Jesus Christ.

Man is the suitable subject for the covenant, because he was created "in the image" of God, capable of knowledge and freedom. Christian thought has perceived in man's "likeness" to God the foundation of man's call to participate in the interior life of God—his opening to the supernatural.

In this way, the revealed truth about man, created "in the image and likeness of God,". contains not only all that is *"humanum"* in him, and therefore essential to his humanity, but potentially also what is *"divinum,"* and therefore gratuitous. That is to say, it contains also what God—Father, Son and Holy Spirit—had *de facto* foreseen for man as the supernatural dimension of his existence, without which man could not attain all the fullness destined for him by the Creator.

General audience of April 23, 1986

DIVINE PROVIDENCE

Faith in Divine Providence Strengthens Our Reasons for Hope

"I believe in one God, the Father Almighty, Creator of heaven and earth." The first article of the creed has not finished revealing to us its extraordinary riches. Faith in God as the Creator of the world (of "things visible and invisible"), is organically linked to the revelation of divine Providence.

In our reflection on creation we begin today a series of catecheses whose theme lies both at the heart of the Christian faith, and in the heart of the person called to faith. It is the theme of divine Providence. It concerns God who, as a wise and omnipotent Father, is present and active in the world and in the history of every creature. He does this so that every creature, and specifically man, God's image, may be able to live life as a journey under the guidance of truth and love toward the goal of eternal life in God.

The Christian tradition of catechesis asks the question "Why has God created us?" Enlightened by the great faith of the Church, we repeat, whether as adults or children, these or similar words: "God created us to know and love him in this life and to be happy with him forever in the next."

This extraordinary truth of God guides our history with serene countenance and sure hand. Paradoxically, it finds a twofold and conflicting sentiment in the heart of man. On the one hand, he is led to accept and to entrust himself to this Provident God, as the Psalmist says: "I have calmed and quieted my soul, like a child quieted at its mother's breast" (Ps 131:2). On the other hand, man fears and hesitates to abandon himself to God, as Lord and Savior of his life. This is either because he is perplexed by things and forgets the Creator, or because of suffering he has doubts about God as Father. In both cases man calls divine Providence into question. Such is the human condition, that even in Sacred Scripture, Job does not hesitate to complain before God with frank confidence. In this way the word of God indicates that Providence is expressed even in the complaint of his children. Afflicted in body and heart, Job said: "Oh, that I knew where I might find him, that I might come even to his seat! I would lay my case before him, and fill my mouth with arguments" (Job 23:3-4).

Throughout the whole of human history, whether in the thought of philosophers, in the teachings of the great religions, or in the simple reflection of the person in the street, human beings have not lacked reasons to seek to understand, or rather to justify God's action in the world.

Different solutions are proposed. Clearly, not all are acceptable and none is fully exhaustive. From ancient times, some have appealed to blind and capricious fate or destiny, to blind-folded fortune. Others have compromised man's free will in their affirmation of God. Especially in our contemporary age, others think that the affirmation of man and his freedom implies the denial of God. These extreme and unilateral solutions at least make us understand what profound problems of life enter into play when we speak of "divine Providence." How can God's omnipotence be reconciled with our freedom, and our freedom with his infallible decrees? What will our future destiny be? How are we to interpret and recognize his infinite wisdom and goodness in the face of the evils of the world—the moral evil of sin and the suffering of the innocent? This history of ours, unfolding through centuries of events, of terrible catastrophes and of sublime acts of greatness and of sanctity...what is the meaning of it all? Is it an eternal, fatalistic return of everything to the point of departure with no point of arrival, if not a final cataclysm that will bury all life for ever? Or, on the contrary—and here the heart feels that it has reasons greater than those that its puny logic can provide—is there a provident and positive being? Is there this being whom we call God, who surrounds us with his intelligence, tenderness and wisdom, and guides "with a strong and gentle touch" this existence of ours—reality, the world, history, even our rebellious wills, if they consent to him—toward the "seventh day's" rest of a creation which has finally arrived at its fulfillment?

Here, on the razor's edge between hope and despair, we have the word of God to immensely strengthen our reasons for hope. Ever new though repeatedly called upon, that word of God is so marvelous as to be almost incredible from the human point of view. Never does the word of God assume such greatness and attraction as when man's greatest demands confront it. God is here, he is Emmanuel, God with us (Is 7:4). In Jesus of Nazareth, risen from the dead, Son of God and our brother, God shows that "he has made his dwelling among us" (Jn 1:14). We can well say that the whole story of the Church in time consists in the constant and ardent search to find, to examine and to propose the signs of God's presence. The Church is guided in this by the example of Christ and by the power of the Spirit. For this reason the Church can, the Church wishes, the Church must proclaim and give to the world the grace and the meaning of divine Providence. The Church does this for the love of man, to rescue him from the crushing weight of the enigma and to entrust him to a mystery of a great, immeasurable, decisive love such as God is. So the Christian vocabulary is enriched with simple expressions which constitute, today as in the past, the patrimony of faith and culture of

Christ's disciples: God sees, God knows, God willing, to live in the presence of God, may his will be done, God writes straight with crooked lines...in short—divine Providence.

The Church announces divine Providence not through her own invention, however inspired by thoughts of humanity, but because God has revealed himself thus. He revealed in the history of his people that his creative action and his salvific intervention were indissolubly united, that they formed part of a single plan decreed from eternal ages. Thus Sacred Scripture becomes, in its globality, the supreme document of divine Providence. It manifests God's intervention in nature by creation and his still more wonderful intervention by redemption, which makes us new creatures in a world renewed by the love of God in Christ. The Bible speaks of divine Providence in the chapters on creation and in those more specifically concerned with the work of salvation—in Genesis, and in the Prophets, especially in Isaiah, in the so-called psalms of creation and in the profound meditations of Paul on the inscrutable divine plans at work in history (cf. especially Ephesians and Colossians), in the Wisdom Books, so keen to find the sign of God in the world, and in the Book of Revelation completely intent on finding in God the meaning of the world. In the end it appears that the Christian concept of Providence is not simply a chapter of religious philosophy, but that faith provides an answer to the great questions of Job and of all those like him. It does so with the completeness of a vision which, by favoring the rights of reason, does justice to reason itself by anchoring it in the more stable certainties of theology.

In this regard our path will meet with the untiring reflection of faith on the Tradition to which we shall opportunely refer. Within the sphere of the perennial truth, we shall avail ourselves of the Church's effort to be a companion to man who questions himself ever anew and in new terms about Providence. Each in its own way, the First and Second Vatican Councils are precious voices of the Holy Spirit, not to be ignored but to be meditated on. We need not let ourselves be frightened by the depth of the thought, but welcome the life-giving sap of the truth that does not die.

Every serious question should receive a serious, well-reasoned and sound answer. For this reason we shall touch on various aspects of the single theme. We shall see especially how divine Providence enters into the great work of creation and is its affirmation which places in evidence the manifold and actual riches of the divine action. From this, it follows that Providence is manifested as transcendent Wisdom which loves man and calls him to participate in God's plan as the first recipient of his loving care, and at the same time as his intelligent cooperator.

The relationship between divine Providence and human freedom is not one of antithesis, but of a communion of love. Even the profound problem of our future destiny finds a providential light in divine revelation, specifically in Christ. While preserving the mystery intact, it guarantees for us the Father's salvific will. In this perspective divine Providence, far from being denied by the presence of evil and suffering, becomes a bulwark of our hope. It enables us to perceive how it can draw forth good even from evil. Finally we shall recall the great light which Vatican II sheds on the Providence of God in regard to the evolution and progress of the world, taking up at the end in the transcendent vision of the growing kingdom the final point of the unceasing and wise action of a provident God in the world.

"Whoever is wise let him understand these things; whoever is discerning, let him know them; for the ways of the Lord are right, and the upright walk in them, but transgressors stumble in them" (Hos 14:9).

General audience of April 30, 1986

Divine Providence
Continues to Care for Creation

Today we continue the catechesis on divine Providence. By creating, God called into being from nothing all that began to exist outside himself. But God's creative act does not end here. What comes forth from nothing would return to nothing if it were left to itself and not conserved in being by the Creator. Having created the cosmos, God continues to create it, by maintaining it in existence. Conservation is a continuous creation *(conservatio est continua creatio).*

We can say that understood in the most generic sense, divine Providence is expressed especially in this "conservation," namely, in maintaining in existence all that has had being from nothing. In this sense Providence is a constant and unending confirmation of the work of creation in all its richness and variety. It implies the constant and uninterrupted presence of God as Creator in the whole of creation. It is a presence which continually creates and reaches the deepest roots of everything that exists. It operates there as the first cause of being and of action. This presence of God continually expresses the same eternal will to create and to conserve what has been created. It is a supremely and fully sovereign will. By means of it, according to the very nature of goodness which is proper to him in an absolute way *(bonum diffusivum sui),* God continues to declare himself, as in the first moment of creation, in favor of being as opposed to nothing, in favor of life as opposed to death, in favor of "light" as opposed to "darkness" (cf. Jn 1:4-5). In a word, it is a will in favor of the truth, goodness and beauty of all that exists. The mystery of Providence prolongs uninterruptedly and irreversibly the judgment contained in the Book of Genesis: "God saw that it was good...that it was very good" (Gen 1:25, 31). That constitutes the fundamental and unshakeable affirmation of the work of creation.

This essential affirmation is not affected by any evil deriving from the limitation inherent in everything of the cosmos, or which is produced, as has happened in the history of mankind, in sad contrast with that original "God saw that it was good...that it was very good" (Gen 1:25, 31). Divine Providence implies the recognition that in God's eternal plan, in his creative design, evil originally had no place. But once committed by man and permitted by God, evil is, in the last analysis, subordinated to the good: "Everything works for good" as the Apostle says (cf. Rom 8:28). But this is a problem to which we shall have to return.

The truth of divine Providence is present in the whole of revelation. We can even say that it pervades the whole of revelation, as does the truth of creation. With this it constitutes the first and fundamental point of reference in all that God "in many and various ways" wished to say "by the prophets and in these last days...through his Son" (Heb 1:1). It is necessary to reread this truth both in the texts where revelation speaks of it directly, and also where Sacred Scripture bears witness to it indirectly.

It is found right from the beginning, as a fundamental truth of faith, in the ordinary Magisterium of the Church, even though it was only the First Vatican Council that pronounced on it in the context of the solemn Dogmatic Constitution *Dei Filius*, in regard to the truth about creation. Vatican I stated: "All that God created, he conserves and directs by his Providence 'reaching from end to end mightily and governing all things well' (cf. Wis 8:1). 'All lies bare and exposed to his eyes' (cf. Heb 4:13), even what will take place through the free initiative of creatures" *(DS* 3003).

The Council's concise text was dictated by the particular needs of the times (the 19th century). The Council wished first of all to confirm the constant teaching of the Church on Providence, and then the immutable doctrinal tradition linked to the entire biblical message, as is proved by the Old and New Testament passages contained in the text. By confirming this constant teaching of the Christian faith, the Council intended to oppose the errors of materialism and deism of that time. Materialism denies the existence of God, while deism maintains that God is not at all concerned with the world he has created, though admitting the existence of God and the creation of the world. It is precisely the doctrine of deism that directly attacks the truth about divine Providence.

The separation of the work of creation from divine Providence, typical of deism, and still more the total negation of God proper to materialism, open the way to materialistic determinism, to which mankind and human history are completely subordinated. Theoretical materialism is transformed into historical materialism. In this context, the truth about the existence of God, and in particular about divine Providence, constitutes the fundamental and definitive guarantee of man and of his liberty in the cosmos. Already in the Old Testament, Sacred Scripture indicates this when it sees God as a strong and indestructible support: "I love you, O Lord, my strength, O Lord, my rock, my fortress, my deliverer. O God, my rock of refuge, my shield, the horn of my salvation, my stronghold!"

(Ps 18:3). God is the unshakeable foundation on which man rests with his whole being: "You it is who hold fast my lot" (Ps 16:5).

On the part of God, divine Providence is a sovereign affirmation of the whole of creation and, in particular, of man's pre-eminence among creatures. Providence constitutes the fundamental guarantee of the sovereignty of man himself in regard to the world. This does not imply the cancellation of the immanent determination of the laws of nature. But it excludes that materialistic determinism which reduces the whole of human existence to the "domain of necessity," practically annihilating the "domain of freedom" which the Creator on the contrary destined for man. God by his Providence never ceases to be the ultimate support of the "domain of freedom."

Faith in divine Providence obviously remains strictly connected with the basic concept of human existence, with the meaning of human life. Man can face up to his own existence in an essentially different way, when he has the certainty that he is not at the mercy of a blind destiny (fate), but depends on someone who is his Creator and Father. Therefore faith in divine Providence is inscribed in the first words of the Apostles' Creed: "I believe in God, the Father Almighty." This faith frees human existence from the different forms of fatalistic thought.

In the wake of the constant tradition of the Church's teaching and in particular of the teaching of the First Vatican Council, the Second Vatican Council also spoke many times about divine Providence. From the texts of its Constitutions it follows that God is he who "has fatherly care of all" *(GS* 24), and in particular "of the human race" *(DV* 3). An expression of this care is also found in the "divine law itself—eternal, objective and universal, whereby God orders, directs and governs the entire universe and all the ways of the human community" *(DH* 3). "For man would not exist were he not created by

God's love and constantly preserved by it; and he cannot live fully according to truth unless he freely acknowledges that love and devotes himself to his Creator" *(GS* 19).

General audience of May 7, 1986

Divine Providence Carries out
an Eternal Plan of Wisdom and Love

To the recurring query, and one at times indicative of doubt—whether and how God is present in the world today—the Christian faith replies with luminous and firm certainty: "all that God has created, he watches over and governs by his Providence." In these concise words the First Vatican Council formulated the revealed doctrine on divine Providence. In the Old and New Testaments, we find ample expression of this revelation. According to it, two elements are present in the concept of divine Providence: the element of caring for and at the same time that of authority. These two elements permeate each other. God as Creator has supreme authority *(dominium altum)* over all creation, as is said by analogy with the sovereign power of earthly princes. All that is created, by the very fact of having been created, belongs to God its Creator, and consequently, depends on him. In a certain sense every being pertains more "to God" than "to itself." It is first "of God" and then "of itself." This is so in a radical and total manner which infinitely surpasses all the analogies of relationship between authority and subjects on earth.

The Creator's authority is expressed as the Father's care. This other analogy contains in a certain sense the heart of the truth about divine Providence. To express the same truth, Sacred Scripture uses the comparison: "The Lord is my shepherd, there is nothing I shall want" (Ps 23:1). What a stupendous image! The ancient creeds and the Christian tradition of the early centuries expressed the truth about Providence with the term: *"Omnipotens,"* corresponding to the Greek *"Pantokrator."* But this concept does not do justice to the depth and beauty of the biblical "shepherd," as revealed truth communicates it to us in such a vivid sense. Divine Providence is an "authority full of solicitude" which carries out an eternal plan of wisdom and love in governing the created world and in particular "the ways of human society" (cf. Second Vatican Council, *DH* 3). It is a "caring authority," full of power and of goodness at the same time. According to the text of the Book of Wisdom cited by the First Vatican Council, it "reaches from end to end mightily *(fortiter)* and governs all things well *(suaviter)"* (Wis 8:1)—that is, it embraces, sustains, cares for and in a certain sense nourishes the whole of creation, according to another biblical comparison.

The Book of Job expresses it thus:

"Behold God is sublime in his power, what teacher is there like him?... He holds in check the waterdrops that filter in rain through his mists, till the skies run with them and the showers rain down on mankind. For by these he nourishes the nations, and gives them food in abundance" (Job 36:22, 27-28, 31).

"With hail, also, the clouds are laden, as they scatter their flashes of light. He it is who changes their rounds, according to his plans, in their task upon the surface of the earth" (Job 37:11-12).

Likewise the Book of Sirach:

"By his command he sends the driving snow and speeds the lightnings of his judgment" (Sir 43:13).

The Psalmist exalted "the power of your wonderful

deeds," "the abundant goodness," the "splendor of the glorious majesty" of God, who "is good to all and has compassion over all he has made," and proclaimed:

"The eyes of all look hopefully to you and you give them their food in due season. You open your hand and satisfy the desire of every living thing" (Ps 145:5, 6, 7, 9, 15-16).

And again:

"You raise grass for the cattle, and the vegetation for men's use, producing bread from the earth, and wine to gladden men's hearts, so that their faces gleam with oil, and bread fortifies the hearts of men" (Ps 104:14-15).

In many passages Sacred Scripture praises divine Providence as the supreme authority over the world. Full of care for all creatures, and especially for human beings, it avails itself of the efficient power of created causes. This manifests the creative wisdom which is supremely far-seeing, by analogy with an essential quality of human prudence. God infinitely transcends all that is created. At the same time, he ensures that the world presents that marvelous order which can be observed both in the macrocosm and in the microcosm. It is precisely Providence as the transcendent Wisdom of the Creator that ensures that the world is not "chaos," but "cosmos."

"You have disposed all things by measure and number and weight" (Wis 11:20).

The Bible's mode of expression refers the government of things directly to God. Nevertheless, the difference between the action of God the Creator as First Cause, and the action of creatures as secondary causes is sufficiently clear. Here we come up against a question which very much occupies the mind of modern man. It concerns the autonomy of the creature, and therefore the role of efficient cause in the world which man thinks to carry out.

According to the Catholic faith, it pertains to the Creator's transcendent wisdom to ensure that God is present in the world as Providence, and at the same time that the created world possesses that "autonomy" of which the Second Vatican Council speaks. On the one hand, God, by maintaining all things in existence, makes them what they are: "For by the very circumstance of their having been created, all things are endowed with their own stability, truth, goodness, proper laws and order" *(GS* 36).

On the other hand, because of the manner in which God rules the world, the latter is in a situation of real autonomy, which "harmonizes with the will of the Creator" *(GS* 36).

Divine Providence is expressed precisely in such "autonomy of created things," which manifests both the power and the "gentleness" proper to God. That autonomy confirms that as a transcendent and mysterious wisdom, the Creator's Providence comprises everything ("it reaches from end to end"). It is realized in everything with its creative power and its regulating strength *(fortiter).* But it leaves intact the role of creatures as secondary causes, immanent, in the dynamism of the formation and development of the world, as in that *suaviter* the Book of Wisdom indicates.

In what regards the immanent formation of the world, man possesses a very special place. He has this from the very beginning and constitutively, inasmuch as he is created in the image and likeness of God. According to the Book of Genesis, he is created to "have dominion," to "subdue the earth" (cf. Gen 1:28). By participating, as a rational and free subject, but always as a creature, in the Creator's dominion over the world, man becomes in a certain sense "providence" for himself, according to the beautiful expression of St. Thomas (cf. *Summa Theol.,* I, 22, 2 ad 4). For the same reason, however, there falls on him from the beginning a particular responsibility both before God and creatures, and especially before other people.

The New Testament confirms and enriches these notions about divine Providence which are offered to us by the biblical tradition of the Old Testament. Of all Jesus' words on this theme, those recorded by the evangelists Matthew and Luke are particularly touching: "Therefore do not be anxious saying, 'What shall we eat?' or 'What shall we drink?' or 'What shall we wear?' For the Gentiles seek all these things; and your heavenly Father knows that you need them all. But seek first his kingdom and his righteousness, and all these things shall be yours as well" (Mt 6:31-33; cf. also Lk 12:29-31).

"Are not two sparrows sold for a penny? Not one of them will fall to the ground without your Father's will. But even the hairs of your head are all numbered. Fear not, therefore; you are of more value than many sparrows" (Mt 10:29-31; cf. also Lk 21:18).

"Look at the birds of the air; they neither sow nor reap nor gather into barns, and yet your heavenly Father feeds them. Are you not of more value than they?... And why are you anxious about clothing? Consider the lilies of the field, how they grow; they neither toil nor spin; yet I tell you, not even Solomon in all his glory was arrayed like one of these. But if God so clothes the grass of the field, which today is alive and tomorrow is thrown into the oven, will he not much more clothe you, O you of little faith?" (Mt 6:26-30; cf. Lk 12:24-28).

With these words the Lord Jesus not only confirmed the teaching on divine Providence contained in the Old Testament. He entered more deeply into the subject as regards humanity, every single person, treated by God with the exquisite delicacy of a father.

Without doubt the verses of the Psalms which exalted the Most High as the refuge, protection and strength of man were magnificent. For example, Psalm 91 states: "He who dwells in the shelter of the Most High, who abides in the shadow of the Almighty, will say to the Lord, 'My refuge and my fortress; my God in whom I trust'...because you have made the Lord your refuge, the Most High your habitation...because he cleaves to me in love, I will deliver him; I will protect him, because he knows my name. When he calls me, I will answer him; I will be with him in trouble" (Ps 91:1-2, 9, 14-15).

These are beautiful expressions; but Christ's words reach still greater fullness of meaning. They are said by the Son who, "scrutinizing" all that has been said on the subject of Providence, bears perfect witness to the mystery of his Father, a mystery of Providence and of paternal care which embraces every creature, even the most insignificant, like the grass of the field or the sparrows. How much more, therefore, human beings! Christ especially wishes to emphasize this. If divine Providence is so generous in regard to creatures inferior to man, how much more will it have care for him! In this page of the Gospel on Providence we find the truth about the hierarchy of values which is present from the beginning of the Book of Genesis, in the description of creation—man has primacy over things. He has that primacy in his nature and in his spirit, he has it in the attention and care of Providence, he has it in the heart of God!

Moreover, Jesus insistently proclaimed that man, so privileged by his Creator, is duty-bound to cooperate with the gift received from Providence. He cannot be satisfied with the mere values of sense, of matter and of utility. He must seek above all "the kingdom of God and his righteousness" because "all these things (namely, earthly goods) shall be yours as well" (cf. Mt 6:33).

Christ's words direct our attention to this particular dimension of Providence, at the center of which is man, a rational and free being. We shall return to this subject in the following reflections.

General audience of May 14, 1986

Divine Providence and Human Freedom

In our journey into the depths of the mystery of God as Providence, we frequently face the question: if God is present and operating in everything, how can man be free? Above all, what meaning and task does his freedom have? How are we to understand in the light of divine Providence that evil fruit of sin which derives from an abuse of freedom?

Let us take up again the solemn statement of Vatican I: "All that God created, he conserves and directs by his Providence 'reaching from end to end mightily and governing all things well' (cf. Wis 8:1). 'All lies bare and exposed to his eyes' (cf. Heb 4:13), even what will take place through the free initiative of creatures" *(DS* 3003).

The mystery of divine Providence is deeply inscribed in the whole work of creation. As the expression of God's eternal wisdom, the plan of Providence precedes the work of creation. As the expression of his eternal power, it presides over it and puts it into effect. In a certain sense it can be said that Providence is realized in it. It is a transcendent Providence, but at the same time immanent in things, in all things. According to the text of the Council that we have read, this is valid especially in the order of creatures endowed with intelligence and free will.

While comprising "mightily and disposing well" the whole of creation, Providence embraces in a particular way those creatures made in the image and likeness of God. They enjoy, through the freedom granted to them by the Creator, "the autonomy of created beings," in the sense understood by the Second Vatican Council (cf. *GS* 36). Created beings of a purely spiritual nature should be included within the sphere of these creatures. We shall speak about them later. They constitute the invisible world. In the visible world, man is the object of particular attention on the part of divine Providence. According to the teaching of Vatican II, man "is the only creature on earth which God has willed for itself" *(GS* 24), and it is precisely for this reason that "man...cannot fully find himself except through a sincere gift of himself" (cf. *GS* 24).

God's loving wisdom

The fact that the visible world is crowned by the creation of man, opens up before us completely new perspectives on the mystery of divine Providence. That is indicated by the dogmatic statement of the First Vatican Council when it emphasizes that to the eyes of divine wisdom and knowledge all lies "bare" ("open"), and in a certain sense naked—even what the rational creature does by virtue of his freedom. This involves that which results from a conscious choice, and a free decision of the human person. Even in regard to this sphere, divine Providence preserves its superior creative and regulating causality. It is the transcendent superiority of the Wisdom which loves, and through love it acts mightily and gently. It is a Providence which solicitously and paternally guides, sustains and leads to its end his own creature, so richly endowed, while respecting its freedom.

In this meeting point of God's creative eternal plan with human freedom, a mystery as inscrutable as it is adorable indubitably looms up. The mystery consists in the intimate relation, first of all ontological and then psychological, between the divine action and human self-determination. We know that this freedom of decision pertains to the natural dynamism of the rational creature. We also know by experience the fact of human freedom, authentic even though wounded and weak. As regards its relation to divine causality, it is opportune to recall St. Thomas Aquinas' emphasis on the concept of Providence as the expression of divine Wisdom which orders all things to their proper end: *ratio ordinis rerum in finem,* "the rational ordering of things to their end" (cf. *Summa Theol.,* I, 22, 1). All that God creates receives this finality, and therefore becomes the object of divine Providence (cf. *Summa Theol.,* I, 22, 2). In man—created in the image of God—the whole visible creation should draw near to God, finding again the way of its definitive fulfillment. This thought already was expressed, among others, by St. Irenaeus *(Adv. Haer.,* 4, 38; 1105-1109). It is echoed by the teaching of Vatican Council II on the development of the world by the work of humanity (cf. *GS* 7). Man is called upon to carry out a true development in the world. This progress should have a character which is not merely "technological," but especially "ethical," in order to bring the kingdom of God to fulfillment in the created world (cf. *GS* 35, 43, 57, 62).

Created in the image and likeness of God, man is the sole visible creature that the Creator has "willed for itself" *(GS* 24). In the world subject to God's transcendent wisdom and power, man is also a being which is an end in itself, though having his finality in God. As a person he possesses his own finality (auto-teleology), by virtue of which he tends to self-realization. Man is enriched with a gift which is also a duty. He is wrapped up in the mystery of divine Providence. We read in the Book of Sirach:

"The Lord created man out of earth....

he granted them authority over
the things upon the earth....
He forms men's tongues and eyes and ears,
and imparts to them an understanding heart.
With wisdom and knowledge he fills them;
good and evil he shows them.
He looks with favor upon their hearts,
and shows them his glorious works....
He has set before them knowledge,
a law of life as their inheritance..." (Sir 17:1-2, 5-7, 9).

Endowed with such "existential" equipment, man sets out on his journey in the world. He begins to write his own history. Divine Providence accompanies him throughout his journey. Again we read in the Book of Sirach:

"Their ways are ever known to him,
they cannot be hidden from his eyes....
All their actions are clear as the sun to him,
his eyes are ever upon their ways" (Sir 17:13, 15).

The Psalmist gives to this same truth a touching expression:

"If I take the wings of the dawn,
if I settle at the farthest limits of the sea,
even there your hand shall guide me,
and your right hand hold me fast" (Ps 139:9-10).

"You know me full well;
nor was my frame unknown to you..." (Ps 139:14-15).

Divine Providence, then, makes itself present in human history, in the history of thought and freedom, in the history of hearts and consciences. In man and with man the action of Providence acquires a "historical" dimension. It does this in the sense that it follows the rhythm and adapts itself to the laws of development of human nature, while remaining unchanged and unchangeable in the sovereign transcendence of its subsisting being. Providence is an eternal presence in the history of humanity—of individuals and communities. The history of nations and of the whole human race unfolds beneath the "eye" of God and under his almighty action. All that is created is "cared for" and governed by Providence. Full of paternal solicitude, God's authority implies full respect for freedom in regard to rational and free beings. In the created world, this freedom is an expression of the image and likeness to the divine Being itself, to divine freedom itself.

Respect for created freedom is so essential that God in his Providence even permits human sin (and that of the angels). Pre-eminent among all but always limited and imperfect, the rational creature can make evil use of freedom, and can use it against God, the Creator. It is an agonizing subject for the human mind, and the Book of Sirach has reflected on it in words of great depth

> "When God, in the beginning, created man,
> he made him subject to his own free choice.
> If you choose you can keep the commandments;
> it is loyalty to do his will.
> There are set before you fire and water;
> to whichever you choose, stretch forth your hand.
> Before man are life and death,
> whichever he chooses shall be given him.
> Immense is the wisdom of the Lord;
> he is mighty in power, and all-seeing.
> The eyes of God see all he has made;
> he understands man's every deed.
> No man does he command to sin,
> to none does he give strength for lies" (Sir 15:14-20).

"Who can detect failings?" the Psalmist asked (cf. Ps 19:13). Yet divine Providence sheds its light even on this unheard of rejection by man (through sin) so that we may learn not to commit it.

Sin was not only possible in the world in which man was created as a rational and free being, but it has been shown as an actual fact "from the very beginning." Sin is radical opposition to God. It is decidedly and absolutely not willed by God. However, he has permitted it by creating free beings, by creating the human race. He has permitted sin which is the consequence of the abuse of created freedom. This fact is known from revelation and experienced in its consequences. From it, we can deduce that from the viewpoint of God's transcendent Wisdom, in the perspective of the finality of the entire creation, it was more important that there should be freedom in the created world, even with the risk of its abuse, rather than to deprive the world of freedom by the radical exclusion of the possibility of sin.

By God's Providence, however, if on the one hand he has permitted sin, on the other, with the loving solicitude of a father, he has foreseen from eternity the way of reparation, of redemption, of justification and of salvation through love. Freedom is ordained to love. Without freedom there cannot be love. In the conflict between good and evil, between sin and redemption, love has the last word.

General audience of May 21, 1986

The Mystery of
Predestination in Christ

The question about one's own destiny is a deep concern of the human heart. It is a great, difficult, but decisive question: "What will happen to me tomorrow?" There is the risk that mistaken replies may lead to forms of fatalism, desperation, or even a proud and false sense of security. "Fool! This night your soul is required of you," God warns (Lk 11:20). But the inexhaustible grace of divine Providence is manifested precisely here. Jesus provides an essential light. Speaking of divine Providence in the Sermon on the Mount, he ended with the following exhortation: "Seek first the kingdom of God and his righteousness, and all these things shall be yours as well" (Mt 6:33; cf. also Lk 12:31). In the previous catechesis we reflected on the profound relation between God's Providence and human freedom. Jesus addresses the words on the kingdom of God and on the necessity of seeking it above everything else precisely to man, first of all to man, created in the image of God.

This link between Providence and the mystery of the kingdom of God directs our thought to the truth of man's destiny—his predestination in Christ. The predestination of man and of the world in Christ, the eternal Son of the Father, confers on the whole doctrine of divine Providence a decisive soteriological and eschatological characteristic. The Divine Master himself indicated it in his conversation with Nicodemus: "For God so loved the world that he gave his only Son, that whoever believes in him should not perish but have eternal life" (Jn 3:16).

These words of Jesus constitute the nucleus of the doctrine on predestination, which we find in the teaching of the apostles and especially in St. Paul's letters.

We read in the Letter to the Ephesians:

"God, the Father of our Lord Jesus Christ...chose us in him before the foundation of the world, that we should be holy and blameless before him in love, having destined us to be his children through Jesus Christ, according to the purpose of his will, to the praise of his glorious grace" (Eph 1:3-6).

These luminous statements explain authentically and authoritatively what predestination consists in. (Christian terminology calls this "predestination" from the Latin term *praedestinatio.*) It is important to clarify this term from those erroneous or even imprecise and non-essential meanings which have entered into common use—predestination as a synonym for "blind fate" or the capricious "anger" of an envious divinity. In divine revelation the word "predestination" means God's eternal choice, a paternal, intelligent and positive choice, a choice prompted by love.

Chosen in the Eternal Son

Together with the decision that puts it into effect, namely, the plan of creation and redemption, this choice pertains to the intimate life of the most Holy Trinity. It is made from eternity by the Father together with the Son in the Holy Spirit. It is a choice which, according to St. Paul, precedes the creation of the world, ("before the foundation of the world," Eph 1:4), and of humanity in the world. Even before being created, man is "chosen" by God. This choice takes place in the eternal Son ("in him," Eph 1:4), that is, in the Word of the eternal Mind. Man is chosen in the Son to participate in the same sonship by divine adoption. The essence of the mystery of predestination consists in this. It manifests the Father's eternal love ("in love, having destined us to be his sons through Jesus Christ," Eph 1:4-5). Predestination contains man's eternal vocation to participate in the very nature of God. It is a vocation to holiness, through the grace of adoption as sons ("to be holy and blameless before him" Eph 1:4).

In this sense predestination precedes "the foundation of the world," namely, creation, since creation is realized in the perspective of man's predestination. By applying the temporal analogies of human language to the divine life, we can say that God "first" willed to communicate himself in his divinity to the human race, called to be his image and likeness in the created world. "First," he chose man, in the eternal and consubstantial Son, to participate in his sonship through grace. Only "afterward" ("in its turn") God willed creation; he willed the world to which humanity belongs. In this way the mystery of predestination enters "organically" in a certain sense into the whole plan of divine Providence. The revelation of this plan opens up before us the perspective of the kingdom of God and leads us to the heart of this kingdom, where we discover the ultimate finality of creation.

We read in the Letter to the Colossians: "With joy give thanks to the Father, who has qualified us to share in the inheritance of the saints in light. He has delivered us from the dominion of darkness and transferred us to the kingdom of his beloved Son, in whom we have redemption, the forgiveness of sins" (Col 1:12-14). God's kingdom is the kingdom of the "beloved Son" in the eternal plan of the Triune God. This is so particularly because the "redemption" and "the remission of sins" is accomplished through the Son. The Apostle's words allude also to human "sin." Predestination, that is, adoption as sons of the eternal Son, operates therefore not only in relation to the creation of the world, but in relation to the redemption, carried out by the Son, Jesus Christ. Redemption becomes the expression of Providence, that is, of the solicitous governance which God the Father exercises particularly in regard to creatures endowed with freedom.

In the Letter to the Colossians we find that the truth of "predestination" in Christ is closely connected with the truth of "creation in Christ." St. Paul wrote: "He is the image of the invisible God, the first-born of all creation; for in him all things were created..." (Col 1:15-16). Thus, the world created in Christ the eternal Son, bears in itself from the beginning, as the first gift of Providence, the call, or the pledge of predestination in Christ. The finality of the world is joined to this, as the fulfillment of the definite eschatological salvation, and first of all of humanity. "For in him [Christ] all the fullness of God was pleased to dwell" (Col 1:19). The fulfillment of the finality of the world, and especially of man, takes place precisely by means of this fullness which is in Christ. Christ is the fullness. That finality of the world is fulfilled in him in a certain sense. According to it, divine Providence cares for and governs the things of the world, and in particular, man in the world, his life and his history.

Thus we understand another fundamental aspect of divine Providence—its salvific finality. God "desires all men to be saved and to come to the knowledge of the truth" (1 Tim 2:4). In this perspective it is only right to broaden a certain naturalistic concept of Providence, limited to the good government of physical nature or even of natural moral behavior. In actual fact, divine Providence is expressed in the attainment of the ends which correspond to the eternal plan of salvation. In this process, thanks to the "fullness" of Christ, in him and through him sin is overcome. Sin is essentially opposed to the salvific finality of the world, to the definitive fulfillment which the world and humanity find in God. Speaking of the fullness which has taken up its abode in Christ, the Apostle proclaimed: "For in him all the fullness of God was pleased to dwell, and through him to reconcile to himself all things, whether on earth or in heaven, making peace by the blood of his cross" (Col 1:19-20).

Against the background of these reflections drawn from St. Paul's letters, Christ's exhortation becomes more intelligible, that is, in regard to the Providence of the heavenly Father which embraces everything (cf. Mt 6:33-34 and also Lk 12:22-31). He says: "Seek first the kingdom of God and his righteousness, and all these things shall be yours as well" (Mt 6:33; cf. Lk 12:31). With that "first" Jesus wishes to indicate what God himself wills "first"—that which is his first intention in the creation of the world, and at the same time the final end of the world itself. This is "the kingdom of God and his righteousness" (the righteousness of God). The whole world was created in view of this kingdom, so that it would become a reality in man and in history. By means of this "kingdom" and of this "righteousness," that eternal predestination which the world and man have in Christ may be fulfilled.

St. Peter's words correspond to this Pauline vision of predestination:

"Blessed be the God and Father of our Lord Jesus Christ! By his great mercy we have been born anew to a living hope through the resurrection of Jesus Christ from the dead, and to an inheritance which is imperishable, undefiled, and unfading, kept in heaven for you, who by God's power are guarded through faith for a salvation, ready to be revealed in the last time" (1 Pet 1:3-5).

Truly "blessed be God," who reveals to us how his Providence is his untiring, solicitous intervention for our salvation. It is indefatigably at work until we shall reach "the last time." Then, "the predestination in Christ" of the beginning will be definitively accomplished "through the resurrection in Jesus Christ," who is "the Alpha and the Omega" of our human history (Rv 1:8).

General audience of May 28, 1986

The Presence of Evil and Suffering in the World

Let us take up again the text of the First Letter of Peter to which we referred at the end of the previous catechesis:

"Praised be the God and Father of our Lord Jesus Christ,
he who in his great mercy gave us new birth;
a birth unto hope which draws its life from the
resurrection of Jesus Christ from the dead;
a birth to an imperishable inheritance,
incapable of fading or defilement,
which is kept in heaven for you" (1 Pet 1:3-4).

The same Apostle has another enlightening and consoling statement:

"In this you rejoice, though now for a little while you may have to suffer various trials, so that the genuineness of your faith, more precious than gold which though perishable is tested by fire..." (1 Pet 1:6-7).

From this text one can argue that the revealed truth about the "predestination" in Christ of the created world and especially of the human race *(praedestinatio in Christo),* constitutes the principal and indispensable foundation of the reflections we intend to propose on the theme of the relation between divine Providence and the reality of evil and suffering present under so many forms in human life.

For many this is the principal difficulty in accepting the truth about divine Providence. In some cases this difficulty assumes a radical form when one even accuses God because of the evil and suffering in the world. It can even reach the point of rejecting the truth about God and his existence (that is, atheism). This difficulty is expressed in a less radical, but nonetheless disturbing form, in the numerous critical questions that people ask about God. The doubt, the query or even the contestation arise from the difficulty of reconciling the truth about divine Providence, of God's pastoral solicitude for the created world, with the reality of evil and suffering experienced by people in different ways.

We can say that the vision of the reality of evil and suffering is present in all its fullness in the pages of Sacred Scripture. The Bible is, above all, a great book about suffering. This enters fully within the scope of the things which God wished to say to humanity, "in varied ways...through the prophets, but in these last days...through his Son" (cf. Heb 1:1). It enters in the context of God's self-revelation and in the context of the Gospel, or the Good News of salvation. For this reason the only adequate method to find a response to the question about evil and suffering in the world is to seek it in the context of the revelation offered by the word of God.

Evil is multiform

But first of all we must be quite clear about evil and suffering. In itself it is multiform. Generally one distinguishes evil in the physical sense from that in the moral sense. Moral evil is distinguished from physical evil, first of all by the fact that it implies guilt. It depends on free will, and it is always an evil of a spiritual nature. It is distinguished from physical evil, because the latter does not necessarily and directly include man's will, even though this does not mean that it cannot be caused by man or result from his fault. Physical evil caused by him appears in many forms. At times it results from ignorance or lack of prudence, and at other times from neglecting opportune precautions or even by inappropriate and harmful actions. But it must be added that many cases of physical evil in the world happen independently of human causes. Suffice it to mention, for example, natural disasters or calamities, and also all the forms of physical disability or of bodily or psychological diseases for which people are not blameworthy.

Suffering is engendered in human beings by the experience of these multiple forms of evil. In some ways it can also be found in animals inasmuch as they are endowed with senses and a relative sensitivity. But in man, suffering reaches the dimension proper to the spiritual faculties he possesses. It can be said that human suffering is interiorized, intimately known, and experienced in the whole dimension of one's being and capacities of action and reaction, of receptivity and rejection. It is a terrible experience, before which, especially when without guilt, man brings forward those difficult, tormenting, and at times dramatic questions. Sometimes they constitute a complaint, sometimes a challenge, and sometimes a cry of rejection of God and his Providence. They are questions and problems which can be summed up thus: how can evil and suffering be reconciled with that paternal solicitude, full of love, which Jesus Christ attributes to God in the Gospel? How are they to be reconciled with the transcendent wisdom and omnipotence of the Creator? And in a still more dialectical form—in the presence of all the experience of evil in the world, especially when confronted with the suffering of the innocent, can we say that God does not will evil? And if he wills it, how can we believe that "God is love?"—all the more so since this love is omnipotent?

Faced with these questions we too, like Job, feel how difficult it is to give an answer. Let us not seek it in ourselves, but with humility and confidence in the Word of God. Already in the Old Testament we find the striking and significant statement: "against wisdom evil does not prevail. She reaches mightily from one end of the earth to the other, and she orders all things well" (Wis 7:30; 8:1). The Old Testament already bears witness to the primacy of wisdom and of the goodness of God, and to his divine Providence in the presence of the multiform experience of evil and suffering in the world. The Book of Job outlines and develops this attitude. This book is completely dedicated to the theme of evil and suffering seen as a sometimes tremendous trial for the just, but overcome by the certainty, laboriously acquired, that God is good.

From this text we become aware of the limit and transience of created things. Certain forms of physical "evil" (due to the lack or limitation of the good) belong to the very structure of created beings, which by their nature are contingent and passing, and therefore corruptible. Besides, we know that material beings are in a close relation of interdependence as expressed by the old saying: "the death of one is the life of another" *(corruptio unius est generatio alterius)*. So then, in a certain sense death serves life. This law refers also to man inasmuch as he is at the same time an animal and spiritual being, mortal and immortal. In this regard, however, St. Paul's words open up much wider horizons: "Though our outer nature is wasting away, our inner nature is being renewed every day" (2 Cor 4:17). And again: "For this slight momentary affliction is preparing us for an eternal weight of glory beyond all comparison" (2 Cor 4:17).

Sacred Scripture assures us that: "against wisdom evil does not prevail" (Wis 7:30). This strengthens our conviction that in the Creator's providential plan in regard to the world, in the last analysis evil is subordinated to good. Moreover, in the context of the integral truth about divine Providence, one is helped to better understand the two statements: "God does not will evil as such" and "God permits evil." In regard to the first it is opportune to recall the words of the Book of Wisdom: "God did not make death, and he does not delight in the death of the living. For he created all things that they may exist" (Wis 1:13-14). As regards the permission of evil in the physical order, e.g., the fact that material beings (among them also the human body) are corruptible and undergo death, it must be said that this belongs to the very structure of the being of these creatures. In the present state of the material world, it would be difficult to think of the unlimited existence of every individual corporeal being. We can therefore understand that, if "God did not make death," as the Book of Wisdom states, he nonetheless permitted it in view of the overall good of the material cosmos.

In the case of moral evil, however, that is, of sin and guilt in their different forms and consequences also in the physical order, this evil decisively and absolutely is not willed by God. Moral evil is radically contrary to God's will. If in human history this evil is present and at times overwhelming, if in a certain sense it has its own history, it is only permitted by divine Providence because God wills that there should be freedom in the created world. The existence of created freedom (and therefore the existence of man, and the existence of pure spirits such as the angels, of whom we shall speak later), is indispensable for that fullness of creation which corresponds to God's eternal plan (as we already said in a previous catechesis). By reason of that fullness of good which God wills to be realized in creation, the existence of free beings is for him a more important and fundamental value than the fact that those beings may abuse their freedom against the Creator, and that freedom can therefore lead to moral evil.

Undoubtedly it is a great light we receive from reason and revelation in regard to the mystery of divine Providence which, while not willing the evil, tolerates it in view of a greater good. However, the definitive light can come to us only from the victorious cross of Christ. We shall devote our attention to that in the following catechesis.

General audience of June 4, 1986

In Jesus the Redeemer,
Divine Providence Overcomes Evil

In the previous catechesis we dealt with the question posed by people in every age concerning divine Providence, in the face of evil and suffering. God's word luminously and conclusively states: "against the wisdom (of God), evil does not prevail" (Wis 7:30). It indicates that God permits evil in the world for higher ends, but does not will it. Today we desire to listen to Jesus Christ who offers the full and complete answer to this tormenting question, in the context of the paschal mystery.

Let us reflect first of all on the fact that St. Paul announced Christ crucified as "the power of God and the wisdom of God" (1 Cor 1:24), in whom salvation is granted to believers. Certainly, his power is marvelous if it is manifested in the weakness and humiliation of the passion and death of the Cross. It is a sublime wisdom, unknown outside divine revelation. In God's eternal plan, and in his providential action in human history, every evil, and in particular moral evil—sin— is subjected to the good of the redemption and salvation precisely through the cross and resurrection of Christ. It can be said that in him God draws forth good from evil. He does it in a certain sense from the very evil of sin, which was the cause of the suffering of the Immaculate Lamb and of his terrible death on the cross as a victim for the sins of the world. The Church's liturgy does not hesitate even to speak, in this regard, of the "happy fault" *(felix culpa;* cf. *Exsultet* of the Easter Vigil Liturgy).

Thus a definitive answer cannot be given to the question about the reconciliation of evil and suffering with the truth of divine Providence, without reference to Christ. On the one hand, Christ, the Incarnate Word, confirmed through his own life—in poverty, humiliation and toil—and especially through his passion and death, that God is with every person in his suffering. Indeed God takes upon himself the multiform suffering of man's earthly existence. At the same time Jesus Christ reveals that this suffering possesses a redemptive and salvific value and power. That "imperishable inheritance" of which St. Peter spoke in his first letter is prepared through this suffering: "an imperishable inheritance kept in heaven for you" (1 Pet 1:4). The truth of Providence acquires, through the "power and wisdom" of the cross of Christ, its definitive eschatological sense. The definitive answer to the question about the presence of evil and suffering in our earthly existence is offered by divine revelation in the perspective of "predestination in Christ," in the perspective of man's vocation to eternal life, to participation in the life of God himself. Christ has provided this answer, confirming it by his cross and resurrection.

In this way everything, even the evil and suffering present in the created world, and especially in human history, are subjected to that inscrutable wisdom, concerning which St. Paul exclaimed in rapture: "O the depths of the riches and wisdom and knowledge of God! How unsearchable are his judgments and inscrutable his ways..." (Rom 11:33). In the whole context of salvation, it is that "wisdom against which evil does not prevail" (Wis 7:30). It is a wisdom full of love, since "God so loved the world that he gave his only Son..." (Jn 3:16).

Tested like gold

The apostolic writings occupy themselves precisely with this wisdom, rich in compassionate love for the suffering, in order to help the afflicted to recognize God's grace. Thus St. Peter wrote to the Christians of the first generation: "In this you rejoice, though now for a little while you may have to suffer various trials" (1 Pet 1:6). He added: "So that the genuineness of your faith, more precious than gold which though perishable is tested by fire, may redound to praise and glory and honor at the revelation of Jesus Christ" (1 Pet 1:7). These last words refer to the Old Testament, particularly to the Book of Sirach in which we read: "For gold is tested in the fire, and acceptable men in the furnace of humiliation" (Sir 2:5). Taking up again the same idea of testing, Peter continued in his letter: "But rejoice in so far as you share in Christ's sufferings, that you may also rejoice and be glad when his glory is revealed" (1 Pet 4:13).

The apostle St. James expressed himself in a similar way when he exhorted Christians to face up to trials with joy and patience: "Count it all joy, my brethren when you meet various trials, for you know that the testing of your faith produces steadfastness. And let steadfastness have its full effect in you" (Jas 1:2-4). Finally, in the Letter to the Romans, St. Paul compared human and cosmic sufferings to a kind of "groaning in travail" of the whole creation, emphasizing the "inward groaning" of those "who have the first fruits of the Spirit" and wait for the fullness of adoption, that is, "the redemption of our bodies" (cf. Rom 8:22-23). But he added: "We know that in everything God works for good with those who love him..." (Rom 8:28) and: "Who shall separate us from the love of Christ? Shall tribulation, or distress, or persecution, or famine, or nakedness, or peril, or the sword? (Rom 8:35). Finally, he concluded: "For I am sure that neither death, nor life...nor anything else in creation, will be able to separate us from the love of God in Christ Jesus our Lord" (Rom 8:38-39).

Alongside the fatherhood of God, the divine pedagogy also appears, manifested by divine Providence: "It is the discipline *(paideia,* that is, education) that you have to endure. God is treating you as sons; for what son is there whom his father does not discipline?... God disciplines us for our good, that we may share his holiness" (Heb 12:7, 10).

Suffering, therefore, viewed with the eyes of faith, even if it can still appear as the most obscure aspect of man's destiny on earth, permits us to see the mystery of divine Providence contained in Christ's revelation, and in particular, in his cross and resurrection. Doubtlessly it can still happen that while asking himself the age-old questions on evil and suffering in a world created by God, man may not find an immediate answer, especially if he doesn't have a living faith in the paschal mystery of Jesus Christ. Gradually, however, with the help of faith nourished by prayer, he discovers the true meaning of suffering which everyone experiences in his own life. It is a discovery which depends on the word of divine revelation and on the "word of the Cross" (cf. 1 Cor 1:18) of Christ, which is "the power of God and the wisdom of God" (1 Cor 1:24). As the Second Vatican Council stated: "Through Christ and in Christ, the riddles of sorrow and death grow meaningful. Apart from his Gospel, they overwhelm us" *(GS* 22). If through faith we discover this power and this "wisdom," we are on the salvific path of divine Providence. The meaning of the Psalmist's words are confirmed:

"The Lord is my shepherd...
Even though I walk in the dark valley
I fear no evil: for you are at my side" (Ps 23:1, 4).

In this way divine Providence is revealed as God walking alongside man.

In conclusion, the truth about Providence, which is intimately connected with the mystery of creation, must be understood in the context of the whole of revelation, of the whole creed. Thus one sees that the revelation of the "predestination" *(praedestinatio)* of man and of the world in Christ, the revelation of the whole economy of salvation and its realization in history, enter organically into the truth of Providence. The truth of divine Providence is also closely linked to the truth of the kingdom (cf. Mt 6:33; cf. Lk 12:31). The truth about divine Providence, about God's transcendent government of the created world, becomes intelligible in the light of the truth about the kingdom of God, about that kingdom which God has eternally intended to realize in the created world on the basis of the "predestination in Christ" who is "the first-born of all creation" (Col 1:15).

General audience of June 11, 1986

Divine Providence in the Light of Vatican II

The truth about divine Providence appears as a point of convergence of the many truths contained in the statement: "I believe in God, the Father Almighty, Creator of heaven and earth." Because of its richness and ever present topicality it deserved treatment from the entire Magisterium of the Second Vatican Council, which discussed it in an excellent manner. In many documents of the Council we find appropriate references to this truth of faith, and it is present in a particular way in the Constitution *Gaudium et Spes*. By setting that out in relief we summarize the previous catecheses on divine Providence.

As is known, the Constitution *Gaudium et Spes* treats of the Church in the modern world. From the first paragraphs, however, one sees clearly that it is impossible to treat this subject on the basis of the Church's Magisterium without going back to the revealed truth on the relationship of God with the world, and in the last analysis to the truth of divine Providence.

We read: "The council focuses its attention on the world of men, the whole human family...that world which is the theater of man's history, and the heir of his energies, his tragedies and his triumphs; that world which the Christian sees as created and sustained by its maker's love, fallen indeed into the bondage of sin, yet emancipated now by Christ, who was crucified and rose again to break the stranglehold of personified evil, so that the world might be fashioned anew according to God's design and reach its fulfillment" *(GS 2)*.

This "description" involves the whole doctrine of Providence, understood both as God's eternal plan in creation, and as the carrying out of this plan in history. It is also understood as the salvific and eschatological finalization of the universe and especially of the human world according to its "predestination in Christ," the center and pivot of all things. This repeats in other terms the dogmatic statement of the First Vatican Council: "All that God created, he conserves and directs by his Providence 'reaching from end to end mightily and governing all things well' (cf. Wis 8:1). 'All lies bare and exposed to his eyes' (cf. Heb 4:13), even what will take place through the free initiative of creatures" *(DS* 3003). More specifically, right from the very beginning, *Gaudium et Spes* focuses on a question as pertinent to our subject as it is of interest to modern man—how to reconcile the "growth" of God's kingdom with the development (evolution) of the world. We shall now follow the main lines of this exposition, precisely indicating its principal assertions.

Protagonists of development

In the visible world men and women are the protagonists of historical and cultural development. They are in a certain sense "providence" for themselves, since they are created in the image and likeness of God, conserved in being by him and guided with fatherly love in the task of "exercising dominion" over other creatures. "Throughout the course of the centuries, men have labored to better the circumstances of their lives through a monumental amount of individual and collective effort. To believers, this point is settled: considered in itself, this human activity accords with God's will. For man, created in God's image, received a mandate to subject to himself the earth and all it contains, and to govern the world with justice and holiness; a mandate to relate himself and the totality of things to him who was to be acknowledged as the Lord and Creator of all. Thus, by the subjection of all things to man, the name of God would be wonderful in all the earth" *(GS* 34).

Previously, the same conciliar document had stated: "Man is not wrong when he regards himself as superior to bodily concerns, and as more than a speck of nature or a nameless constituent of the city of man. For by his interior qualities he outstrips the whole sum of mere things. He plunges into the depths of reality whenever he enters into his own heart; God, who probes the heart, awaits him there; there he discerns his proper destiny beneath the eyes of God" *(GS* 14).

The development of the world toward economic and cultural orders ever more suited to the integral requirements of man is a task which enters into man's vocation to exercise dominion over the earth. Therefore the real successes of modern scientific and technological civilization, no less than those of humanistic culture and of the "wisdom" of the centuries, enter into the scope of the "providence" shared with man for the implementation of God's plan in the world. The Council sees and recognizes the value and function of the culture and work of our time in this light. The Constitution *Gaudium et Spes* describes the new cultural and social condition of humanity, with its distinctive notes and its possibilities for such rapid advancement as to occasion amazement and hope (cf. *GS*, 53-54). The Council does not hesitate to witness to man's wonderful achievements, setting them in the framework of the divine plan and command, and linking them with the Gospel of brotherhood preached by Jesus Christ: "When man develops the earth by the work of his hands or with the aid of technology, in order that it might bear fruit and become a dwelling worthy of the whole human family and when he consciously takes part in the life of social groups, he carries out the design of God manifested at the beginning of time, that he should subdue the earth, perfect creation and develop himself. At the same time he obeys the commandment of Christ that he place himself at the service of his brethren" *(GS* 57; cf. also *GS* 63).

However, the Council did not close its eyes to the immense problems concerning man's development today, whether in his dimension as a person, or in that of community. It would be illusory to believe that these problems can be ignored, just as it would be an error to formulate them in an inadequate or insufficient manner, under the pretext of omitting the necessary reference to God's providence and will. The Council said: "Though mankind is stricken with wonder at its own discoveries and its power, it often raises anxious questions about the current trend of the world, about the place and role of man in the universe, about the meaning of its individual and collective strivings, and about the ultimate destiny of reality and of humanity" *(GS* 3). And it explained: "This transformation has brought serious difficulties in its wake. Thus while man extends his power in every direction, he does not always succeed in subjecting it to his own welfare. Striving to probe more profoundly into the deeper recesses of his own mind, he frequently appears more unsure of himself. Gradually and more precisely he lays bare the laws of society, only to be paralyzed by uncertainty about the direction to give it" *(GS* 4).

The Council spoke expressly of the "contradictions and imbalances" begotten by a "rapid and disorderly" evolution in socio-economic conditions, in the way of life, the culture, and in the outlook and conscience of man, in the family, in social relations, in relations between groups, communities and nations, with the consequent "mutual distrust, enmities, conflicts and hardships. Of such man is at once the cause and the victim" (cf. *GS* 8-10). Finally the Council arrived at the root of the problem when it stated "that the imbalances under which the modern world labors are linked with that more basic imbalance which is rooted in the heart of man" *(GS* 10).

Value and function of culture

In the presence of this situation in the world today, there is no justification for that mentality according to which the "dominion" which man claims is absolute and radical and can be realized without any reference to divine Providence. It is a vain and dangerous illusion to build one's own life and to make the world the realm of one's happiness, by relying exclusively on one's own powers. It is the great temptation into which the modern world has fallen, unmindful of the fact that the laws of nature also govern the industrial and post-industrial civilization (cf. *GS* 26-27). But it is easy to be dazzled by a supposed self-sufficiency of the progressive "dominion" of the forces of nature, to the point of forgetting God or of setting oneself in his place. Today in some circles this claim leads to forms of biological, genetic, and psychological manipulation. If this is not governed by criteria of the moral law (and consequently by the finalization of the kingdom of God) it can result in the domination of man over man with tragically disastrous consequences. Recognizing contemporary man's greatness, but also his limitation, in the legitimate autonomy of created things (cf. *GS* 36), the Council reminded him of the truth of divine Providence which comes to his assistance and help. In this relationship with God the Father, Creator and Providence, man can ever discover anew the basis of his salvation.

General audience of June 18, 1986

Divine Providence and
the Growth of the Kingdom of God

Today also, as in the previous catechesis, we draw on the abundant reflections of Vatican II on the historical condition of modern man. On the one hand, he is sent by God to have dominion over creation and subdue it, and on the other, he himself, as a creature, is subject to the loving presence of God the provident Father and Creator.

Today more than at any other time, man is particularly sensitive to the greatness and autonomy of his task as investigator and ruler of the forces of nature. One must however note that there is a serious obstacle in the development and progress of the world. It is constituted by sin and by the closure which it implies, that is, by moral evil. The conciliar Constitution *Gaudium of Spes* provides ample witness to this.

The Council stated: "Although he was made by God in a state of holiness, from the very onset of his history man abused his liberty, at the urging of the evil one. Man set himself against God and sought to attain his goal apart from God" *(GS* 13). Hence, as an inevitable consequence, "while human progress is a great advantage to man, it brings with it a strong temptation. For when the order of values is jumbled and bad is mixed with the good, individuals and groups pay heed solely to their own interests, and not to those of others. Thus it happens that the world ceases to be a place of true brotherhood. In our own day, the magnified power of humanity threatens to destroy the race itself" *(GS* 37).

Ethical significance of evolution

Modern man is rightly aware of his own role, but, "if the expression, the independence of temporal affairs, is taken to mean that created things do not depend on God, and that man can use them without any reference to their Creator, anyone who acknowledges God will see how false such a meaning is. For without the Creator the creature would disappear. For their part, however, all believers of whatever religion always hear his revealing voice in the discourse of creatures. When God is forgotten, however, the creature itself grows unintelligible" *(GS* 36).

We especially recall a text which enables us to grasp the "other dimension" of the world's historical evolution at which the Council was always looking. The Constitution states: "God's Spirit, who with a marvelous providence directs the unfolding of time and renews the face of the earth, is not absent from this development" *(GS* 26). To overcome evil is at the same time to will man's moral progress, whereby human dignity is safeguarded, and to give a response to the essential requirements for a "more human" world. In this perspective God's kingdom which is developing in history finds in a certain way its "matter" and the signs of its effective presence.

The Second Vatican Council has emphasized with great clarity the ethical significance of evolution, showing how the ethical ideal of a "more human" world is in line with the Gospel teaching. While making a precise distinction between the development of the world and the history of salvation, it sought at the same time to point out in all their fullness the bonds that exist between them: "While earthly progress must be carefully distinguished from the growth of Christ's kingdom, to the extent that the former can contribute to the better ordering of human society, it is of vital concern to the kingdom of God. For after we have obeyed the Lord, and in his Spirit nurtured on earth the values of human dignity, brotherhood and freedom, and indeed all the good fruits of our nature and enterprise, we will find them again, but freed of stain, burnished and transfigured, when Christ hands over to the Father: 'a kingdom eternal and universal, a kingdom of truth and life, of holiness and grace, of justice, love and peace.' On this earth that kingdom is already present in mystery. When the Lord returns it will be brought into full flower" *(GS* 39).

Encouragement of unity

The Council expressed the conviction of believers when it proclaimed: "The Church recognizes that worthy elements are found in today's social movements, especially an evolution toward unity, a process of wholesome socialization and of association in civic and economic realms. The promotion of unity belongs to the innermost nature of the Church, for she is, 'thanks to her relationship with Christ, a sacramental sign and an instrument of intimate union with God, and of the unity of the whole human race.' Thus she shows the world that an authentic union, social and external, results from a union of minds and hearts, namely from that faith and charity by which her own unity is unbreakably rooted in the Holy Spirit. For the force which the Church can inject into the modern society of man consists in that faith and charity put into vital practice, not in any external dominion exercised by merely human means" *(GS* 42).

For this reason a profound bond and even an elementary identity is created between the principal sectors of the "world's" history and evolution and the history of salvation. The plan of salvation sinks its roots in the most real aspirations and in the finalities of humanity. Redemption also is continually directed toward humanity "in the world." The Church always comes in contact with the "world" in the sphere of these aspirations and finalities of humanity. In like manner the history of salvation runs its course in the riverbed of the world's history, considering it in a certain way as its own. And vice versa—the real conquests of humanity, the authentic victories of the world's history, are also the "substratum" of the kingdom of God on earth (cf. Card. Karol Wojtyla, *At the Sources of Renewal*, Study on the implementation of the Second Vatican Council, Collins, London, 1981, pp. 166-178).

In this regard we read in the Constitution *Gaudium et Spes:* "Human activity, to be sure, takes its significance from its relationship to man. Just as it proceeds from man, so it is ordered toward man.... Rightly understood this kind of growth is of greater value than any external riches which can be garnered. A man is more precious for what he is than for what he has. Similarly, all that men do to obtain greater justice, wider brotherhood, a more humane disposition of social relationships has greater worth than technical advances.... Hence, the norm of human activity is this: that in accord with the divine plan and will, it harmonize with the genuine good of the human race, and that it allow men as individuals and as members of society to pursue their total vocation and fulfill it" (cf. *GS* 35; cf. also *GS* 59).

The same document also states: "This social order requires constant improvement. It must be founded on truth, built on justice and animated by love; in freedom it should grow every day toward a more humane balance. An improvement in attitudes and abundant changes in society will have to take place if these objectives are to be gained. God's Spirit, who with a marvelous providence directs the unfolding of time and renews the face of the earth, is not absent from this development" *(GS* 26).

The adaptation to the guidance and action of the Spirit of God in the unfolding of history is brought about through the continual appeal and the consistent and faithful response to the voice of conscience: "In fidelity to conscience, Christians are joined with the rest of men in the search for truth, and for the genuine solution to the numerous problems which arise in the life of individuals from social relationships. Hence the more right conscience holds sway, the more persons and groups turn aside from blind choice and strive to be guided by the objective norms of morality" *(GS* 16).

The Council realistically recalled the presence, in the actual human situation, of the most radical obstacle to the true progress of man and humanity—moral evil, sin, as a result of which "man is split within himself. As a result, all of human life, whether individual or collective, shows itself to be a dramatic struggle between good and evil, between light and darkness. Indeed, man finds that by himself he is incapable of battling the assaults of evil successfully, so that everyone feels as though he is bound by chains" *(GS* 13).

The whole of human history has been the story of "a monumental struggle against the powers of darkness [which] pervade the whole history of man. The battle was joined from the very origins of the world and will continue until the last day, as the Lord has attested (cf. Mt 24:13; 13:24-30; 36-43). Caught in this conflict, man is obliged to wrestle constantly if he is to cling to what is good, nor can he achieve his own integrity without great efforts and the help of God's grace" *(GS* 37).

In conclusion we can say that, if the growth of God's kingdom is not identified with the evolution of the world, it is nonetheless true that the kingdom of God is in the world, and first of all in man, who lives and works in the world. The

Christian knows that with his commitment for the progress of history and with the help of God's grace he cooperates in the growth of the kingdom, toward the historical and eschatological fulfillment of the plan of divine Providence.

General audience of June 25, 1986

THE ANGELS

Creator of All Things, Seen and Unseen

We cannot conclude our catechesis on God, Creator of the world, without devoting adequate attention to a precise item of divine revelation—the creation of purely spiritual beings which Sacred Scripture calls "angels." This creation appears clearly in the creeds, especially in the Nicene-Constantinopolitan Creed: "I believe in one God, the Father Almighty, Creator of heaven and earth, of all things (that is *entia* or beings) seen and unseen." We know that man enjoys a unique position within the sphere of creation. By his body he belongs to the visible world, while by his spiritual soul which vivifies the body, he is as it were on the boundary between the visible and invisible creation. According to the creed which the Church professes in the light of revelation, other beings which are purely spiritual belong to the invisible creation. Therefore they are not proper to the visible world, even though present and working therein. They constitute a world apart.

Today, as in times past, these spiritual beings are discussed with greater or lesser wisdom. One must recognize that at times there is great confusion. The risk arises of passing off as the Church's faith on the angels what does not pertain to it, or, vice versa, of neglecting some important aspect of the revealed truth. The existence of spiritual beings, which Sacred Scripture usually calls "angels," was denied already in Christ's time by the Sadducees (cf. Acts 23:8). It is denied also by materialists and rationalists of every age. But, as a modern theologian acutely observed, "if one wishes to get rid of the angels, one must radically revise Sacred Scripture itself, and with it the whole history of salvation" (A. Winklhofer, *Die Welt der Engel*, Ettal 1961, p. 144, note 2; in *Mysterium Salutis*, II, 2, p. 726). The whole of Tradition is unanimous on this point. The Church's creed basically echoes what Paul wrote to the Colossians: "for in him (Christ) all things were created, in heaven and on earth, visible and invisible, whether thrones or dominations or principalities or authorities—all things were created through him and for him" (Col 1:16). As the Son-Word, eternal and consubstantial with the Father, Christ is the first-born of all creation (Col 1:15). He is at the center of the universe, as the reason and cornerstone of all creation, as we have already seen in previous catecheses, and as we shall see later when we shall speak more directly of him.

The reference to the "primacy" of Christ helps us to understand that the truth about the existence and activity of the angels (good and bad) is not the central content of the word of God. In revelation God speaks first of all "to men...and lives among them, so that he may invite and take them into fellowship with himself," as we read in the Constitution *Dei Verbum* of the Second Vatican Council *(DV* 2). Thus "the deepest truth...both about God and the salvation of man" is the central content of the revelation which "shines out" more fully in the person of Christ (cf. *DV* 2). The truth about the angels is in a certain sense "collateral," though inseparable from the central revelation, which is the existence, the majesty and the glory of the Creator which shines forth in all creation ("seen" and "unseen") and in God's salvific action in the history of the world. The angels are not creatures of the first order, in the reality of revelation. However, they fully belong to it, so much so that sometimes we see them carrying out fundamental tasks in the name of God himself.

All this that pertains to creation enters, according to revelation, into the mystery of divine Providence. Vatican I, which we have quoted several times, stated it in an exemplary concise manner: "All that God created, he conserves and directs by his Providence 'reaching from end to end mightily and governing all things well' (cf. Wis 8:1). 'All lies bare and exposed to his eyes' (cf. Heb 4:13), even what will take place through the free initiative of creatures" *(DS* 3003). Providence then also embraces the world of pure spirits, which are intellectual and free beings still more fully than men. In Sacred Scripture we find important references to them. There is also the revelation of a mysterious, though real, drama concerning these angelic creatures, without anything escaping divine wisdom, which strongly *(fortiter)* and at the same time gently *(suaviter)* brings all to fulfillment in the kingdom of the Father, Son and Holy Spirit. We recognize above all that Providence, as the loving Wisdom of God, was manifested precisely in the creation of purely spiritual beings, so as to express better the likeness of God in them. They are superior to all that is created in the visible world, including man, who is also the indelible image of God. God who is absolutely perfect Spirit, is reflected especially in spiritual beings which by nature, that is, by reason of their spirituality, are nearer to him than material creatures, and which constitute as it were the closest "circle" to the Creator. Sacred Scripture offers abundant explicit evidence of this maximum closeness to God of the angels, who are spoken of figuratively as the "throne" of God, as his "legions," his "heaven." It has inspired the poetry and art of the Christian centuries which present the angels to us as the "court of God."

General audience of July 9, 1986

Creator of the Angels
Who Are Free Beings

Today we continue our catechesis on the angels whose existence, willed by an act of God's eternal love, we profess in the words of the Nicene-Constantinopolitan Creed: "I believe in one God, the Father Almighty, Creator of heaven and earth, of all that is, seen and unseen."

The angels are called from the beginning, by virtue of their intelligence, and in the perfection of their spiritual nature, to know the truth and to love the good which they know in the truth in a more full and perfect way than is possible to human beings. This love is an act of a free will, and therefore for the angels also freedom implies a possibility of choice for or against the Good which they know, that is, God himself. It must be repeated here what we already mentioned earlier in regard to man—by creating free beings, God willed that there should be realized in the world true love which is possible only on the basis of freedom. He willed therefore that the creature, constituted in the image and likeness of the Creator, should be able in the greatest degree possible to render himself similar to God who "is love" (1 Jn 4:16). By creating the pure spirits as free beings, God in his Providence could not but also foresee the possibility of the angels' sin. But precisely because Providence is eternal wisdom which loves, God would have been able to draw from the history of this sin, incomparably more radical inasmuch as it was the sin of a pure spirit, the definitive good of the whole created cosmos.

Revelation clearly states that the world of the pure spirits is divided into good angels and bad ones. This division is not the work of God's creation, but is based on the freedom proper to the spiritual nature of each one of them. It is the result of choice which for purely spiritual beings possesses an incomparably more radical character than human choice, and it is irreversible given the degree of intuitiveness and penetration of the good wherewith their intelligence is endowed. In this regard it must also be said that the pure spirits were subjected to a test of a moral character. It was a decisive test regarding first of all God himself, a God known in a more essential and direct way than is possible to man, a God who granted to these spiritual beings the gift of participating in his divine nature, before doing so to the human race.

A radical and irreversible choice

In the case of the pure spirits, the decisive choice regarded first of all God himself, the first and supreme Good, accepted or rejected in a more essential and direct way, than could happen within the scope of action of human free will. The pure spirits have a knowledge of God incomparably more perfect than human knowledge. By the power of their intellect, not conditioned nor limited by the mediation of sense knowledge, they see to the depths the greatness of infinite Being, of the first Truth, of the supreme Good. To this sublime capacity of knowledge of the pure spirits God offered the mystery of his divinity, making them thus partakers, through grace, of his infinite glory. Precisely as beings of a spiritual nature they had in their intellect the capacity, the desire of this supernatural elevation to which God had called them. It made them, long before man, "partakers of the divine nature" (2 Pet 1:4), partakers of the intimate life of him who is Father, Son and Holy Spirit, of him who in the communion of the three divine Persons, "is love" (1 Jn 4:16). God had admitted all the pure spirits, before and to a greater extent than man, to the eternal communion of love.

The choice made on the basis of the truth about God, known in a higher way because of the clarity of their intellects, has divided the world of pure spirits into the good and the bad. The good chose God as the supreme and definitive Good, known to the intellect enlightened by revelation. To have chosen God means that they turned to him with all the interior force of their freedom, a force which is love. God became the total and definitive scope of their spiritual existence. The others instead turned their backs on God, contrary to the truth of the knowledge which indicated him as the total and definitive good. Their choice ran counter to the revelation of the mystery of God, to his grace which made them partakers of the Trinity and of the eternal friendship with God in communion with him through love. On the basis of their created freedom they made a radical and irreversible choice on a parity with that of the good angels, but diametrically opposed. Instead of accepting a God full of love, they rejected him. They were inspired by a false sense of self-sufficiency, of aversion and even of hatred which is changed into rebellion.

How are we to understand such opposition and rebellion against God in beings endowed with such profound and enlightened intelligence? What can be the motive for such a radical and irreversible choice against God? Of a hatred so profound as to appear solely the fruit of folly? The Fathers of the Church and theologians do not hesitate to speak of a "blindness" produced by the overrating of the perfection of their own being, driven to the point of ignoring God's supremacy, which requires instead an act of docile and obedient subjection. All this is summed up concisely in the words: "I will not serve" (Jer 2:20), which manifest the radical and irreversible refusal to take part in the building up of the kingdom of God in the created world. Satan, the rebellious spirit, wishes to have his own kingdom, not that of God. He rises up as the first "adversary" of the Creator, the opponent of Providence, and antagonist of God's loving wisdom. From Satan's rebellion and sin, and likewise from that of man, we must conclude by accepting the wise experience of Scripture which states: "In pride there is ruin" (Tob 4:13).

General audience of July 23, 1986

Creator of Things Unseen—
the Angels

In the previous catechesis we dwelt on the article of the creed in which we proclaim and confess God as Creator not only of the whole visible world, but also of the "things unseen." We treated of the question of the existence of the angels who were called upon to make a decision for God or against God by a radical and irreversible act of acceptance or rejection of his salvific will.

According to Sacred Scripture the angels are purely spiritual creatures. They are presented for our reflection as a special realization of the "image of God," the most perfect Spirit, as Jesus himself reminded the Samaritan woman in the words: "God is spirit" (Jn 4:24). From this point of view the angels are the creatures closest to the divine exemplar. The name given to them by Sacred Scripture indicates that what counts most in revelation is the truth concerning the tasks of the angels in regard to humanity—angel *(angelus)* means "messenger." Used in the Old Testament, the Hebrew *malak* signifies more precisely "delegate" or "ambassador." The angels, spiritual creatures, have a function of mediation and of ministry in the relationships between God and man. Under this aspect the Letter to the Hebrews says that Christ has been given a "name," and therefore a ministry of mediation, far superior to that of the angels (cf. Heb 1:4).

Care and solicitude

The Old Testament especially emphasizes the special participation of the angels in the celebration of the glory which the creator receives as a tribute of praise on the part of the created world. The Psalms are the interpreters of this voice in a special way, when, for example, they proclaim: "Praise the Lord from the heavens praise him in the heights! Praise him all his angels..." (Ps 148:1-2). Similarly in Psalm 103: "Bless the Lord, O you his angels, you mighty ones who do his word, hearkening to the voice of his word!" (Ps 103:20). This last verse of Psalm 103 indicates that the angels take part, in a way proper to themselves, in God's government of creation. They are "the mighty ones who do his word" according to the plan established by divine Providence. A special care and solicitude for people is entrusted to the angels in particular, whose requests and prayers they present to God, as mentioned, for example, in the Book of Tobit (cf. especially Tob 3:17 and 12:12). Psalm 91 proclaims: "For to his angels he has given command about you...upon their hands they shall bear you up, lest you dash your foot against a stone" (Ps 91:11-12). Following the Book of Daniel it can be said that the tasks of angels as ambassadors of the living God extend not only to individual human beings and to those who have special duties, but also to entire nations (Dan 10:13-21).

The New Testament highlights the role of the angels in Christ's messianic mission, and first of all in the mystery of the incarnation of the Son of God. We observe this in the account of the announcement of the birth of John the Baptist (cf. Lk 1:11), of Christ himself (cf. Lk 1:26), in the explanations and orders given to Mary and Joseph (cf. Lk 1:30-37; Mt 1:20-21), in the indications given to the shepherds on the night of the Lord's birth (Lk 2:9-15), and in the protection of the newborn child from the danger of persecution by Herod (cf. Mt 2:13).

The Gospels also speak of the presence of the angels during Jesus' forty days of fast in the desert (cf. Mt 4:11) and during his prayer in Gethsemane (cf. Lk 22:43). After Christ's resurrection an angel appeared under the form of a young man, who said to the women who had hastened to the tomb and were surprised to find it empty: "Do not be amazed; you seek Jesus of Nazareth, who was crucified. He has risen, he is not here...go, tell his disciples..." (Mt 16:5-7). Two angels were seen also by Mary Magdalene, who was privileged with a personal apparition of Jesus (Jn 20:12-17; cf. also Lk 24:4). The angels appeared to the apostles after Christ's ascension, and said to them: "Men of Galilee, why do you stand here looking up into heaven? This Jesus, who was taken up from you into heaven, will come in the same way as you saw him go into heaven" (Acts 1:10-11). They are the angels of him who as St. Peter writes, "has gone into heaven and is at the right hand of God, with angels, authorities, and powers subject to him" (1 Pet 3:22).

If we pass to the second coming of Christ, in the Parousia, we find that all the Synoptic Gospels note that "the Son of man...will come in the glory of the Father with the holy angels" (thus Mk 8:38; as also Mt. 16:27; and Mt 25:31 in the description of the last judgment; and Lk 9:26; cf. also St. Paul in 2 Thess 1:7). The angels, as pure spirits, not only participate in the holiness of God himself, in the manner proper to them, but in the key moments they surround Christ and accompany him in the fulfillment of his salvific mission in regard to the human race. In the same way the whole of Tradition and the ordinary Magisterium of the Church down the centuries have attributed to the angels this particular character and this function of messianic ministry.

General audience of July 30, 1986

Angels Participate
in the History of Salvation

In recent catecheses we have seen how the Church has professed throughout the centuries the truth about the existence of the angels as purely spiritual beings. Illuminated by the light that comes from Sacred Scripture, the Church has professed this with the Nicene-Constantinopolitan Creed, and has confirmed it in the Fourth Lateran Council (1215), whose formulation was repeated by the First Vatican Council in the context of the doctrine on creation: "God at the beginning of time created from nothing both creatures together, the spiritual and the corporeal, that is, the angelic and the earthly, and thus he created human nature as having both, since it is made up of spirit and of body" (Const. *Dei Filius, DS* 3002). In other words, God created both realities from the very beginning— the spiritual reality and the corporeal, the earthly world and the angelic world. He created all this at one and the same time with a view to the creation of man, constituted of spirit and matter and set, according to the biblical narrative, in the framework of a world already established according to his laws and already measured by time.

The faith of the Church recognizes not only the existence of the angels, but certain distinctive characteristics of their nature. Their purely spiritual being implies first of all their non-materiality and their immortality. The angels have no "body" (even if, in particular circumstances, they reveal themselves under visible forms because of their mission for the good of people). Therefore they are not subject to the laws of corruptibility which are common to the material world. Referring to the condition of the angels, Jesus himself said that in the future life, those who are risen "cannot die any more, because they are equal to the angels" (Lk 20:36).

As creatures of a spiritual nature, the angels are endowed with intellect and free will, like human beings, but in a degree superior to them, even if this is always finite because of the limit which is inherent in every creature. The angels are therefore personal beings and, as such, are also "in the image and likeness" of God. Sacred Scripture also refers to the angels by using terms that are not only personal (like the proper names of Raphael, Gabriel, Michael) but also "collective" (like the titles seraphim, cherubim, thrones, powers, dominions, principalities), just as it distinguishes between angels and archangels. While bearing in mind the analogous and representative character of the language of the sacred text, we can deduce that these beings and persons are as it were grouped together in society. They are divided into orders and grades, corresponding to the measure of their perfection and to the tasks entrusted to them. The ancient authors and the liturgy itself speak also of the angelic choirs (nine, according to Dionysius the Areopagite). Especially in the patristic and medieval periods, theology has not rejected these representations. It has sought to explain them in doctrinal and mystical terms, but without attributing an absolute value to them. St. Thomas preferred to deepen his researches into the ontological condition, the epistemological activity and will and also the loftiness of these purely spiritual creatures. He did this both because of their dignity in the scale of beings and also because he could investigate more deeply in them the capacities and the activities that are proper to the spirit in the pure state. From this he deduced much light to illuminate the basic problems that have always agitated and stimulated human thought—knowledge, love, liberty, docility to God, and how to reach his kingdom.

The theme which we have touched on may seem "far away" or "less vital" to the modern mentality. But the Church believes that she renders a great service when she proposes sincerely the totality of the truth about God the Creator and also about the angels. Man nurtures the conviction that it is he (and not the angels) who is at the center of the divine revelation in Christ, man and God. It is precisely the religious encounter with the world of the purely spiritual beings that becomes valuable as a revelation of his own being not only as body but also as spirit, and of his belonging to a design of salvation that is truly great and efficacious within a community of personal beings who serve the providential design of God for man and with man.

Let us note that Sacred Scripture and Tradition give the proper name of angels to those pure spirits who chose God, his glory and his kingdom in the fundamental test of their liberty. They are united to God by the consummate love which flows from the beatific vision, face to face, of the most Holy Trinity. Jesus himself told us this: "The angels in heaven always see the face of my Father who is in heaven" (Mt 18:10). "To see the face of the Father always" in this way is the highest manifestation of the adoration of God. One can say that this constitutes the "heavenly liturgy," carried out in the name of the entire universe. The earthly liturgy of the Church is incessantly joined with it, especially in its culminating moments. Let it suffice here to record the act with which the Church, every day and every hour, in the whole world, before beginning the Eucharistic Prayer in the center of the Mass, appeals "to the angels and the archangels" to sing the glory of the thrice-holy God. She unites herself thus to those first adorers of God, in the worship and the loving knowledge of the unspeakable mystery of his holiness.

According to revelation, the angels who participate in the life of the Trinity in the light of glory are also called to play their part in the history of human salvation, in the moments established by divine Providence. "Are they not all ministering spirits sent forth to serve, for the sake of those who are to possess salvation?" asked the author of the Letter to the Hebrews (1:14). The Church believes and teaches this on the basis of Sacred Scripture. From it, we learn that the task of the good angels is to protect people and be solicitous for their salvation.

We find these expressions in various passages of Sacred Scripture, such as Psalm 91 which has already been quoted several times: "He will give his angels charge of you, to keep you in all your ways. On their hands they will bear you up, lest you dash your foot against a stone" (Ps 91:11-12). Speaking of children and warning against giving them scandal, Jesus himself referred to "their angels" (Mt 18:10). Besides this, he attributed to the angels the function of witnesses in the last divine judgment about the fate of those who have acknowledged or denied Christ: "Whoever acknowledges me before men, the Son of Man likewise will acknowledge him before the angels of God; but whoever denies me before men will be denied before the angels of God" (Lk 12:8-9; cf. Rev 3:5). These words are significant because, if the angels take part in the judgment of God, then they are interested in human life. This interest and participation seem to be accentuated in the eschatological discourse, in which Jesus has the angels appear in the Parousia, that is, in the definitive coming of Christ at the end of history (cf. Mt 24:31; 25:31-41).

Among the books of the New Testament, the Acts of the Apostles especially shows us some facts that bear witness to the solicitude of the angels for human beings and for their salvation. Thus the angel of God liberated the apostles from prison (cf. Acts 5:18-20) and first of all Peter, when he was threatened with death at the hands of Herod (cf. Acts 12:5-10). He guided the activity of Peter with regard to the centurion Cornelius, the first pagan to be converted (Acts 10:3-8; 11:1-12), and analogously the activity of the deacon Philip along the road from Jerusalem to Gaza (Acts 8:26-29).

From these few facts which we have cited as examples, we understand how the Church could come to the conviction that God has entrusted to the angels a ministry in favor of human beings. Therefore the Church confesses her faith in the guardian angels, venerating them in the liturgy with an appropriate feast and recommending recourse to their protection by frequent prayer, as in the invocation "Angel of God." This prayer seems to draw on the treasure of the beautiful words of St. Basil: "Every one of the faithful has beside him an angel as tutor and pastor, to lead him to life" (cf. St. Basil, *Adv. Eunomium,* III, 1; cf. also St. Thomas, *Summa Theol.,* q. 11, a. 3).

Finally, it is appropriate to note that the Church honors the figures of three angels with a liturgical cult—those which Sacred Scripture calls by name. The first is Michael the Archangel (cf. Dan 10:13-20; Rv 12:7; Jude 9). His name is a synthesis that expresses the essential attitude of the good spirits. *Mica-El* means "Who is like God?" This name expresses the salvific choice thanks to which the angels "see the face of the Father" who is in heaven. The second is Gabriel, a figure bound especially to the mystery of the incarnation of the Son of God (cf. Lk 1:19-26). His name means "my power is God" or "power of God," as if to say that at the culmination of creation, the incarnation is the supreme sign of the omnipotent Father. Finally, the third archangel is called Raphael. *Rafa-El* means "God heals." He is made known to us by the story of Tobias in the Old Testament (cf. Tob 12:15-20 ff.), which is so significant for what it says about entrusting to the angels the little children of God, who are always in need of custody, care and protection.

If we reflect well, we see that each one of these three figures, *Mica-El, Gabri-El* and *Rafa-El* reflects in a particular way the truth contained in the question posed by the author of the Letter to the Hebrews: "Are they not all ministering spirits sent forth to serve, for the sake of those who are to possess salvation?" (Heb 1:14).

General audience of August 6, 1986

The Fall of
the Rebellious Angels

Today we continue the theme of the previous catecheses, which were dedicated to the article of the faith that concerns the angels, God's creatures. We shall begin today to explore the mystery of the freedom which some of them have turned against God and his plan of salvation for humanity.

As the evangelist Luke testified, when the disciples returned to the Master full of joy at the fruits they had gathered in their first missionary attempt, Jesus uttered a sentence that is highly evocative: "I saw Satan fall from heaven like lightning" (Lk 10:18). With these words, the Lord affirmed that the proclamation of the kingdom of God is always a victory over the devil. But at the same time, he also revealed that the building up of the kingdom is continuously exposed to the attacks of the spirit of evil. When we consider this, as we propose to do with today's catechesis, it means that we prepare ourselves for the condition of struggle which characterizes the life of the Church in this final time of the history of salvation (as the Book of Revelation asserts—cf. 12:7). Besides this, it will permit us to clarify the true faith of the Church against those who pervert it by exaggerating the importance of the devil, or by denying or minimizing his malevolent power.

The preceding catecheses on the angels have prepared us to understand the truth which Sacred Scripture has revealed and which the Tradition of the Church has handed on about Satan, that is, the fallen angel, the wicked spirit, who is also called the devil or demon.

This "fall" has the character of the rejection of God with the consequent state of "damnation." It consists in the free choice of those created spirits who have radically and irrevocably rejected God and his kingdom, usurping his sovereign rights and attempting to subvert the economy of salvation and the order of the entire creation. We find a reflection of this attitude in the words addressed by the tempter to our first parents: "You will become like God" or "like gods" (cf. Gen 3:5). Thus the evil spirit tried to transplant into humanity the attitude of rivalry, insubordination and opposition to God, which has, as it were, become the motivation of Satan's existence.

In the Old Testament, the narrative of the fall of man as related in the Book of Genesis contains a reference to the attitude of antagonism which Satan wishes to communicate to man in order to lead him to sin (Gen 3:5). In the Book of Job too, we read that Satan seeks to generate rebellion in the person who is suffering (cf. Job 1:11; 2:5-7). In the Book of Wisdom (cf. Wis 2:24), Satan is presented as the artisan of death, which has entered human history along with sin.

In the Fourth Lateran Council (1215), the Church taught that the devil (or Satan) and the other demons "were created good by God but have become evil by their own will." We read in the Letter of Jude: "The angels who did not keep their own dignity, but left their own dwelling, are kept by the Lord in eternal chains in the darkness, for the judgment of the great day" (Jude 6). Similarly, in the Second Letter of Peter, we hear of "angels who have sinned" and whom God "did not spare, but...cast in the gloomy abysses of hell, reserving them for the judgment" (2 Pet 2:4). It is clear that if God "does not forgive" the sin of the angels, this is because they remain in their sin. They are eternally "in the chains" of the choice that they made at the beginning, rejecting God, against the truth of the supreme and definitive Good that is God himself. It is in this sense that St. John wrote that "the devil has been a sinner from the beginning..." (1 Jn 3:8). And he has been a murderer "from the beginning," and "has not persevered in the truth, because there is no truth in him" (Jn 8:44).

Satan—cosmic liar and murderer

These texts help us to understand the nature and the dimension of the sin of Satan. It consists in the denial of the truth about God, as he is known by the light of the intellect and revelation as infinite Good, subsistent Love and Holiness. The sin was all the greater, in that the spiritual perfection and the epistemological acuteness of the angelic intellect, with its freedom and closeness to God, were greater. When, by an act of his own free will, he rejected the truth that he knew about God, Satan became the cosmic "liar and the father of lies" (Jn 8:44). For this reason he lives in radical and irreversible denial of God, and seeks to impose on creation—on the other beings created in the image of God, and in particular on people—his own tragic "lie about the good" that is God. In the Book of Genesis, we find a precise description of this lie and falsification of the truth about God, which Satan (under the form of a serpent) tried to transmit to the first representatives of the human race—God is jealous of his own prerogatives and therefore wants to impose limitations on man (cf. Gen 3:5). Satan invites the man to free himself from the impositions of this yoke, by making himself, "like God."

In this condition of existential falsehood, Satan—according to St. John—also becomes a "murderer." That is, he is one who destroys the supernatural life which God had made to dwell from the beginning in him and in the creatures made "in the likeness of God"—the other pure spirits and men. Satan wishes to destroy life lived in accordance with the truth, life in the fullness of good, the supernatural life of grace and love. The author of the Book of Wisdom wrote: "Death has entered the world through the envy of the devil, and those who belong to him experience it" (Wis 2:24). Jesus Christ warned in the Gospel: "Fear rather him who has the power to destroy both soul and body in Gehenna" (Mt 10:28).

As the result of the sin of our first parents, this fallen angel has acquired dominion over man to a certain extent. This is the doctrine that has been constantly professed and proclaimed by the Church, and which the Council of Trent confirmed in its treatise on original sin (cf. *DS* 1511). It finds a dramatic expression in the liturgy of baptism, when the catechumen is asked to renounce the devil and all his empty promises.

In Sacred Scripture we find various indications of this influence on man and on the dispositions of his spirit (and of his body). In the Bible, Satan is called "the prince of this world" (cf. Jn 12:31; 14:30; 16:11), and even "the god of this world" (2 Cor 4:4). We find many other names that describe his nefarious relationship with the human race: "Beelzebul" or "Belial," "unclean spirit," "tempter," "evil one" and even "Antichrist" (1 Jn 4:3). He is compared to a "lion" (1 Pet 5:8), to a "dragon" (in Revelation) and to a "serpent" (Gen 3). Very frequently, he is designated by the name "devil," from the Greek *diaballein* (hence *diabolos*). This means to "cause destruction, to divide, to calumniate, to deceive." In truth, all this takes place from the beginning through the working of the evil spirit who is presented by Sacred Scripture as a person, while it is declared that he is not alone. "There are many of us," as the devils cried out to Jesus in the region of the

Gerasenes (Mk 5:9); and Jesus, speaking of the future judgment, spoke of "the devil and his angels" (cf. Mt 25:41).

According to Sacred Scripture, and especially the New Testament, the dominion and the influence of Satan and of the other evil spirits embraces the entire world. We may think of Christ's parable about the field (the world), about the good seed and the bad seed that the devil sows in the midst of the wheat, seeking to snatch away from hearts the good that has been "sown" in them (cf. Mt 13:38-39). We may think of the numerous exhortations to vigilance (cf. Mt 26:41; 1 Pet 5:8), to prayer and fasting (cf. Mt 17:21). We may think of the strong statement made by the Lord: "This kind of demon cannot be cast out by any other means than prayer" (Mk 9:29). The action of Satan consists primarily in tempting people to evil, by influencing their imaginations and higher faculties, to turn them away from the law of God. Satan even tempted Jesus (cf. Lk 4:3-13), in the extreme attempt to thwart what is demanded by the economy of salvation, as this has been pre-ordained by God.

It is possible that in certain cases the evil spirit goes so far as to exercise his influence not only on material things, but even on the human body, so that one can speak of "diabolical possession" (cf. Mk 5:2-9). It is not always easy to discern the preternatural factor operative in these cases, and the Church does not lightly support the tendency to attribute many things to the direct action of the devil. But in principle it cannot be denied that Satan can go to this extreme manifestation of his superiority in his will to harm and lead to evil.

To conclude, we must add that the impressive words of the apostle John, "The whole world lies under the power of the evil one" (1 Jn 5:19), allude also to the presence of Satan in the history of humanity. This presence becomes all the more acute when man and society depart from God. The influence of the evil spirit can conceal itself in a more profound and effective way. It is in his "interests" to make himself unknown. Satan has the skill in the world to induce people to deny his existence in the name of rationalism and of every other system of thought which seeks all possible means to avoid recognizing his activity. But this does not signify the elimination of man's free will and responsibility, and even less the frustration of the saving action of Christ. It is, rather, a case of a conflict between the dark powers of evil and the powers of redemption. The words that Jesus addressed to Peter at the beginning of the Passion are eloquent in this context: "Simon, behold, Satan has sought to sift you like wheat; but I have prayed for you, that your faith may not fail" (Lk 22:31).

This helps us to understand why Jesus, in the prayer that he taught us, the "Our Father," terminated it almost brusquely, unlike so many other prayers of his era, by reminding us of our condition as people exposed to the snares of evil and of the evil one. Appealing to the Father with the Spirit of Jesus and invoking his kingdom, the Christian cries with the power of faith: let us not succumb to temptation, free us from evil, from the evil one. O Lord, let us not fall into the infidelity to which we are seduced by the one who has been unfaithful from the beginning.

General audience of August 13, 1986

Christs Victory Conquers Evil

Our catecheses on God, the Creator of the things "that are unseen," have brought fresh light and strength to our faith concerning the truth about the evil one, or Satan. He is certainly not willed by God, who is supreme love and holiness, and whose wise and strong Providence knows how to guide our existence to victory over the prince of darkness. The Church's faith teaches us that the power of Satan is not infinite. He is only a creature—powerful, in that he is pure spirit, but nevertheless always a creature, with the limits proper to creatures, subordinated to the will and dominion of God. If Satan is at work in the world because of his hatred of God and of his kingdom, this is permitted by divine Providence. God directs the history of humanity and of the world with power and goodness *(fortiter et suaviter)*. It is certainly true that Satan's action causes much damage, to individuals and to society, both of a spiritual kind and also indirectly of a material kind. But he is not able ultimately to neutralize the definitive end toward which man and all creation tend—the Good. He cannot block the construction of the kingdom of God, in which at the end there will be full realization of the righteousness and

313

the love of the Father for the creatures who are eternally "predestined" in Jesus Christ, his Son and Word. Indeed, we can say with St. Paul that the work of the evil one cooperates for the good (cf. Rom 8:28) and that it helps to build up the glory of the "chosen" ones (cf. 2 Tim 2:10).

Total salvation

Thus, the whole history of humanity can be considered as serving total salvation which means the victory of Christ over the "prince of this world" (Jn 12:31; 14:30; 16:11). "You shall bow down only before the Lord your God, you shall adore him alone" (Lk 4:8), Christ says eternally to Satan. At a dramatic moment of Jesus' ministry, when he was openly accused of casting out demons because of his alliance with Beelzebul, the chief of the demons, Jesus replied with these words that are at once severe and comforting: "Every kingdom that is divided falls into ruin, and no city or family that is divided can stand upright. Now if Satan drives out Satan, then he is divided in himself. How then can his kingdom stand upright?... And if it is by the power of the Spirit of God that I cast out the demons, then it is certain that the kingdom of God has come among you" (Mt 12:25-26, 28). "When a strong man, well armed, guards his palace, all his goods are secure. But if one stronger than he comes and overpowers him, he takes away the armor in which he trusted, and divides his spoils" (Lk 11:21-22). The words which Christ speaks about the tempter find their historical fulfillment in the cross and resurrection of the Redeemer. As we read in the Letter to the Hebrews, Christ became a sharer in human nature even to the cross "in order to reduce to powerlessness, by means of death, the one who has power over death, that is, the devil...and thus to free those who...were held in slavery" (Heb 2:14-15). This is the great certainty of the Christian faith—"the prince of this world has been judged" (Jn

16:11); "the Son of God has appeared, in order to destroy the works of the devil" (1 Jn 3:8), as St. John bears witness. It is therefore the crucified and risen Christ who has revealed himself as that "stronger one" who has overpowered "the strong man," the devil, and has cast him down from his throne.

The Church shares in Christ's victory over the devil, for Christ has given to his disciples the power to cast out demons (cf. Mt 10:1 and parallels; Mk 16:17). The Church uses this victorious power through faith in Christ and prayer (cf. Mk 9:29; Mt 17:19 ff.), which in particular cases can take the form of exorcism.

It is to this historical phase of the victory of Christ that the announcement and the beginning of the final victory, the Parousia, belongs. This is the second and definitive coming of Christ at the close of history, and it is toward this that the life of the Christian is oriented. Even if it is true that earthly history continues to unfold under the influence of "that spirit who now is at work in the rebellious," as St. Paul says (Eph 2:2), believers know that they have been called to struggle for the definitive triumph of the good. "For our battle is not against creatures made of blood and flesh, but against the principalities and powers, against those who hold communion over this world of darkness, against the spirits of evil that dwell in the heavenly places" (Eph 6:12).

Definitive victory

As the end of the struggle gradually draws nearer, it becomes in a certain sense ever more violent, as Revelation, the last book of the New Testament, shows in a special emphasis (cf. Rv 12:7-9). But it is precisely this book that emphasizes the certainty that is given to us by all of divine revelation, that the struggle will finish with the definitive victory of the good. In this victory, which is contained in anticipation in the paschal mystery of Christ, there will be the definitive fulfillment of the first announcement in the Book of Genesis, which is significantly called the Proto-Evangelium, when God admonished the serpent: "I will put enmity between you and the woman" (Gen 3:15). In this definitive phase, God will complete the mystery of his fatherly Providence and "will set free from the power of darkness" those whom he has eternally "predestined in Christ" and will "bring them over into the kingdom of his beloved Son" (cf. Col 1:13-14). Then the Son will subject even the whole universe to the Father, so that "God may be all in all" (cf. 1 Cor 15:28).

Here we finish the catecheses on God as the Creator of "the things that are visible and invisible," which are united, in our structuring of the catecheses, with the truth about divine Providence. It is obvious to the eyes of the believer that the mystery of the beginning of the world and of history is joined indissolubly to the mystery of the end, in which the finality of all that has been created reaches its fulfillment. The creed unites so many truths in such an organic manner, that it is truly the harmonious cathedral of the faith.

In a progressive and organic way, we have been able to admire, struck dumb with wonder, the great mystery of the intelligence and love of God, in his action of creation, directed to the cosmos, to the human person, and to the world of pure spirits. We have considered the Trinitarian origin of this action and its wise orientation toward the life of man who is truly the "image of God." He is called in his turn to rediscover fully his own dignity in the contemplation of the glory of God. We have been enlightened about one of the greatest problems that perturb man and characterize his search for truth—the problem of suffering and of evil. At the root, there is no mistaken or wicked decision by God, but rather his choice—and in a certain manner the risk he has undertaken—of creating us free, in order to have us as friends. Evil too has been born of liberty.

But God does not give up, and he predestines us with his transcendent wisdom to be his children in Christ, directing all with strength and sweetness, so that the good may not be overcome by evil.

We must now let ourselves be guided by divine revelation in our exploration of the other mysteries of our salvation. We have now received a truth which must be profoundly important for every Christian—that there are pure spirits, creatures of God, initially all good and then, through a choice of sin, irreducibly separated into angels of light and angels of darkness. The existence of the wicked angels requires of us that we be watchful so as not to yield to their empty promises. Yet we are certain that the victorious power of Christ the Redeemer enfolds our lives, so that we ourselves may overcome these spirits. In this, we are powerfully helped by the good angels, messengers of God's love, to whom, taught by the tradition of the Church, we address our prayer: "Angel of God, who are my guardian, enlighten, guard, govern and guide me, who have been entrusted to you by the heavenly goodness. Amen."

General audience of August 20, 1986

Appendix

Note: This appendix contains some texts which the Pope frequently refers to in his catecheses.

The Nicene-Constantinopolitan Creed

We believe in one God, Father omnipotent, maker of heaven and earth, and of all things visible and invisible. And in one Lord Jesus Christ, the only begotten Son of God, born of the Father before all ages, light of light, true God of true God, begotten not made, consubstantial with the Father, by whom all things were made, who for us men and for our salvation came down and was made flesh by the Holy Spirit and of the Virgin Mary, and became man, and was crucified for us by Pontius Pilate, suffered, and was buried and arose again the third day, according to the Scripture, and ascended into heaven, and sits at the right hand of the Father, and is coming again with glory to judge the living and the dead; of whose kingdom there shall be no end. And in the Holy Spirit, the Lord, the giver of life, who proceeds from the Father, who together with the Father and Son is worshipped and glorified, who spoke through the prophets. In one holy, Catholic, and apostolic Church. We confess one baptism for the remission of sins. We look for the resurrection of the dead, and the life of eternity to come. Amen.

(The Pseudo-Athanasian Symbol *Quicumque)*

Whoever wishes to be saved must of all hold the Catholic faith, for anyone who does not maintain this whole and inviolate will surely be lost eternally.

And the Catholic faith is this, that we worship one God in Trinity, and Trinity in Unity, neither confounding the Persons nor dividing the substance. For there is one person of the Father, another of the Son, and another of the Holy Spirit. But the godhead of the Father, of the Son and of the Holy Spirit is all one, the glory equal, the majesty co-eternal. As the Father is, so is the Son, and so is the Holy Spirit. Uncreated the Father, the Son uncreated, and the Holy Spirit uncreated. The Father immeasurable, the Son immeasurable, and the Holy Spirit immeasurable. The Father eternal, the Son eternal, and the Holy Spirit eternal. And yet there are not three eternals but one eternal. Just as there are not three uncreated nor three immeasurables, but one uncreated and one immeasurable. Likewise the Father is almighty, the Son is almighty, and the Holy Spirit is almighty; yet not three almighties, but one almighty. Thus God the Father, God the Son, and God the Holy Spirit; yet not three Gods but one God. Thus the Father is Lord, the Son is Lord, and the Holy Spirit is Lord; yet there are not three Lords, but one Lord. For as we are compelled by Christian truth to acknowledge that each Person by himself is God and Lord, we are forbidden by the true Catholic religion to say that there are three Gods or Lords. The Father is made by none, nor created nor begotten. The Son is from the Father alone, not made nor created but begotten. The Holy Spirit is from the Father and the Son, not made nor created nor begotten but proceeding. So there is one Father, not three Fathers; one Son, not three Sons; and one Holy Spirit, not three Holy Spirits. And in this Trinity none is before or after another, none is greater or less, but all three Persons are co-eternal with one another and co-equal. So that in all things, as has already been said above, both Unity in Trinity and Trinity in Unity are to be adored. Therefore whoever will be saved must believe this of the Trinity. For eternal salvation it is further necessary that we faithfully believe in the incarnation of our Lord Jesus Christ. The right faith is therefore this: that we believe and confess that our Lord Jesus Christ the Son of God is both God and man; God of the substance of the Father, begotten before time, and man of the substance of his mother born in time; perfect God and perfect man, consisting of a rational soul and human body; equal to the Father in his divinity, less than the Father in his humanity; who, although both God and man is not two but one Christ; one, however, not by the conversion of the Godhead into flesh but by the assumption of manhood into God. Wholly one, not by fusion of substance but by unity of person. For as the rational soul and the body are one man, so God and man are one Christ. Who suffered for our salvation, descended into hell, rose again from the dead on the third day, ascended into heaven, sits at the right hand of the Father, whence he will come to judge the living and the dead. When he comes, all men will rise again with their bodies and give an account of their own deeds, and those who have done good will enter into eternal life, and those who have done evil into eternal fire. This is the Catholic faith. And if anyone shall not faithfully and firmly believe it, he cannot be saved.

Text of the Dogmatic Constitution
Dei Filius of Vatican Council I

Chapter 1—God, the Creator of All Things

DS 3001   The holy, Catholic Roman Church believes and confesses that there is one God, true and living, Creator and Lord of heaven and earth, almighty, eternal, immense, incomprehensible, infinite in his intellect and will and in all perfection. As he is one unique and spiritual substance, entirely simple and unchangeable, we must proclaim him distinct from the world in existence and essence, blissful in himself and from himself, and ineffably exalted above all things that exist or can be conceived besides him.

DS 3002   This one and only true God, of his own goodness and almighty power, not for the increase of his own happiness, nor for the acquirement of his perfection, but in order to manifest his perfection through the benefits which he bestows on creatures, with absolute freedom of counsel, "from the beginning of time made at once *(simul)* out of nothing both orders of creatures, the spiritual and the corporeal, that is, the angelic and the earthly, and then *(deinde)* the human creature, who as it were shares in both orders, being composed of spirit and body."

DS 3003   By his providence God protects and governs all things which he has made, "reaching mightily from one end of the earth to the other, and ordering all things well" (Wis 8:1). For "all are open and laid bare to his eyes" (cf. Heb 4:13), also those things which are yet to come to existence through the free action of creatures.

Chapter 2—Revelation

DS 3004   God, the beginning and end of all things, can be known with certainty from the things that were created, through the natural light of human reason, for "ever since the creation of the world his invisible nature has been clearly perceived in the things that have been made" (Rom 1:20); but that it pleased his wisdom and bounty to reveal himself and his eternal decrees in another and a supernatural way, as the apostle says, "In many and various ways God spoke of old to our fathers by the prophets; but in these last days he has spoken to us by the Son" (Heb 1:1-2).

DS 3005   It is to be ascribed to this divine revelation that such truths among things divine as of themselves are not beyond human reason can, even in the present condition of mankind, be known by everyone with facility, with firm certitude and with no admixture of error. It is, however, not for this reason that revelation is to be called absolutely necessary, but because God in his infinite goodness has ordained man to a supernatural end, viz., to share in the good things of God which utterly exceed the intelligence of the human mind, for "no eye has seen, nor ear heard, nor the heart of man conceived, what God prepared for those who love him" (1 Cor 2:9).

DS 3006   Further, this supernatural revelation, according to the universal belief of the Church, declared by the sacred Synod of Trent, "is contained in the written books and unwritten traditions which have come down to us, having been received by the apostles from the mouth of Christ himself, or from the apostles themselves by the dictation of the Holy Spirit, and have been transmitted as it were from hand to hand." These books of the Old and New Testaments are to be received as sacred and canonical in their integrity, with all their parts, as they are enumerated in the decree of the said Council and are contained in the ancient Latin edition of the Vulgate. These the Church holds to be sacred and canonical, not because, having been carefully composed by mere human industry, they were afterward approved by her authority, nor merely because they contain revelation with no admixture of error, but because, having been written by the inspiration of the Holy Spirit, they have God for their author and have been delivered as such to the Church herself.

DS 3007   However, what the holy Council of Trent has laid down concerning the interpretation of the divine Scripture for the good purpose of restraining undisciplined minds, has been explained by certain men in a distorted manner. Hence we renew the same decree and declare this to be its sense: In matters of faith and morals, affecting the building up of Christian doctrine, that is to be held as the true sense of Holy Scripture which Holy Mother the Church has held and holds, to whom it belongs to judge of the true sense and interpretation of Holy Scriptures. Therefore no one is allowed to interpret the same Sacred Scripture contrary to this sense, or contrary to the unanimous consent of the Fathers.

Chapter 3—Faith

DS 3008   Since man is totally dependent upon God, as upon his Creator and Lord, and since created reason is absolutely subject to uncreated truth, we are bound to yield by faith the full homage of intellect and will to God who reveals himself. The Catholic Church professes that this faith, which is the "beginning of man's salvation," is a supernatural virtue whereby, inspired and assisted by the grace of God, we believe that what he has revealed is true, not because the intrinsic truth of things is recognized by the natural light of reason, but because of the authority of God himself who reveals them, who can neither err nor deceive. For faith, as the apostle testifies, is "the assurance of things hoped for, the conviction of things not seen" (Heb 11:1).

DS 3009   However, in order that the obedience of our faith be nevertheless in harmony with reason (cf. Rom 12:1), God willed that exterior proofs of his revelation, viz., divine facts, especially miracles and prophecies, should be joined to the interior helps of the Holy Spirit; as they manifestly display the omnipotence and infinite knowledge of God, they are the most certain signs of the divine revelation, adapted to the intelligence of all men. Therefore Moses and the prophets, and especially Christ our Lord himself, performed many manifest miracles and uttered prophecies; and of the apostles we read: "They went forth and preached everywhere, while the Lord worked with them and confirmed the message by the signs that attended it" (Mk 16:20); and again it is written: "We have the prophetic word made more sure; you will do well to pay attention to this as to a lamp shining in a dark place" (2 Pet 1:19).

DS 3010   Though the assent of faith is by no means a blind impulse of the mind, still no man can "assent to the Gospel message," as is necessary to obtain salvation, "without the illumination and inspiration of the Holy Spirit, who gives to all joy in assenting to the truth and believing it." Wherefore faith itself, even when it is not working through love (cf. Gal 5:6), is in itself a gift of God, and the act of faith is a work appertaining to salvation, by which man yields voluntary obedience to God himself by assenting to and cooperating with grace, which he could resist.

DS 3011   All those things are to be believed with Catholic faith which are contained in the word of God, written or handed down, and which by the Church, either in solemn judgment or through her ordinary and universal teaching office, are proposed for belief as having been divinely revealed.

DS 3012   But, since "without faith it is impossible to please God" (Heb 11:6) and to attain to the fellowship of his sons, hence, no one is justified without it; nor will anyone attain eternal life except "he shall persevere unto the end in it" (Mt 10:22; 24:13). Moreover, in order that we may satisfactorily perform the duty of embracing the true faith and of continuously persevering in it, God, through his only-begotten Son, has instituted the Church, and provided it with clear signs of his institution, so that it can be recognized by all as the guardian and teacher of the revealed word.

DS 3013   To the sole Catholic Church belong all the manifold and wonderful endowments which by divine disposition are meant to put into light the credibility of the Christian faith. Nay more, the Church by herself, with her marvelous propagation, eminent holiness and inexhaustible fruitfulness in everything that is good, with her Catholic unity and invincible stability, is a great and perpetual motive of credibility and an irrefutable testimony of her divine mission.

DS 3014   Thus, like a standard lifted up among the nations (cf. Is 11:12), she invites to herself those who do not yet believe, and at the same time gives greater assurance to her children that the faith which they profess rests on solid ground.

To this testimony the efficacious help coming from the power above is added. For the merciful Lord stirs up and aids with his grace those who are wandering astray, that they be able to "come to the knowledge of the truth" (1 Tim 2:4), and those whom "He has called out of darkness into his admirable light" (1 Pet 2:9). He confirms them with his grace that they may persevere in this light, for he deserts none who does not desert him. Therefore, the condition of those who by the heavenly gift of faith have embraced the Catholic truth, and of those who led by human opinions follow a false religion, is by no means the same. For, those who have received the faith under the teaching authority of the Church can never have a just reason to change this same faith or to call it into question. For this reason, "giving thanks to God the Father who has qualified us to share in the inheritance of the saints in light" (Col 1:12), let us not neglect so great a salvation, but "looking to Jesus the pioneer and perfecter of our faith" (Heb 12:2), "let us hold fast the confession of our hope without wavering" (Heb 10:23).

Chapter 4—Faith and Reason

DS 3015   The perpetual common belief of the Catholic Church has held and holds also that there is a twofold order of knowledge, distinct not only in its principle but also in its object; in its principle, because in the one we know by natural reason, in the other by divine faith; in its object, because apart from what natural reason can attain, there are proposed to our belief mysteries that are hidden in God, which can never be known unless they are revealed by God. Hence the apostle who, on the one hand, testifies that God is known to the gentiles in the things that have been made (cf. Rom 1:20), on the other hand, when speaking about the grace and truth that came through Jesus Christ (cf. Jn 1:17), proclaims: "We speak the wisdom of God in a mystery, a wisdom which is hidden, which God ordained before the world unto our glory, which none of the princes of this world knew.... But to us God has revealed by his Spirit. For the Spirit searches everything, yes the deep things of God" (1 Cor 2:7-10 Vulg.). The only-Begotten himself praises the Father because he has hidden these things from the wise and understanding and has revealed them to babes (cf. Mt 11:25).

DS 3016   Nevertheless, if reason illumined by faith inquires in an earnest, pious and sober manner, it attains by God's grace a certain understanding of the mysteries, which is most fruitful, both from the analogy with the objects of its natural knowledge and from the connection of these mysteries with one another and with man's ultimate end. But it never becomes capable of understanding them in the way it does truths which constitute its proper object. For divine mysteries by their very nature so excel the created intellect that, even when they have been communicated in revelation and received by faith, they remain covered by the veil of faith itself and shrouded as it were in darkness as long as in this mortal life "we are away from the Lord; for we walk by faith, not by sight" (2 Cor 5:6-7).

DS 3017   However, though faith is above reason, there can never be a real discrepancy between faith and reason, since the same God who reveals mysteries and infuses faith has bestowed the light of reason on the human mind, and God cannot deny himself, nor can truth ever contradict truth. The deceptive appearance of such a contradiction is mainly due to the fact that either the dogmas of faith have not been understood and expounded according to the mind of the Church, or that uncertain theories are taken for verdicts of reason. Thus "we define that every assertion that is opposed to enlightened faith is utterly false" (Lateran V: *DS* 1441).

DS 3018   Further, the Church which, along with the apostolic office of teaching, received the charge of guarding the deposit of faith has also from God the right and the duty to proscribe what is falsely called knowledge (cf. 1 Tim 6:20), lest anyone be deceived by philosophy and vain fallacy (cf. Col 2:8). Hence all believing Christians are not only forbidden to defend as legitimate conclusions of science such opinions which they realize to be contrary to the doctrine of faith, particularly if they have been condemned by the Church, but they are seriously bound to account them as errors which put on the fallacious appearance of truth.

DS 3019   Not only can there be no conflict between faith and reason, they also support each other since right reason demonstrates the foundations of faith and, illumined by its light, pursues the science of divine things, while faith frees and protects reason from errors and provides it with manifold insights. It is therefore far remote from the truth to say that the Church opposes the study of human arts and sciences; on the contrary, she supports and promotes them in many ways. She does not ignore or despise the benefits that human life derives from them. Indeed, she confesses: as they have their origin from God who is the Lord of knowledge (cf. 1 Sam 2:3), so too, if rightly pursued, they lead to God with his grace. Nor does the Church in any way forbid that these sciences, each in its sphere. should make use of their own principles and of the method proper to them. While, however, acknowledging this just freedom, she seriously warns lest they fall into error by going contrary to the divine doctrine, or, stepping beyond their own limits, they enter into the sphere of faith and create confusion.

DS 3020   For the doctrine of faith which God has revealed has not been proposed like a philosophical system to be perfected by human ingenuity, but has been committed to the spouse of Christ as a divine trust to be faithfully kept and infallibly declared. Hence also that meaning of the sacred dogmas is perpetually to be retained which our Holy Mother Church has once declared, and there must never be a deviation from that meaning on the specious ground and title of a more profound understanding. "Therefore, let there be growth and abundant progress in understanding, knowledge and wisdom, in each and all, in individuals and in the whole Church, at all times and in the progress of ages, but only within the proper limits, i.e., within the same dogma, the same meaning, the same judgment."

Canons on Chapter 1

DS 3021   If anyone denies the one true God, Creator and Lord of things visible and invisible, *anathema sit.*

DS 3022   If anyone is not ashamed to assert that nothing exists besides matter, *anathema sit.*

DS 3023   If anyone says that the substance and essence of God and all things is one and the same, *anathema sit.*

DS 3024   If anyone says that finite beings, the corporeal as well as the spiritual, or at least the spiritual ones, have emanated from the divine substance; or that the divine essence becomes all things by self-manifestation or self-evolution; or lastly that God is the universal or indefinite being which, by self-determination, constitutes the universality of beings, differentiated in genera, species and individuals, *anathema sit.*

DS 3025   If anyone refuses to confess that the world and all things contained in it, the spiritual as well as the material, were in their whole substance produced by God out of nothing; or says that God created not by an act of will free from all necessity, but with the same necessity by which he necessarily loves himself; or denies that the world was made for the glory of God, *anathema sit.*

Canons on Chapter 2

DS 3026   If anyone says that the one true God, our Creator and Lord, cannot be known with certainty with the natural light of human reason through the things that are created, *anathema sit.*

DS 3027   If anyone says that it is impossible or useless for man to be taught through divine revelation about God and the cult to be rendered to him, *anathema sit.*

DS 3028   If anyone says that man cannot be called by God to a knowledge and perfection that surpasses the natural, but that he can and must by himself, through constant progress, finally arrive at the possession of all that is true and good, *anathema sit.*

DS 3029   If anyone does not receive as sacred and canonical the books of Holy Scripture, entire and with all their parts, as the sacred Synod of Trent has enumerated them, or denies that they have been divinely inspired, *anathema sit.*

Canons on Chapter 3

DS 3031   If anyone says that human reason is so independent that faith cannot be enjoined upon it by God, *anathema sit.*

DS 3032   If anyone says that divine faith is not distinct from the natural knowledge of God and of moral truths; that, therefore, for divine faith it is not necessary that the revealed truth be believed on the authority of God who reveals it, *anathema sit.*

DS 3033   If anyone says that divine revelation cannot be made credible by outward signs, and that, therefore, men ought to be moved to faith solely by each one's inner experience or by personal inspiration, *anathema sit.*

DS 3034   If anyone says that no miracles are possible, and that, therefore, all accounts of them, even those contained in Holy Scripture, are to be dismissed as fables and myths; or that miracles can never be recognized with certainty, and that the divine origin of the Christian religion cannot be legitimately proved by them, *anathema sit.*

DS 3035   If anyone says that the assent to the Christian faith is not free but is produced with necessity by arguments of human reason; or that the grace of God is necessary only for that living faith which works by love, *anathema sit.*

DS 3036   If anyone says that the condition of the faithful and of those who have not yet attained to the only true faith is the same, so that Catholics could have a just reason for suspending their judgment and calling into question the faith which they have already received under the teaching authority of the Church, until they have completed a scientific demonstration of the credibility and truth of their faith, *anathema sit.*

Canons on Chapter 4

DS 3041   If anyone says that in divine revelation no true and properly so called mysteries are contained but that all dogmas of faith can be understood and demonstrated from natural principles by reason, if it is properly trained, *anathema sit.*

DS 3042   If anyone says that human sciences are to be pursued with such liberty that their assertions, even if opposed to revealed doctrine, may be held as true and cannot be proscribed by the Church, *anathema sit.*

DS 3043   If anyone says that, as science progresses, at times a sense is to be given to dogmas proposed by the Church, different from the one which the Church has understood and understands, *anathema sit.*

DS 3044   Therefore, in fulfillment of our supreme pastoral office, we beseech in the love of Jesus Christ, and we command in the authority of the same God our Savior, all Christian faithful, and especially those who hold authority or are engaged in teaching, to put their zeal and effort in removing and eliminating these errors from the holy Church and in spreading the light of pure faith.

DS 3045   It is, however, not enough to avoid the malice of heresy unless those errors which lead close to it are also carefully avoided. We therefore remind all of their duty to observe also the constitutions and decrees by which such perverse opinions, which are not explicitly enumerated here, are proscribed by this Holy See.

Index

auline
BOOKS & MEDIA

The Daughters of St. Paul operate book and media centers at the following addresses. Visit, call or write the one nearest you today, or find us on the World Wide Web, www.pauline.org

CALIFORNIA
3908 Sepulveda Blvd, Culver City, CA 90230   310-397-8676
5945 Balboa Avenue, San Diego, CA 92111   858-565-9181
46 Geary Street, San Francisco, CA 94108   415-781-5180

FLORIDA
145 S.W. 107th Avenue, Miami, FL 33174   305-559-6715

HAWAII
1143 Bishop Street, Honolulu, HI 96813   808-521-2731
Neighbor Islands call: 800-259-8463

ILLINOIS
172 North Michigan Avenue, Chicago, IL 60601   312-346-4228

LOUISIANA
4403 Veterans Memorial Blvd, Metairie, LA 70006   504-887-7631

MASSACHUSETTS
Rte. 1, 885 Providence Hwy, Dedham, MA 02026   781-326-5385

MISSOURI
9804 Watson Road, St. Louis, MO 63126   314-965-3512

NEW JERSEY
561 U.S. Route 1, Wick Plaza, Edison, NJ 08817   732-572-1200

NEW YORK
150 East 52nd Street, New York, NY 10022   212-754-1110
78 Fort Place, Staten Island, NY 10301   718-447-5071

OHIO
2105 Ontario Street, Cleveland, OH 44115   216-621-9427

PENNSYLVANIA
9171-A Roosevelt Blvd, Philadelphia, PA 19114   215-676-9494

SOUTH CAROLINA
243 King Street, Charleston, SC 29401   843-577-0175

TENNESSEE
4811 Poplar Avenue, Memphis, TN 38117   901-761-2987

TEXAS
114 Main Plaza, San Antonio, TX 78205   210-224-8101

VIRGINIA
1025 King Street, Alexandria, VA 22314   703-549-3806

CANADA
3022 Dufferin Street, Toronto, Ontario, Canada M6B 3T5   416-781-9131
1155 Yonge Street, Toronto, Ontario, Canada M4T 1W2   416-934-3440

¡También somos su fuente para libros, videos y música en español!